MARIN IN OIL

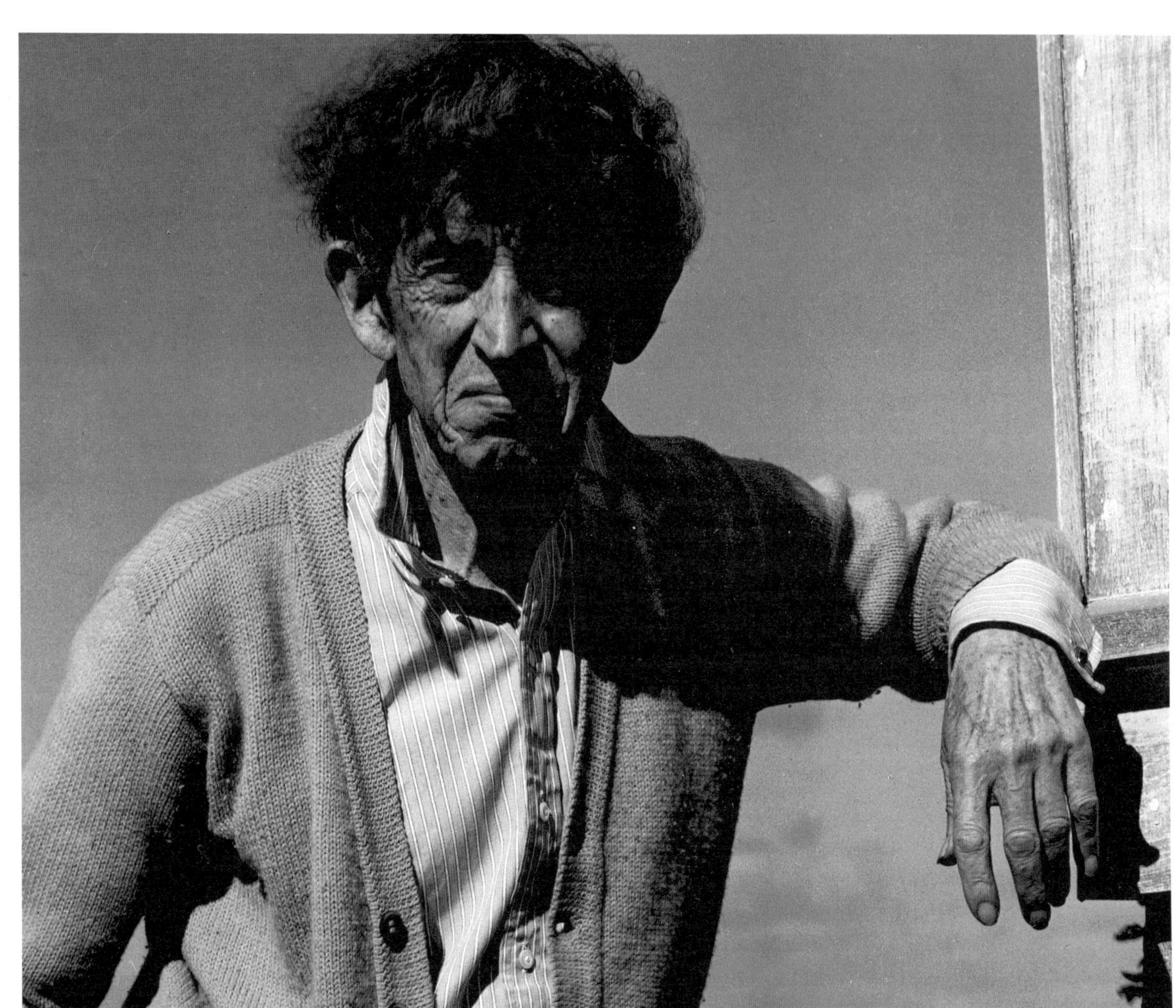

MARIN
IN OIL

KLAUS KERTESS

THE PARRISH ART MUSEUM
Southampton, New York

This exhibition and its accompanying catalogue
have been made possible with support from

The Robert Lehman Foundation
The National Endowment for the Arts,
Washington, D.C., A Federal Agency
The Cowles Charitable Trust
The Betty Parsons Foundation
The New York State Council on the Arts
Suffolk County Office of Cultural Affairs
Kennedy Galleries, Inc.
Mr. and Mrs. George S. Kaufman

Library of Congress Catalog Card Number 86-63058
ISBN 943526-15-9

COVER
Lobster Boat, Cape Split, Maine. 1938.
Oil on canvas, 22 x 28 in.
Collection Mr. and Mrs. Carl D. Lobell, New York
Plate 28

FRONTISPIECE AND BACK COVER
Paul Strand: *John Marin, Cape Split, Maine, 1945.*

CONTENTS

FOREWORD

For much of John Marin's lifetime and thereafter, his significant role during the early phase of modernism has been acknowledged through the attention devoted to his watercolors. The contribution of his oils has been addressed only fleetingly by both his supporters and his critics. The advent of Surrealism may have diminished Marin's achievements in this regard, as did perhaps his distance, both physical and emotional, from the artists who were becoming America's Abstract Expressionists. Thus The Parrish Art Museum's exhibition, *Marin in Oil,* is a new and important chapter in our understanding of Marin. We have a chance to see here and for the first time, a massing of these works and an exceptional and thorough examination of them by Klaus Kertess, the Parrish's Robert Lehman Curator.

For The Parrish Art Museum, Marin has a particular and peculiar relevance. We know that Marin studied at the Pennsylvania Academy of the Fine Arts during William Merritt Chase's tenure as a teacher there; that Marin worked around Peconic Bay sometime in 1911; and that Fairfield Porter was a lender to Marin's retrospective exhibition at The Museum of Modern Art in 1936. The fact that Marin's work serves as a bridge between the Parrish's key holdings of William Merritt Chase and Fairfield Porter–and a precursor as well to American Abstract Expressionist painting, which holds special meaning here on the East End of Long Island–aids us in expanding our perspective on our collection in nineteenth- and twentieth-century American art.

This project was realized by Klaus Kertess, who has continuously found ways for the Parrish to bring new meaning to its collections. We are especially grateful to the Robert Lehman Foundation for supporting his work here, and for their help in purchasing John Marin's *Tunk Mountains, Maine* (oil on canvas, 1946) in 1984.

Special thanks go to our lenders, both private and public collections, who realized the significance of this project and cooperated fully throughout it. Norma and John Marin, Jr. and Lawrence Fleischman of the Kennedy Galleries deserve our most sincere gratitude, since without their generosity and support the exhibition would not have been possible. To Dorothy Norman, Elaine de Kooning, Paul F. Walter, William Rayner, Charles

Cowles, Jan Cowles, Michael Thomas, Philip Isles and Livio Borghese we are grateful for their good counsel in this venture.

We are delighted to have financial support from both public and private sectors. Substantial aid has come from the Robert Lehman Foundation, the Cowles Charitable Trust, and the National Endowment for the Arts, along with help from the New York State Council on the Arts, the Suffolk County Office of Cultural Affairs, the Kennedy Galleries, Inc., the Betty Parsons Foundation, and Mr. and Mrs. George S. Kaufman.

At The Parrish Art Museum, our Registrar, Alicia Longwell, deserves special acknowledgment for her masterful handling of the details of the exhibition and the catalogue publication. We owe much to Dana Levy, its designer, and Sara Blackburn, its editor, for giving shape and beauty to the catalogue; to Maureen O'Brien, Associate Director for Curatorial Affairs; Norma Loehner, Curatorial Secretary; Anke Jackson, Associate Director for Budget and Operations; Robin Box-Klopfer, Installer, thanks go for their thoughtful attention to this project. At Kennedy Galleries, Inc., we are indebted to Registrar F. Frederick Bernaski for his cooperation in facilitating many of the loans for the exhibition.

To those museums that will share in the joys of this endeavor, we are especially grateful: The Norton Gallery and School of Art, West Palm Beach, Florida; The Telfair Academy of Arts and Sciences, Savannah, Georgia; Museum of Art, The Pennsylvania State University, University Park, Pennsylvania; and Albright-Knox Art Gallery, Buffalo, New York.

Importantly, we are thankful to the Trustees of The Parrish Art Museum and its President, Garrick C. Stephenson, for their wholehearted support and enthusiasm for this project.

TRUDY KRAMER
Director
The Parrish Art Museum
March 1987

LENDERS

Archer M. Huntington Art Gallery, The University of Texas at Austin
Dallas Museum of Art
Willard Straight Hall Collection, Cornell University, Ithaca, New York
University of Maine at Machias
Whitney Museum of American Art, New York
San Francisco Museum of Modern Art
The Santa Barbara Museum of Art
Hirshhorn Museum and Sculpture Garden, Smithsonian Institution, Washington, D.C.
The Phillips Collection, Washington, D.C.
Colby College Museum of Art, Waterville, Maine
Norton Gallery of Art, West Palm Beach, Florida

Mr. and Mrs. William C. Bahan, Fort Worth, Texas
Douglass and Fredrica Carmichael, Washington, D.C.
Mr. and Mrs. William Janss, Sun Valley, Idaho
Joseph M. Klein, M.D., Longboat Key, Florida
Dr. and Mrs. William Lannick, New York
Mr. and Mrs. Carl D. Lobell, New York
Mr. and Mrs. John Marin, Jr., New York
Norma Boom Marin, New York
Mr. and Mrs. Irving Moskovitz, New York
Dr. and Mrs. Norman Rosenberg, East Brunswick, New Jersey
Charles Simon, New York
Six private collections

Kennedy Galleries, Inc., New York

SCHEDULE OF THE EXHIBITION

THE PARRISH ART MUSEUM
Southampton, New York
July 18-September 20, 1987

THE NORTON GALLERY AND SCHOOL OF ART
West Palm Beach, Florida
October 11-November 29, 1987

THE TELFAIR ACADEMY OF ARTS AND SCIENCES
Savannah, Georgia
January 20-March 7, 1988

MUSEUM OF ART, THE PENNSYLVANIA STATE UNIVERSITY
University Park, Pennsylvania
March 20-May 18, 1988

ALBRIGHT-KNOX ART GALLERY
Buffalo, New York
July 16-September 4, 1988

CHRONOLOGY

1870 Born in Rutherford, New Jersey, December 23.

1899–1901 Studied at Pennsylvania Academy of Fine Arts; beginning of lifelong friendship with Arthur B. Carles.

1905 Arrived in Paris, September 27.

1907 Exhibited in Salon d'Automne and Salon des Indépendants.
Traveled in Italy.

1908 Founding member of New Society of American Artists in Paris.
Exhibited in Salon d'Automne.

1909 Exhibited at Stieglitz's 291 with Alfred Maurer.
Returned briefly to United States.

1910 Returned to Europe; worked in Paris and Austrian Tyrol.
Returned to the United States in summer.
First one-person exhibition at 291.

1912 Married Marie Jane Hughes, December 12.

1913 Participated in Armory Show.

1914 First trip to Maine.
Birth of only child, John C. Marin III (John Marin, Jr.).

1920 Purchased house in Cliffside, New Jersey.
Began to summer regularly in Maine.

1929–1930 Spent two summers around Taos, New Mexico, at the invitation of Mable Dodge Luhan.
Included in "Painting by Nineteen Living Americans," Museum of Modern Art, New York.

1934 Purchased house on Cape Split, Maine.

1936 Major retrospective at Museum of Modern Art, New York.

1945 Death of Marie Jane Marin in Cliffside, New Jersey.

1946 Death of Alfred Stieglitz.

1947 Second major retrospective at Institute of Modern Art,* Boston: Phillips Memorial Gallery, Washington, D.C.; Walker Art Center, Minneapolis.

1950 First all-oil painting exhibition, at An American Place, March 20–May 6.
Retrospective at XXV Biennale, Venice.

1953 Died October 2 on Cape Split, Maine.

*Changed in 1948 to Institute of Contemporary Art

MARIN IN OIL

MARIN IN OIL

Klaus Kertess

The word "new" began to acquire real meaning in the vocabulary of American art in the year 1908. In New York, a group of painters led by Robert Henri banded together under the title of their number, The Eight. Across the Atlantic, another group of artists, led by the painter and photographer Edward (then Eduard) Steichen, formed the New Society of American Artists in Paris. Neither group professed a clear program or a single style, as the French Impressionists and Fauves had done before them, but each group was seeking a new independence and vitality for its native culture. Both were reacting against the often stilted bravura that marked the works of many elders who had been enraptured by the varnished lavishness of the Hals-and-Velásquez-inspired School of Munich. And both groups included students of William Merritt Chase, America's most prominent Munich proponent.

The innovations of The Eight were largely in subject matter and attitude; those of the New Society of American Painters in Paris were more formal in their radicalness. Robert Henri, John Sloan, George Luks, and Edward Shinn of The Eight continued to engage in the painterliness of their immediate predecessors, but they rejected the pomp and pose of the studio as well as the sunny civilities of country sojourns. They focused instead on the democratic grittiness of working-class street life and entertainment. What constituted their newness were their concerted efforts to give America's burgeoning urbanism its first image; their easygoing socialism would reach its apogee in the thirties. While Robert Henri's naturalism and somber palette are testament to his lifetime opposition to modernism, the enthusiasm of his fellow member Maurice Prendergast for Cézanne and pointillism represented a more cosmopolitan Americanism that directly challenged the prevailing academic conception of painting. Prendergast was America's only Postimpressionist, and he had more in common with the younger artists in the group concurrently being formed in Paris by Steichen than he did with The Eight.

Although Edward Steichen's paintings would remain enshrouded in symbolist and Whistlerian mists, he was an enthusiast of Cézanne and the early-twentieth-century modernism of Matisse and Brancusi. In his association with Alfred Stieglitz, Steichen became the major conduit for transmitting Parisian modernism to the frontiers of the American art scene. In Europe, he rallied his young countrymen to form the New Society of American Artists in Paris. They did not promote themselves as a group or even exhibit as one; like The Eight, they formed primarily to protest the conservatism of the elder establishment—in this case, the Society of American Artists. What the "New" in the group's title connoted was an interest in the antiestablishment Parisian artists who were exhibiting regularly in the Salon d'Automne and the Salon des Indépendants. In 1905 most of the group was already in Paris to witness the coloristic fireworks of the Fauves, who, led by Matisse, Vlaminck, and Derain, were given center stage at that year's Salon d'Automne. There too, one could see in depth the earlier work of Van Gogh and Seurat. Three of the new Americans were represented in the Salon d'Automne of 1907, which included almost every major French artist from the late 1880s to the present, from Gauguin and Cézanne to Matisse, Braque, and Rouault. The New Society included Patrick Henry Bruce, Arthur B. Carles, Alfred Maurer, and Max Weber; their individual and varied assimilations of Cézanne, Matisse, and the newly crystallizing tenets of Cubism would shortly have a major impact on the formation of modernism in America. Their international Americanism would be concurrent with and generally opposed to the more conservative and isolationist Americanism of The Eight's Henri and Sloan.

One of the three members of the soon-to-be-formed New Society who exhibited in the 1907 Salon d'Automne was John Marin; the other two were Bruce and Weber. Unlike his compatriots, Marin was not so anxious to add "new" to his vocabulary. Matisse's junior by one year and Picasso's senior by eleven, Marin was still primarily involved in the making of technically expert but rather conventional etchings. In this year of 1907, when Picasso painted the brutally beautiful and pivotal *Demoiselles d'Avignon,* Marin was etching Venetian and Parisian architectural views that were influenced by Whistler and, to a lesser extent, by the French etcher Charles Meryon. By 1910 his preoccupation with line would increasingly extend into strokes of watercolor, his major medium prior to 1905. The architecture of the subject would be slowly submerged in the architecture of the plane of the paper support. Marin's profound joy in both his subjects and materials as well as in the procedures of making resulted in some of the most compelling watercolors of the twentieth century and earned him a reputation as one of America's greatest painters. His exuberant painterliness was blended with his belated absorption of the Parisian avant-garde and extended the American landscape painting of the nineteenth century into the twentieth.

The uniqueness of Marin's almost Oriental, liquid Cubism was nurtured and promoted as an indigenous phenomenon by America's first and foremost impresario of modernism, Alfred Stieglitz. Stieglitz promoted Marin as a watercolorist, but neither Stieglitz nor America was fully prepared to accept him as a painter in the denser medium of oil. Marin had painted sporadically in oil all along, but after 1930, it became his major preoccupation. Then, going back to and expanding upon a singular group of small oils he had completed around 1916, he started painting with an intense, visceral, physical agitation and a painterly clarity that were all but unparalleled in America—and in Europe—until the advent of Abstract Expressionism. If the frenetic energy of New York's rapidly rising skyscrapers had sparked Marin's Cubist dynamics in the second decade of this century, now the ocean's rolling rhythms energized the greater body of his strokes. The dialogue that took place between the mediums of oil and watercolor attained a lyrical synthesis in Marin's final paintings of the late forties and early fifties. He died with seemingly but one disappointment: that his oils had not been accorded their due regard. The intention of the exhibition that this essay accompanies is to analyze and to celebrate Marin's achievements in the medium of oil, posthumously according at least some of the acclaim that has been denied them.

Marin was fond of signing himself the "Ancient Mariner," but he might as accurately have signed his many letters the "Modernist Mariner." Instead, like most of his contemporary supporters, he chose to emphasize his Yankee roots. His own and his early biographers' defensiveness about the French impedes the already difficult task of an analysis of his stylistic complexity, but this is a fact that must be regarded as an integral part of American culture's still-youthful growth in the first half of the twentieth century. Marsden Hartley, who proclaimed his own debts to Berlin and Paris not only visually but verbally, was consequently regarded with suspicion throughout much of his career. Marin's energetically elliptical, and considerable, writing is forceful about the physical pleasures of paint and painting, but it is quite reticent about outside influences other than skyscrapers, mountains, and ocean. If what follows seems occasionally to overcompensate for this reticence, its purpose is certainly not to deny Marin's deeply intuitive empathy with his subjects or his alchemical skills in transforming the dynamics of the observed into the visible dynamics of painting.[1]

"He is a small slender man with unusually long, fine hands. He has probably the longest hair of any contemporary American artist.... That day he had on a high starched collar and an untied necktie that was simply held together by a pearl stickpin.... His face was a deep weather-beaten brown covered with a crosswork of fine wrinkles; from under his thick bangs his piercing eyes looked out warily.... Marin's old friends say that his face had the appearance of a puckered winter apple even when he was half his present age."[2] This was Marin at seventy-two: part Yankee, part neo-Edwardian bohemian dandy; part city resident, part country dweller. After his return to New York, when he was in his forties, he could as readily have lunch at Holland House in the midst of the Stieglitz circle with the likes of Ethel Barrymore, Mark Twain, and Enrico Caruso at nearby tables as he could fish by himself in the country. His wry humor could engage an eminent writer or a fisherman. He might listen to Bach, Handel, or Mozart or play them on the piano as effortlessly, if not as expertly, as he played billiards. But mostly he guarded his work with an unremarkable regularity that was sheltered by his wife, and after her death, by his son. And the rhythmic flow and crackle of writing, fishing, music, and billiards were all dissolved in paint.

At Marin's birth, in 1870, the United States were barely united and just six years short of their centennial celebration. Eakins was recently returned from Paris and in full pursuit of a rigorous realism shorn of all superfluous aesthetic contrivances; Whistler was in London in full pursuit of a rigorous aestheticism shorn of all superfluous realistic contrivances. The directness and freedom from anecdote of Homer's lyric naturalism, with its frequent parallels to early French Impressionism (to be so named in 1874), was moving the tradition of American genre painting away from the pantheistic pomp of the Hudson River School toward a simpler, secular empiricism. Both Homer and Whistler would become important models to Marin when he finally chose to be a painter.

Marin's mother died nine days after his birth and he was raised in the house of his maternal grandparents, in Weehawken, New Jersey—primarily by his maiden aunts Jenny and Lelia Currey. The Curreys were frugal, God-fearing Yankees whose family had been in America since 1700. Marin looked like a Currey. His father was

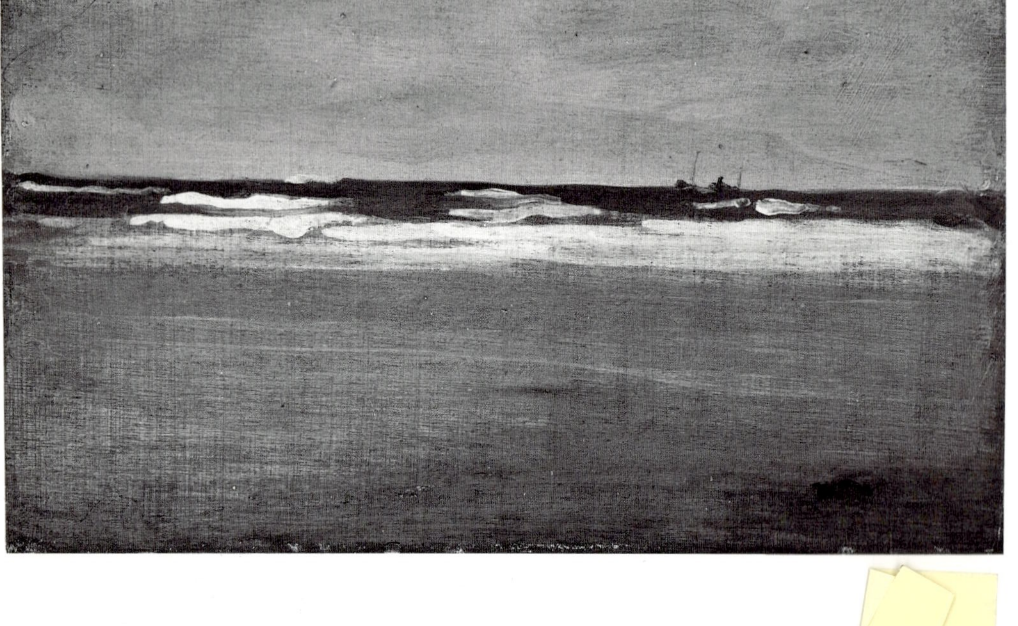

Fig. 1
J.A.M. WHISTLER
The Angry Sea
Oil on wood. 4⅞ x 8½ in.
Freer Gallery of Art,
Smithsonian Institution
Washington, D.C.

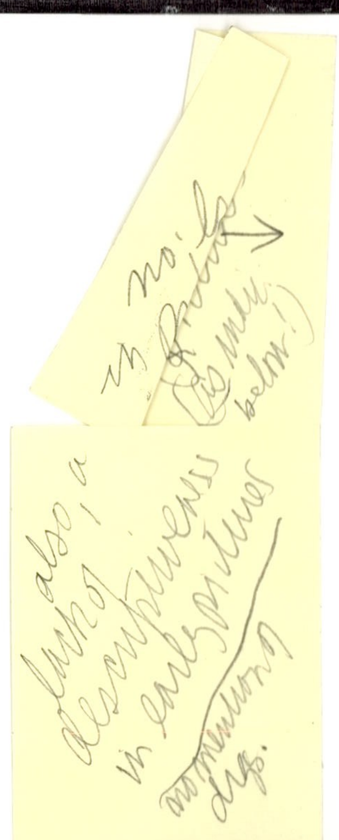

seldom in evidence, although his success as a public accountant and private investment banker provided material support well into his son's adulthood. The devotion of the aunts at least partially compensated for the absence of real parents. Marin's personal life seems to have been almost seamlessly uneventful from beginning to end.

Outdoor activities—sketching, fishing, and hunting—were far more compelling than school. Yielding to conventional family expectations, Marin limited his sketching and painting to Sundays while he tried work, first in a Manhattan wholesale notions company and then, for four years, in a succession of architectural offices. In 1893 he opened his own office and subsequently built six frame houses, in what is now Union City, New Jersey. Finally, in 1899 Marin went to the Pennsylvania Academy of Fine Arts for two years, but even there he resisted formal training. He preferred his outdoor sketching to working from a model in the studio. The Academy was followed by five years of seemingly aimless activity in and around New York, including a year at the Art Students League. In 1905 his father reluctantly agreed to finance the further development of his son's artistic career, in Europe. It was in Paris that Marin's work gradually shifted from views of architecture to architected views of flatness. There, line and stroke were gradually relieved of many of their descriptive duties and freed to create a more dynamic dialogue between what was observed and what was painted.

Marin's work from 1888 to 1905 was almost exclusively in watercolor, frequently of wooded landscape with a house in the middle ground. The simple massing of the house's rectangle respected the plane of the paper; the space is naturalistic but kept quite shallow. The transparent washes, simple massing, and blurred contours indicate some awareness of Impressionism (the rather timid American Impressionists, such as Childe Hassam, could be seen regularly at this time in the exhibitions of the Society of American Artists). At the end of the nineteenth century, Marin's work began to be suffused with the vapors of fin-de-siècle melancholy so prevalent in the expatriate Whistler's work and in the revived romanticism of Inness and Ryder.

Watercolor had already largely lost its stigma as a dilettante's medium of diversion and was beginning to become a major ingredient of American painting. The medium's directness and economy of means and ends, as well as its portability, openness (resistance to high finish), and relative freedom from tradition are characteristics often called American. The founding of the American Society of Painters in Water Colors (later called the American Water Color Society) in 1866 bestowed new legitimacy and visibility on the medium to which Homer would bring a lustrous new mastery after 1875. Homer's watercolors set the standard that Marin's work would be measured against. First Prendergast, then Marin, then Demuth, Sheeler, and Burchfield focused major attention on the freshness that was inherent in this medium previously regarded as minor. Cézanne's expertness in watercolor notwithstanding, and with the possible exception of Signac, Parisian painters continued in their preference for the weightiness of oil. In Germany in the first decade of the century, watercolor's spontaneity and directness became an important vehicle of the Die Brücke group's expressiveness, and the medium's transparency would entrance Klee from the century's second decade to his death. In the late forties and early fifties, such American artists as Brooks, Frankenthaler, and Louis would absorb many of the qualities of watercolor into painting on canvas ("stain" paintings, as they are frequently referred to, were for the most part created with newly developed water-based paint). John Marin would be credited with being America's major celebrant of watercolor in the twentieth century. He translated the medium into a specifically American language, but Paris would provide much of the grammar for his vocabulary.

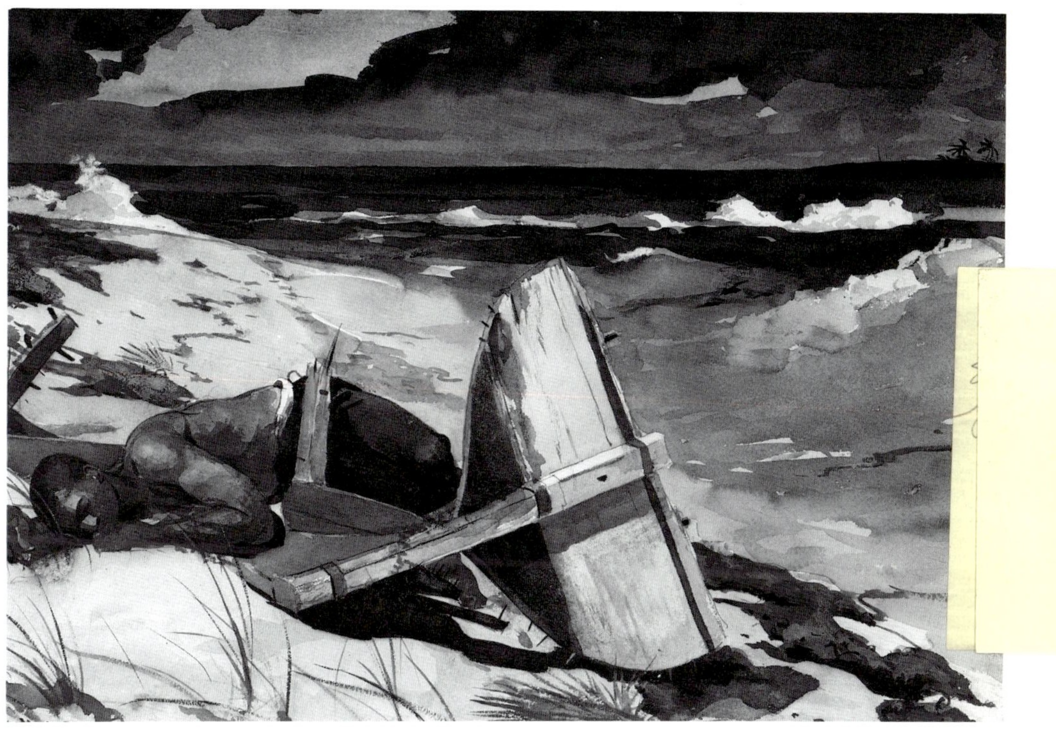

FIG. 2
WINSLOW HOMER
After the Tornado, 1899
Watercolor on paper. 14 15/16 x 21 3/8 in.
The Art Institute of Chicago

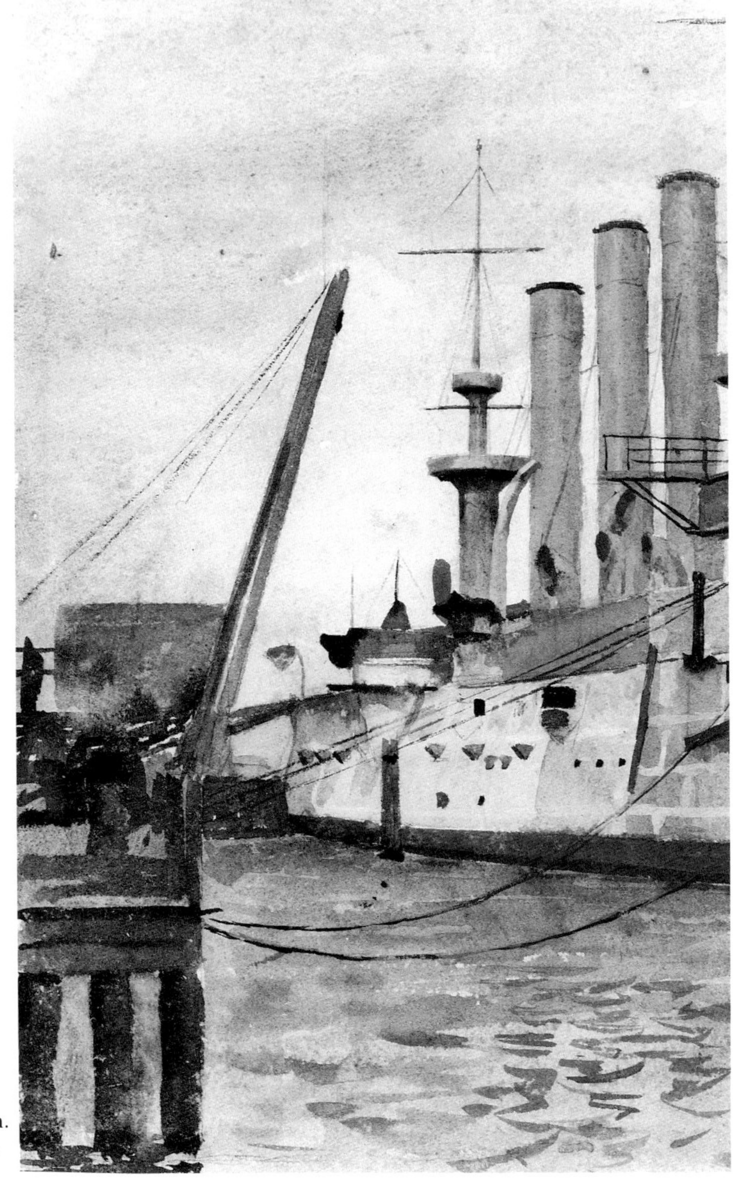

Fig. 3
THOMAS ANSHUTZ
Industrial Boat Scene, ca. 1895
Watercolor on paper. 13 x 8 in.
Courtesy Graham Gallery,
New York

(Opposite)
Fig. 4
JOHN MARIN
Country, France, 1908
Watercolor on paper. $13\frac{5}{8}$ x $12\frac{1}{2}$ in.
Courtesy Kennedy Galleries, Inc.,
New York

When Marin entered the Pennsylvania Academy in 1899, the students' allegiances were largely split between Sargent (and Boldini) and Whistler; the more progressive, including Marin, favored the latter. William Merritt Chase's personal flamboyance, wit, and energy, as well as the traditional (often eclectic) bravura of his painting, had already earned him the role as America's major teacher of painting. His strong emphasis on painterliness dominated the Academy. Chase's own work had by then relinquished some of the varnished flashiness of Munich to an Impressionist-derived lightness and brightness. Marin, however, was more strongly drawn to the simpler openness of Thomas Anshutz's painting and person. While best known as a teacher and a precursor of The Eight's Henri and Sloan, Anshutz created many marine watercolors after 1892 that, like his teaching, stressed the architecture of the plane. While he generally retained blended local colors, Anshutz also made some experiments with broken strokes and let some Impressionist light into his watercolors.

With the exception of Prendergast, no one in America in the 1890s had yet incorporated the radical techniques and compositions that were already firmly established on French canvases. By the mid-1870s, the Impressionists had depersonalized the unique mark of the brushstroke and atomized the tonally built, sculptural solidity of form, as well as most of the illusion of deep space. A flurry of often unblended short strokes coalesced into an overall membrane of rippling light and color that began to call ever more attention to the flatness of the canvas plane. Seurat and Signac, in the mid-1880s, regimented the variegated Impressionist strokes into a limpid architectural regularity and sought a scientific basis for the light that bristled across their canvases. Van Gogh retained the highly visible accumulation of unitary Neo-Impressionist strokes but lengthened them and propelled them into a new, organic intensity and density. Cézanne reverted to more sculptural form but achieved it with a transparent buildup of squat, overlapping strokes. His forms, at once awkward and momentous, expand and contract their profile and mass, now responding to the pressures of the canvas's flatness, now to the pressures of the observation of the subject. For all of them, choreographing the stroke to the scale and overall unity of the plane rather than to the depiction of the subject, and encouraging the stroke to reveal the mechanics of making rather than the expertise of the maker became paramount. The stage for twentieth-century modernism was set.

The daring brashness of the Fauves eulogized and extended the structural flatness of Cézanne, Van Gogh, and Seurat. Their polychromatic festivities inaugurated the new century and greeted Marin upon his arrival in Paris in 1905. He was not particularly eager to make their acquaintance; Whistler still held sway, and Marin's assimilation, first of Fauvism, then of Cubism, was slower than that of peers like Maurer and Weber. Ultimately, however, it would prove to be deeper and more convincing. The traditional commitment of American painting to a specificity of place would, around 1913, be fully integrated with a modernist painterliness unique to Marin and seldom matched until the late 1940s.

Whistler's radicalness resides in his extreme simplification rather than in the invention of new means. His tiny seascapes of the 1880s and 1890s are hovering haikus of water and atmosphere, but their blended, aerated strokes still look back to the seascapes he made at Courbet's side in 1865. Marins' early Parisian watercolors generally retain the subdued, near-monochrome atmospherics of Whistler; the very few oils he produced in Europe are even moodier in their mistiness. The etchings, too, are bathed in (ink) washes of picturesque, Whistlerian tones.

Marin's earliest confidence was in pure line. The lines of the etchings that were his primary preoccupation until 1910 (two-thirds of them would be done by

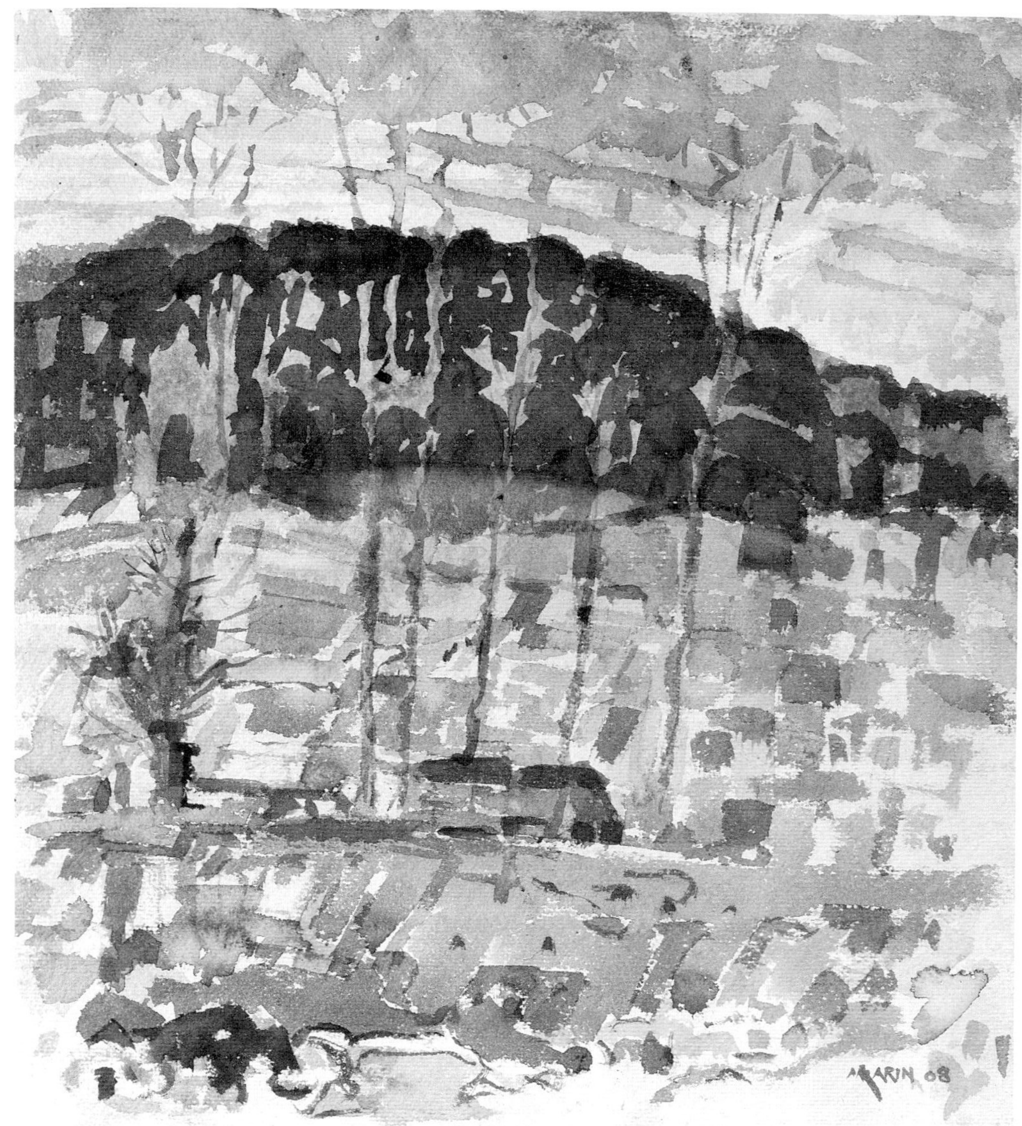

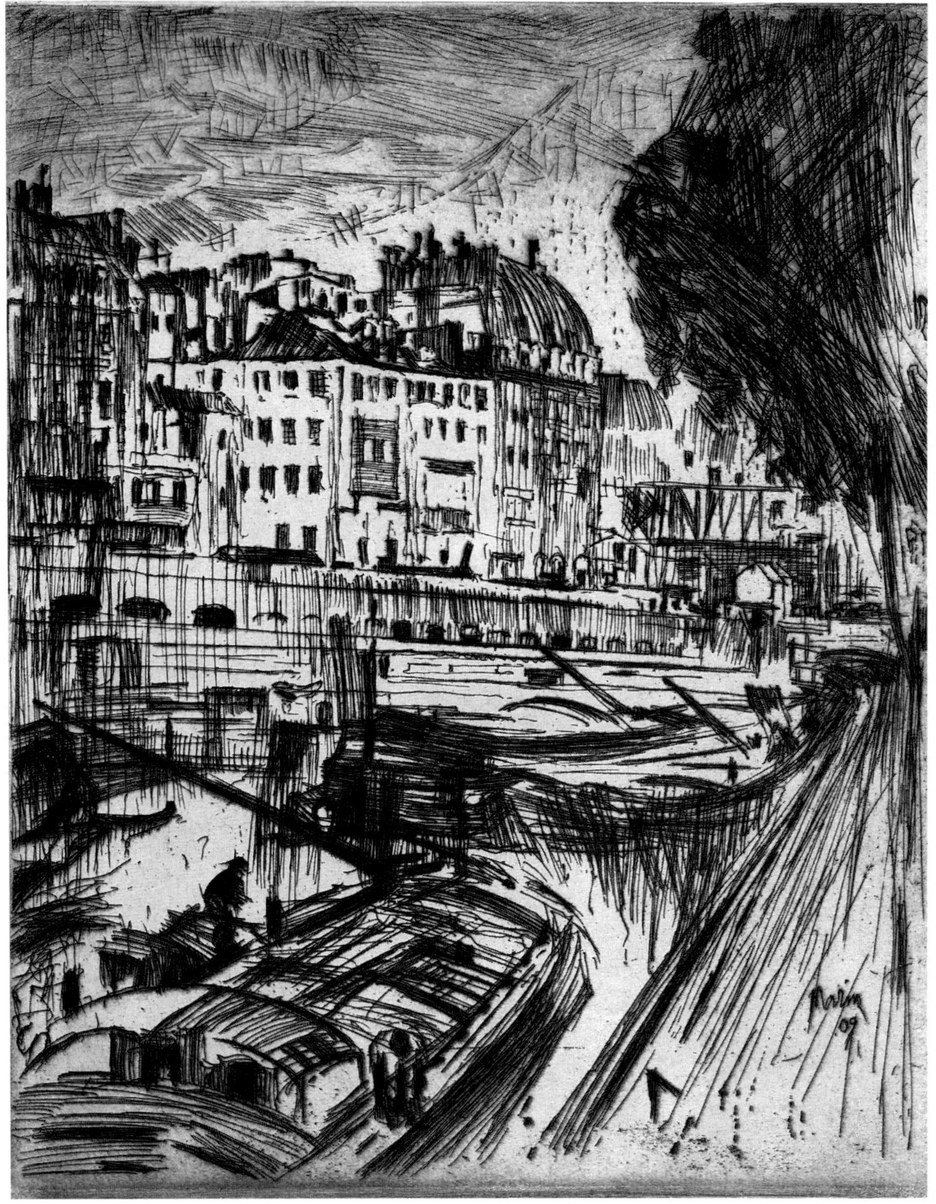

1913) move out of Whistlerian languor to acquire an indepedent energy of their own. The increasing spontaneity and variety of marks made directly on the plate slowly begin to subvert the conventional views of architecture that configure all of the etchings Marin did in Europe. In his drawings he encouraged his line to assume an even more assertive independence.

By 1908 Marin had begun to purge the picturesque with a bolder drive to structure the overall plane of the surface. The silvery wetness of the watercolors began to be more emphatically punctuated by brushstrokes, occasionally in broken tracks of tile-like marks that were similar to those in the pointillist-derived works the Fauves had done in 1904. The color remained tonal and muted, but Marin was taking greater advantage of the medium's transparency and beginning to exploit the paper's raw whiteness as a more active protagonist in composition. In watercolor, more than in the etching, he began to abbreviate landscape and city spontaneously—either into a simple, central massing or into a fusing horizontality. In sky and water (mostly the Seine), paint's liquidity was granted its own liberty.

The subdued, atmospheric space of these early watercolors is still beholden to Whistler, but the improvisatory simplifications, spontaneous strokes, and more holistically integrated composition surely owe a debt to the Fauves. The tracks of broken strokes give the most visible clue. Marin's early critics and biographers, however, had a tendency to compare him, often defensively and with considerable Francophobia, to Cézanne.[3] Marin himself occasionally compromised his feisty independence with defensiveness and claimed to have had no knowledge of Cézanne until he saw his 1911 exhibition at Stieglitz's gallery, 291.[4] Perhaps this was simply the protectionist hostility of the youthful underdog culture trying to compete with the Parisian Goliath.

The issue of Cézanne is perhaps more germane to the development of modernist criticism than to the development of Marin's style. For many, especially those who found the Cubism Cézanne partially inspired unpalatable, Cézanne would remain *the* Artist of Europe. His conjunction of stroke and form internally scaled to the actual size and plane of the canvas, and his radical incorporation of bare canvas or paper, should certainly have had an impact on Marin in Paris. And credulity is further strained at the claim that Marin could have missed seeing Cézanne's posthumous retrospective at the 1907 Salon d'Automne in which he himself was represented. Nevertheless, Cézanne's dense and deliberate construction (and deconstruction) of massive form was alien to the lyric intuitiveness of Marin's intentions. He would have been more inclined to the looser and smoother optical flow attained by Matisse. Matisse, who seldom stopped praising Cézanne, might well have passed his lessons, as well as those of Signac's Neo-Impressionism, on to Marin. Indeed, the tenets of Matisse and the Fauves became increasingly visible in Marin's work through 1914, and together with his equally belated but unique assimilation of Cubism they would mark much of Marin's painting throughout his maturity.

Marin's wry self-effacement would have one believe that he was more preoccupied with billiards than with the paintings of his peers; but even if he never set foot in Gertrude Stein's rue de Fleurus salon, Matisse and the Fauves were still unavoidable. They were the talk and the sight of Paris from 1905 to 1907, when the group broke up and Cubism began to move to the fore. Marin's friend from the Pennsylvania Academy, Arthur B. Carles, arrived in Paris in 1907, and Carles made the introduction to Steichen that led to Marin's joining the New Society of American Artists there. Many of the group's members, including Carles, were Fauve devotees. Max Weber was partially responsible for prevailing upon Matisse to open a school, in 1908; among others, Alfred Maurer attended the classes and

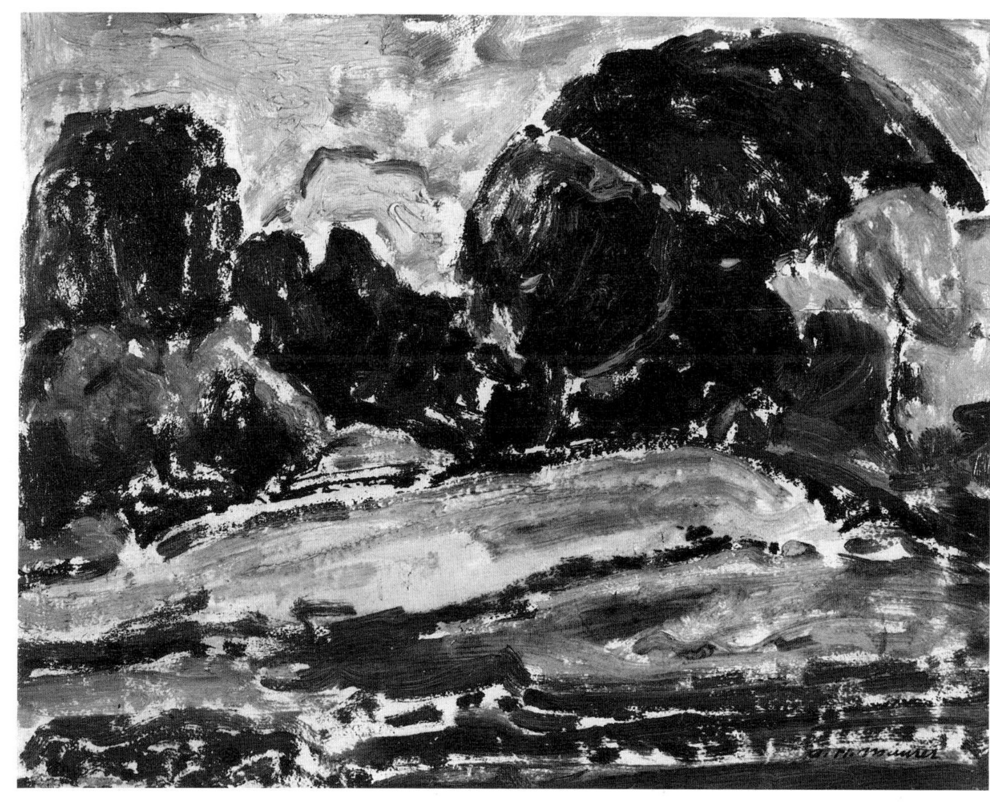

FIG. 6
ALFRED H. MAURER
Landscape with Trees, ca. 1908
Oil on canvas. 31⅞ x 24⅜ in.
University Art Museum,
University of Minnesota, Minneapolis
Gift of Ione and Hudson Walker

(Opposite)
FIG. 5
JOHN MARIN
Quay, Seine, Paris, 1909
Etching, 9¾ x 7¾ in.
The Metropolitan Museum of Art, New York
The Alfred Steiglitz Collection, 1949

quickly became one of Matisse's most avid disciples. Steichen would be responsible for introducing Marin, and Matisse as well, to America.

In 1908 The Little Galleries of the Photo-Secession at 291 Fifth Avenue in New York, which Steichen and Stieglitz had opened together in 1905 to promote the art of photography, became simply 291. The resident proprietor's controversial fame as a photographer would now be joined and often overshadowed by the fame (and scorn) he earned as America's first and foremost impresario of modernism. The names of the American artists—Marin, O'Keeffe, Demuth, Dove, and to a lesser extent Hartley—who were gradually to replace the Europeans at Stieglitz's various galleries are to this day seldom mentioned without the accompaniment of his name. More savant than dealer, part Buddha, part Bergson, part Barnum, Stieglitz was a major force in American culture's real entry into the twentieth century. At first Steichen taught Stieglitz, and Stieglitz taught the world; but then the pupil overtook the teacher and himself became the gospel. Under its new name and the advice of Steichen, the gallery introduced first Rodin (watercolors) and then Matisse to an incredulous America. In March of 1909, for the gallery's first presentation, Steichen chose to present two of the Americans working in Paris, Alfred Maurer and John Marin.

The oil sketches Maurer showed in 1909 already evinced his every effort to let pure color and form clear away the muted Whistlerian tones of his earlier work. His broad simplifications, strong color, and raw strokes still retained more vestiges of representational space and modeling than the paintings of the Fauves, but his landscapes looked—and were derisively greeted—like the work of an American wild man, compared with the tamer watercolors that Marin exhibited. The nuanced atmosphere of Marin's watercolors, still visibly influenced by Whistler, drew more favor, not only from Steichen, but from the critics as well. The energetic buildup of strokes into simple configurations and the increasingly visible dynamics of watercolor's wet-on-wet transparencies already declared Marin's mastery of his chosen medium, but not yet the full independence of his intentions.

When Stieglitz met Marin in Paris for the first time later in 1909, he preferred the bolder, more abbreviated works, and these were shown in Marin's first one-person exhibition at 291 in 1910. Marin's relationship with Stieglitz became one of total trust—a trust that was for the most part justified. Until his death, Stieglitz would be in virtual control of Marin's career; he was permitted to choose whatever Marin work he wanted not only for himself, but also for Marin's personal reserve. Stieglitz was not a man in search of financial gain; any doubts about his ethics were more than dispelled by the vastness of the bequest of his collection, upon his death, to five American museums.

A second Matisse show succeeded Marin's 1910 exhibition and was followed by a group exhibition ("Younger American Painters in Paris") drawn from the New Society of American Artists (including Carles, Marin, Maurer, Steichen, and Weber). Stieglitz added Hartley and included Dove, who was exhibiting for the first time anywhere. The circle awaited the arrival of Demuth and O'Keeffe to be complete. Weber briefly became a powerful influence on Stieglitz and displaced some of Steichen's more conservative influence, but Weber's intractable ego would shortly precipitate his fall from Stieglitz's grace. By 1914 the growing rift partially caused by Steichen's antipathy to the increasing influence of Cubism and Picasso would leave Stieglitz happily alone in the center of 291's circle.

Marin interrupted his European sojourn to return to America in 1909 and stayed through part of 1910; he moved back permanently later that year. His 1911 exhibition included the last works he had produced in Europe and the first new ones done in America; both series were

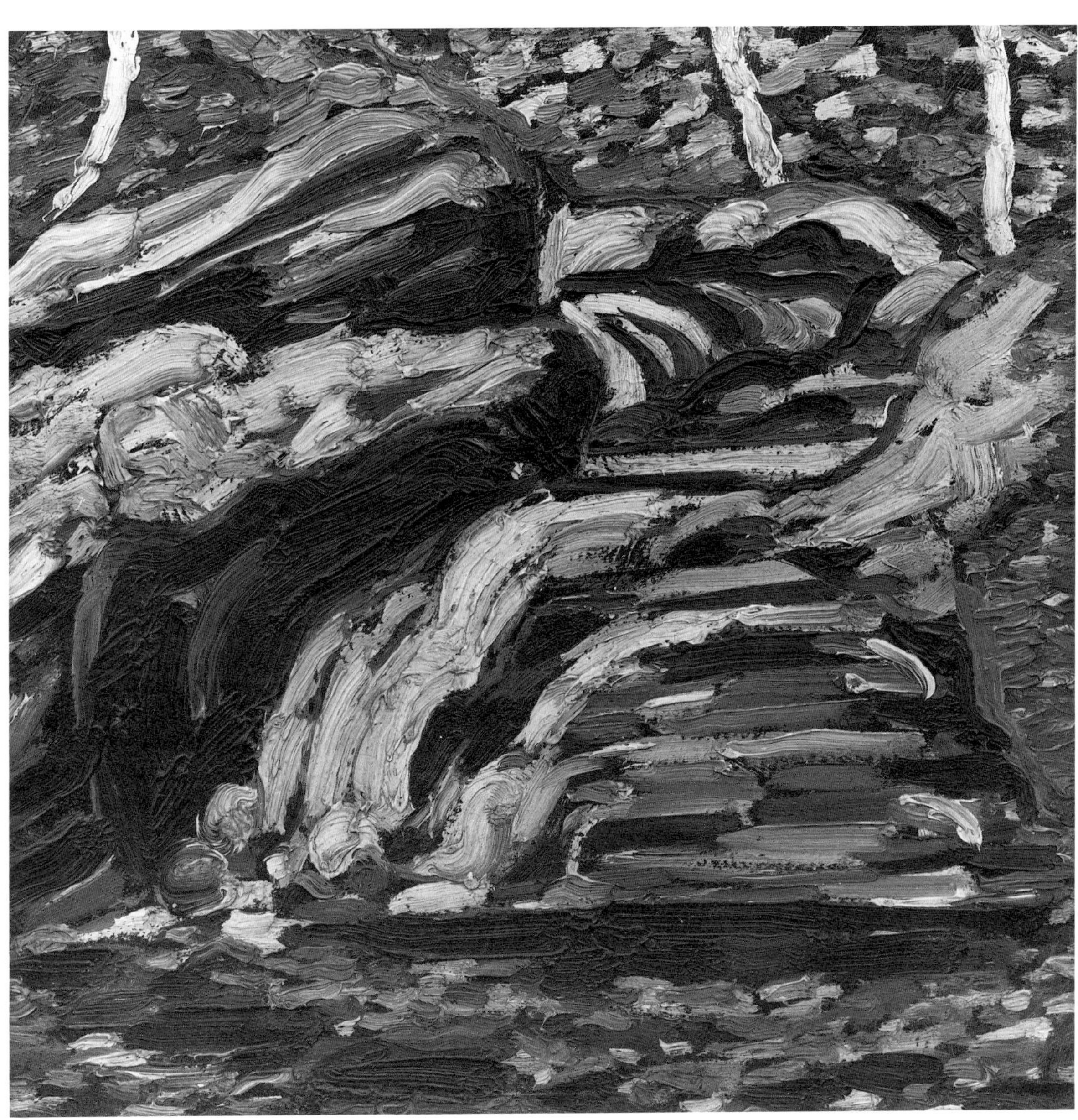

Fig. 7
MARSDEN HARTLEY
Waterfall, 1909
Oil on academy board. 12 x 12 in.
University Art Museum,
University of Minnesota, Minneapolis
Bequest of Hudson Walker from the Ione and
Hudson Walker Collection

Fig. 8
JOHN MARIN
Austrian Tyrol, 1910
Watercolor on paper. 18½ x 15½ in.
The Art Institute of Chicago,
The Alfred Stieglitz Collection

charged with a limber expansiveness and economy of means that accompanied watercolor's ascendance as Marin's major medium. New openness joined with new subjects. The downtown of the ever-newer New York and the Brooklyn Bridge replaced Paris, Venice, Rouen, and various French villages. Broader cubic masses, all but free of descriptive detail and modeling, blended liquidly and were held in firmer tension with and on the plane of the paper.

Generous massing characterized Marin's European watercolors as well. The mountains of the Austrian Tyrol replaced the more restricted urban and rural views he had previously preferred. But the watercolors look more Chinese than Austrian. Variety of strokes coupled with an extreme economy of means (so rare in American painting at the time); the virtual renunciation of rendered representational space in favor of a seamless, painterly blend of near and far and high and low perspectives; rhythmic clarity; and the fluid, atmospheric lushness that now more boldly incorporated blank paper as space—all are characteristics the Tyrolean watercolors share with many of the monochrome ink paintings that started to evolve as early as the ninth century in China and continued to develop there, and then in Japan, for some ten centuries. Marin's deep love of nature combined with his growing awareness that painting was not nature and nature was not painting, an understanding that from the outset had been taken for granted by the Chinese; they had always been oblivious to the penchant for representational "truthfulness" that for so long had obsessed the West.

Marin's Orientalism was emphatic at various times in his career, and it did not go unnoticed. Yet the result of any attempt to document his specific knowledge of or influence by Oriental painting must remain, for the moment, at least, as elliptical as his works themselves. The flat, radically cropped compositions and simplifications of form typical of the Japanese woodblock

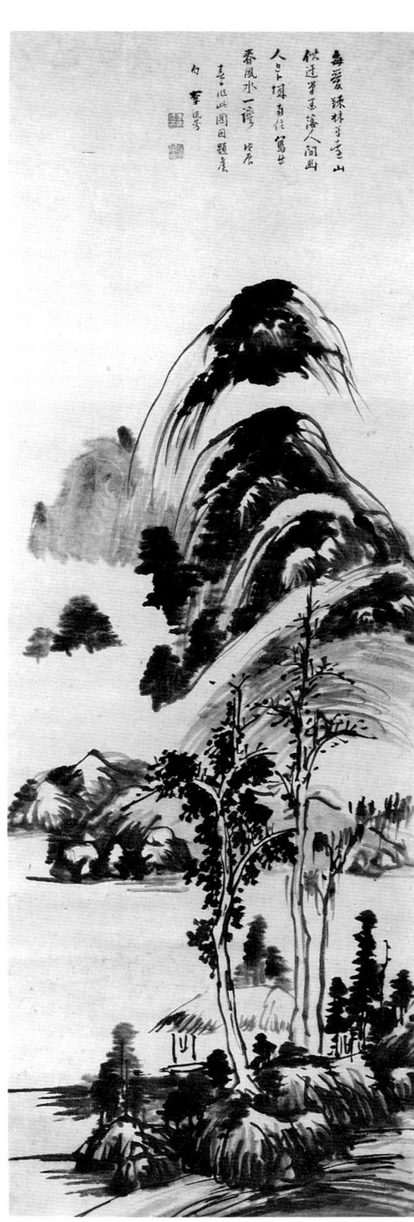

Fig. 9
LI LIU-FANG
Thin Forests and Distant Mountains, 1628
Ink on paper. 45 x 15⅞ in.
The Cleveland Museum of Art,
Purchase, John L. Severance Fund

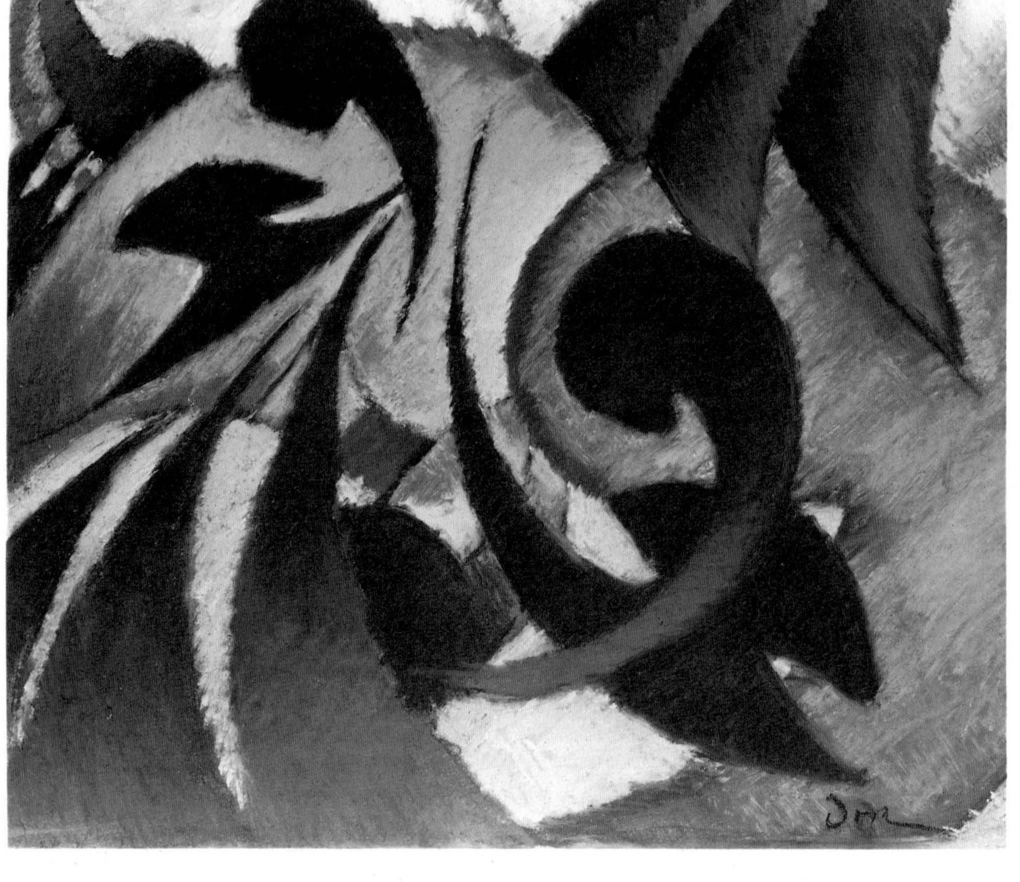

Fig. 10
ARTHUR DOVE
Nature Symbolized, No. 2, 1914
Pastel on paper. 17⅞ x 21½ in.
The Art Institute of Chicago,
The Alfred Stieglitz Collection

prints that were so important to the Impressionists and to artists like Van Gogh were also much admired by Marin,[5] but their relatively unmodulated surfaces bear little resemblance to his variegated strokes—nor do the generally more homogeneous atmospheric fusions of Whistler's hyperaestheticized Japonaisme. Some, but not all, of the similarities to Chinese painting may be accounted for by the closeness of brushed ink to watercolor and by the obvious affinities of modernism with the abstractness of Oriental painting and its conscious pleasure in the procedures of painting.

Marin quite likely saw Chinese painting in Paris and/or in New York. Max Weber, although himself more drawn to African tribal art, may well have encouraged Marin to look at Oriental painting, as he had encouraged Stieglitz to do in Paris in 1909. Weber had been a student of Arthur Dow, who, as a disciple of America's foremost Orientalist, Ernest Fenellosa,[6] avidly professed the merging of East and West. The Metropolitan Museum in New York already had an impressive collection of Chinese painting that ranged from the Sung Dynasty (960–1280) through the eighteenth century.[7] Marin's friend Marsden Hartley, who was one of the most perceptive enthusiasts of his watercolors, claimed for Marin "the same sense of surety of observation and of surety of brush stroke" as the Sung painters.[8] More specific is a conversation quoted by Marin's most opinionated biographer, MacKinley Helm, that briefly documents Marin's awareness of Sung painting.[9] And some of the serendipity of Marin's wetness must be attributed to the Orient. When Cubism, the ocean, and the medium of oil joined the forces of Whistler, the Fauves, Oriental painting, New York City, and the mountains, Marin's vocabulary would be complete.

If his native reticence and his preoccupation with etching had permitted him to stay on the periphery in Paris, Marin's membership in the Stieglitz circle catapulted him into the middle of American modernism and

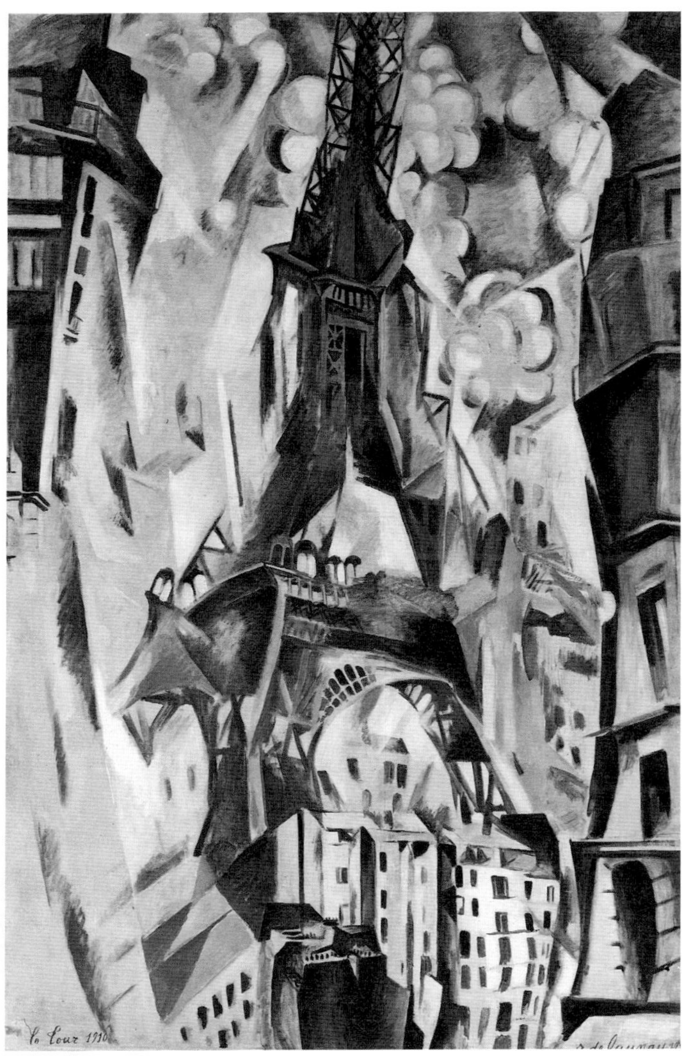

Fig. 11
ROBERT DELAUNAY
Eiffel Tower, 1910
Oil on canvas. 79½ x 54 in.
Solomon R. Guggenheim Museum, New York

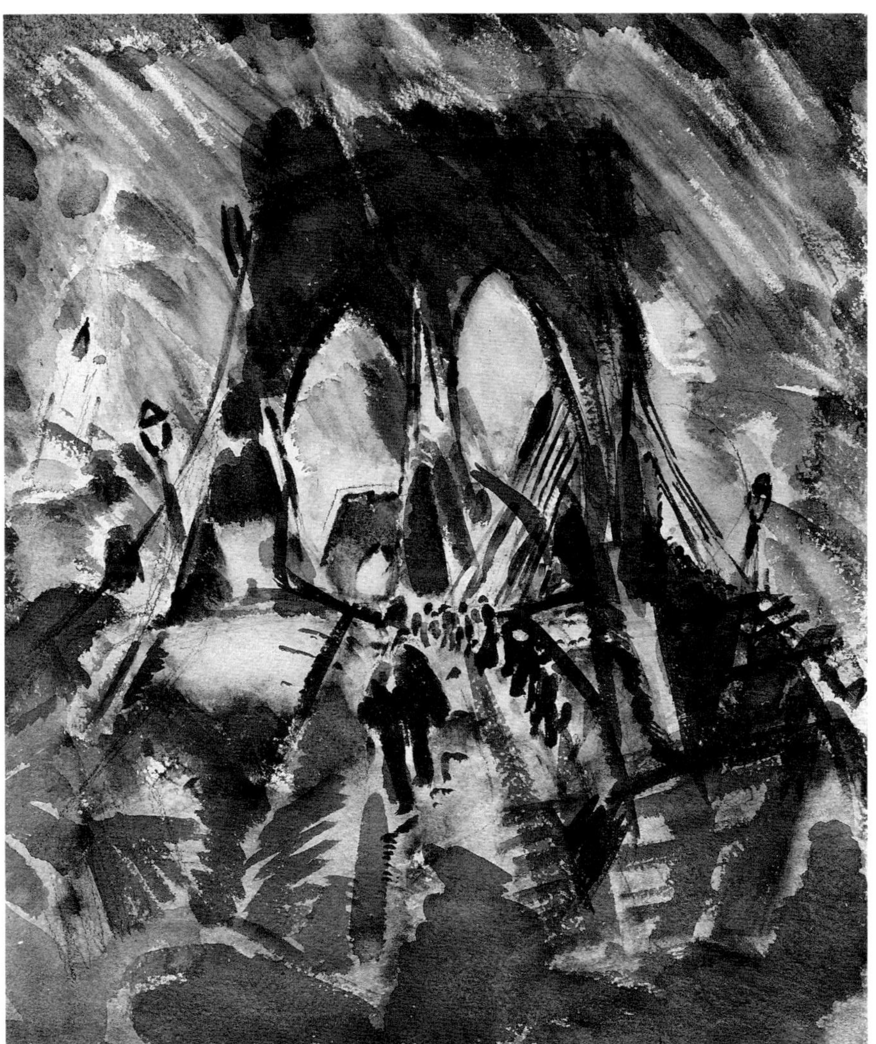

Fig. 12
JOHN MARIN
Brooklyn Bridge, ca. 1912
Watercolor on paper. 18½ x 15½ in.
The Metropolitan Museum of Art, New York
The Alfred Stieglitz Collection, 1949

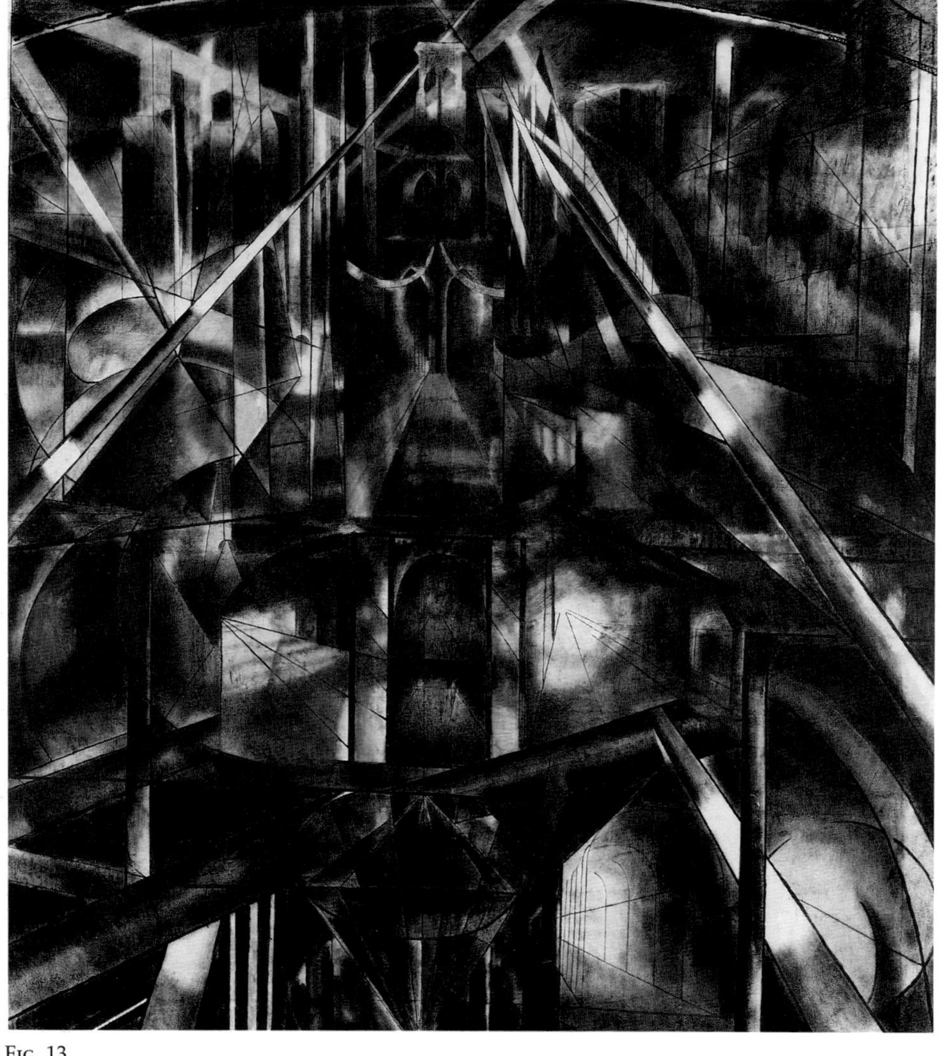

Fig. 13
JOSEPH STELLA
Brooklyn Bridge, 1917–18
Oil on canvas. 84 x 76 in.
Yale University Art Gallery,
Gift of Collection Société Anonyme

most likely made him more responsive to the revolutionary works of his peers. By 1911, Cézanne and Cubism were part of a common international language, not only in France, but in America, Italy, England, and Russia. Concurrently with Kandinsky in Europe, Arthur Dove had already given America its first abstract painting. Weber, back in New York since 1909, was chanting (and painting) the praises of Picasso's proto-Cubism. Hartley was painting Cézannesque still lifes (shown at 291 in 1912) and proto-Cubist landscapes—the former influenced by magazine illustrations of Cézanne's paintings, and the latter by Weber. Stieglitz followed Marin's 1911 exhibition at 291 first with Cézanne watercolors, and then with watercolors and drawings by Picasso.

A jubilation of strokes activates Marin's 1912 watercolors of the Brooklyn Bridge and the Woolworth Building. Charged diagonals break the contours of the architecture and orchestrate the surface with dashing syncopation. The strokes are now totally scaled to the paper; they do not describe, but paraphrase with paint. The planar fusing, the rhythm on the bias, and the centralized configuration are strongly reminiscent of Robert Delaunay's *Eiffel Tower* paintings begun in 1910. Delaunay, together with a number of other Cubists, exhibited in the 1910 Salon des Indépendants, but there is little evidence that Marin saw his paintings (unless in magazine illustrations). As always, Marin's works are openly propelled by intuition: Delaunay's diagonals are more programmatically directed, his planes more precise in their linearity. More likely, Cézanne's watercolors and the variety of Cubist painting visible in New York as well·as the increasing exhilaration of the actual cubistic masses now sculpting the city's skyline joined with each other to catalyze Marin's liquid dynamism.

Marin saw "great forces at work";[10] his desire to express the reaction of these "pull forces" and the "influences of one on another"[11] sounds much like the Futurist Manifesto's exhortation toward a new urban/

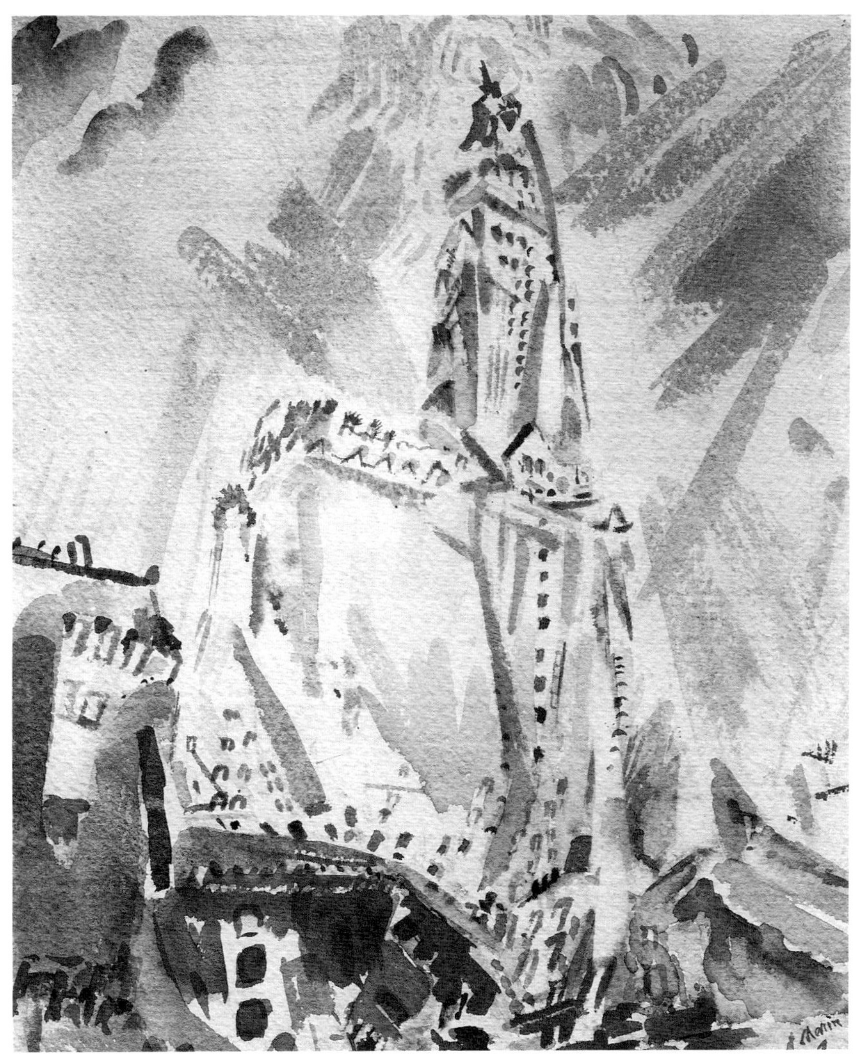

FIG. 14
JOHN MARIN
Woolworth Building, No. 31, 1912
Watercolor on paper. 18 11/16 x 15 11/16 in.
National Gallery of Art, Washington, D.C.,
Gift of Eugene and Agnes E. Meyer

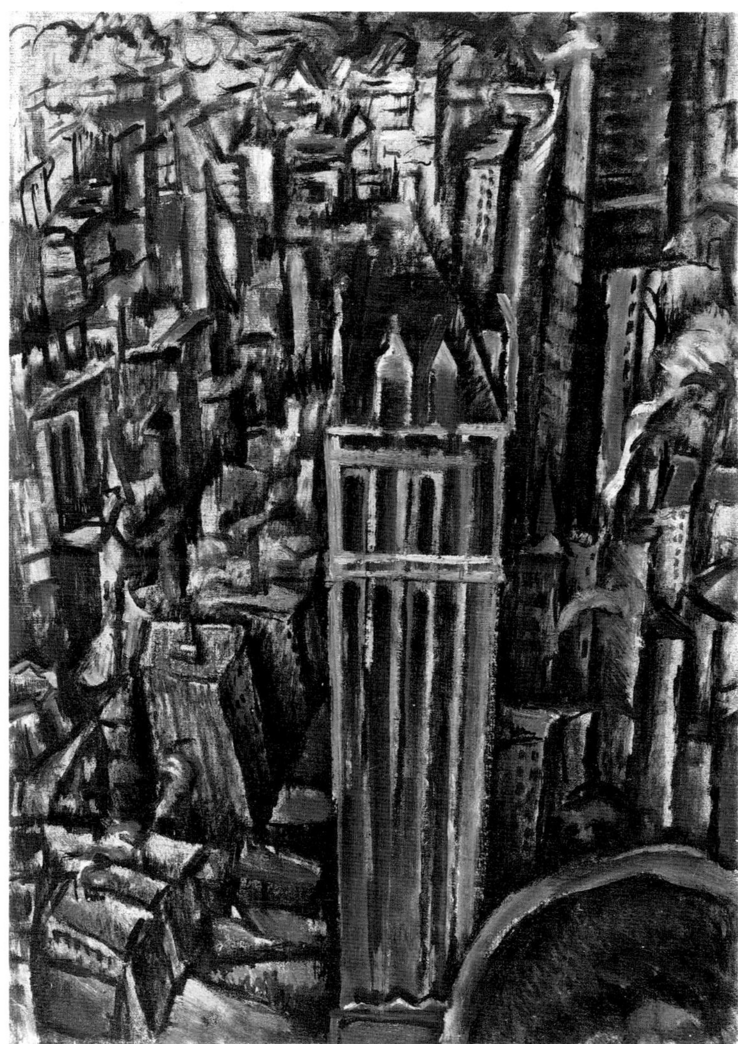

FIG. 15
MAX WEBER
The Woolworth Building, 1912
Oil on canvas. 18 x 12¾ in.
Museum of Fine Arts, Boston
Gift from the Stephen and Sybil Stone Foundation

industrial art but is free of Marinetti's political haranguing.[12] (Marin's familiarity with anything other than Futurist words in 1912 is not likely, since they themselves were just beginning to develop their Cubist-derived vocabulary.)

The impact of Marin's subject matter—whether it was the forces of nature or the forces of the city—upon the mode of making the painting would henceforth be visible. When paint was engaged with the clashing, inorganic angles of New York City, Cubism would predominate. The Woolworth Building's fifty-five stories now exceeded the Eiffel Tower and inaugurated the perpetual round of challenge and crisis that would make New York, and not Paris, the city of the century. By 1928 the skyscraper race had given downtown Manhattan the profile it would largely retain until the building of the World Trade Center in the 1970s. In urban architecture, if not in painting and sculpture, New York was already the leader, and Marin would remain one of its most able chroniclers for the rest of his life. His New York has more vitality than the slightly later, more hieratically decorative representations done by Joseph Stella during his brief Futurist phase. Only the clenched vectors of Max Weber's 1915 Futurist-inspired paintings, such as *Rush Hour,* can match the energy of Marin's maelstrom of strokes.

When they were seen in his 1913 exhibition, Marin's New York watercolors caused a sensation and dismayed his more conservative admirers—as well as Cass Gilbert, the architect of the Woolworth Building, who recoiled at the summary modernization and deletion of all the Gothic detailing inflicted upon his cathedral of commerce. Both Marin's exhibition and the dedication of the Woolworth Building, however, were upstaged by the Armory Show that year. On a grand scale, it consolidated the more private efforts of Stieglitz, who was named an honorary vice president of the exhibition. What the members of the New Society of American Artists in Paris had seen in France was now presented to the American public: Cézanne, Van Gogh, Gauguin, and Matisse were all represented in depth. The Stieglitz circle, except for Dove and Weber, was prominent among the American exhibitors; Marin showed four of his Woolworth Building watercolors. The French Cubists and, to a lesser degree, their American compatriots caused the greatest scandal; Duchamp's *Nude Descending a Staircase* (1912) was the major celebrity. Teddy Roosevelt summed up much of the public's disbelief when he compared the show to P. T. Barnum's fake mermaid. Nonetheless, modernism was now officially established on American soil. Six new galleries opened within two years of the Armory Show, and collectors like Albert Barnes, John Quinn, Agnes Ernst Meyer, and Walter Arensberg helped cushion the coffers of dealers and artists. Even so, Marin was one of the few artists who could actually achieve some material comfort in this new climate. With the exception of a strong backlash in the thirties, Cubism would now dominate much of American art until the late forties and the advent of Abstract Expressionism.

The painterliness that had motivated modernism from the late nineteenth century through the time of the Fauves was now superseded by the tonal, linear planarity of Cubism. Yet it was Cubism's disjunction and increased insistence on the flatness of the canvas that fully liberated Marin's painterliness and permitted him to incorporate its tenets into his brilliant, liquid architecture of the plane. His ability to disperse opticality spontaneously within a Cubist framework accounts for much of his success. Marin was both restless and confident; he moved freely and mostly convincingly from near-representation to near-abstraction and back again, now suppressing Cubism beneath the surface altogether, now turning it into Oriental colophons, now respecting its preference for layering thin, rectangular planes. For many of his peers, Cubism was but a short-lived experiment; for Marin, it was a lifelong partnership. He was forty-three in 1913; his work was beginning to justify and exonerate his slow development.

In 1912 Marin married Marie Jane Hughes, whom he had left waiting while he was in Europe; she has been characterized mainly as kind and caring. Now he settled into the protective pattern that would regulate much of the rest of his life: the warm months spent in the New England countryside, and the cold months near, and occasionally in, New York City. After 1914, Maine became a major part of his life and work. By 1933 he owned homes both in Cliffside, New Jersey, and on Cape Split, in Addison, Maine.

The summer and fall of 1913 were spent in Castorland, New York. Here Cubism and the city were left behind, and the brighter palette that had begun to push through the landscape washes of the previous year was keyed into a Fauvist fanfare. Accompanying the many watercolors, and dependent upon them in their thinness and transparency of paint application as well as their openness and visibly speedy variety of stroke, were some eight paintings in oil. These were not Marin's first efforts in oil, but they were his most sustained attempts to date. The earliest known painting was made in 1901, and only a handful are known to have been painted prior to 1913 (two of them from 1912).

The configuration of these paintings—shallow foreground topped with a wall of foliage and tree forms spreading across most of the canvas—and the frequent dominance of intense primary hues are closely related to the landscapes Matisse painted in 1904–1905. Matisse's brushing of paint is slower and physically denser; his strokes relinquish some of their individual identity as they coagulate on the surface, except where he retained the residual tracks of Neo-Impressionist strokes that had once been but were now no longer visible in Marin's work. The sketchy calligraphy of Marin's strokes is more insistent upon retaining the shape, direction, and velocity of each mark. His bold incorporation of bare canvas, appropriated from his watercolors via the Fauves, breathes light and lightness into the paint. Matisse's unparalleled mastery of color and complexly simple, two-dimensional design hold his surfaces in buoyant tension; Marin's surfaces are set in motion with the vitality and diversity of mark making.

In spite of their energized clarity of structure, the Castorland paintings fall short of the melodic vibrancy of the watercolors. Oil on canvas does not soak and flow with the same fluid ease as watercolor on paper. Canvas gives the brush more resistance than paper; even thinned-down oil is denser than watercolor. Marin's understanding of the need for lightness of touch—his refusal to bruise and muddy the paper's fragile surface—is a major component of the success of his watercolors. Oil and canvas mandate more muscle, more building; only after pushing oil into viscous thickness would Marin also be able to build with thinness.

In 1914 Marin went to Maine for the first time. That year his only child, John, Jr., was born, and he began to enjoy the success that would turn into stardom in his old age. Maine introduced him to the grandness of the ocean, but his brush was not yet ready to assimilate its motions. For the moment wooded landscape still predominated. In one of the few oils probably done in this year (an 8″ x 10″ undated landscape on canvas board), Marin began more consciously to occupy himself with oil's opacity. The paint is still thinned, but the drag of the brush against the weave of the canvas becomes more viscerally visual. Broad, bristle-striated strokes cursorily define and give generous scale to the craggy coastline. The wet paint is drawn into and through to the white canvas below (probably with the tip of the brush handle). This drawing by removing paint activates clouds and punctuates the contours of pine trees and would not be possible in watercolor. Marin was painting almost exclusively outdoors; he painted quickly, fre-

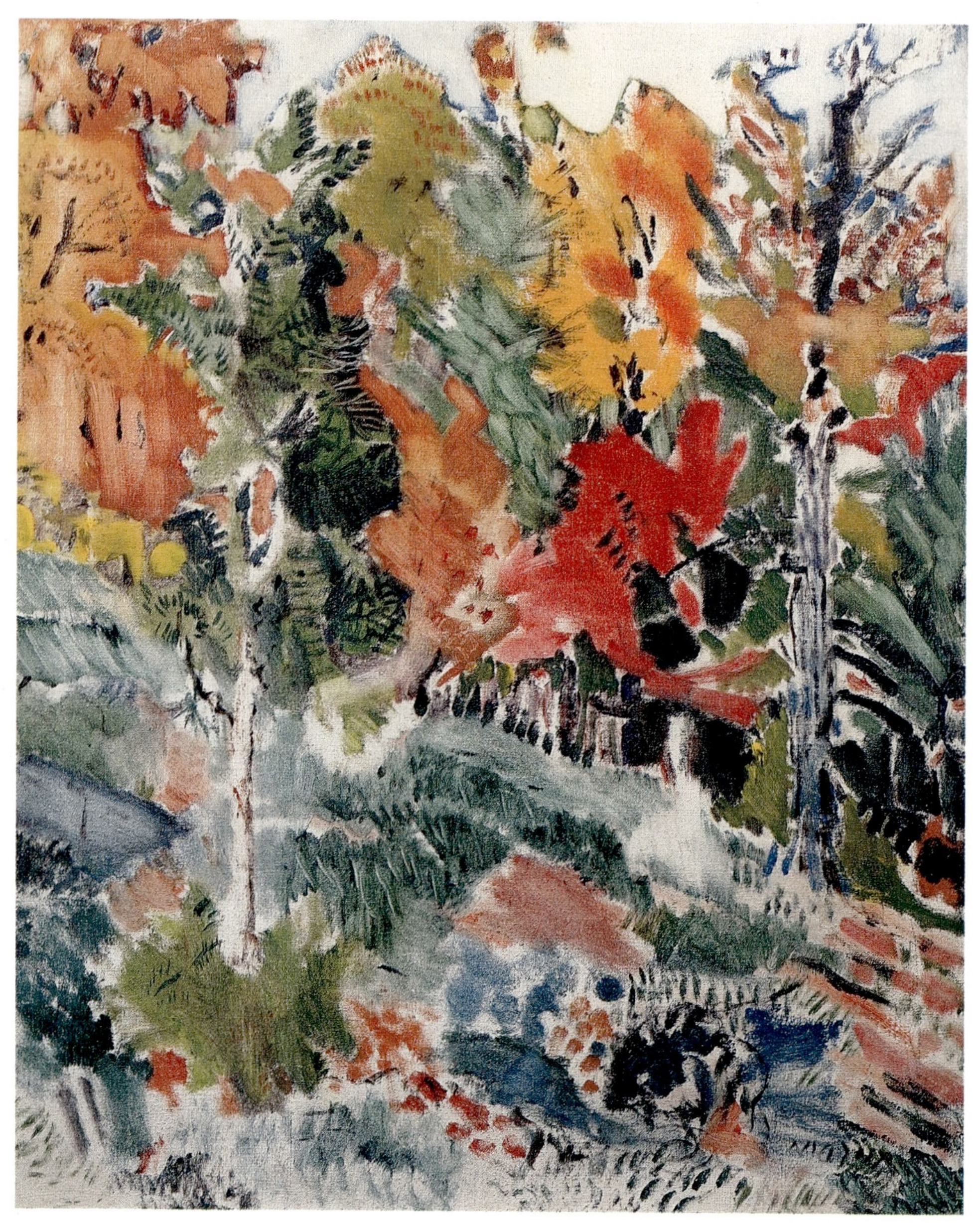

Fig. 16
JOHN MARIN
Autumn, Castorland, 1913
Oil on canvas. 28¼ x 22 in.
Collection Mr. and Mrs. Irving
Moskovitz, New York

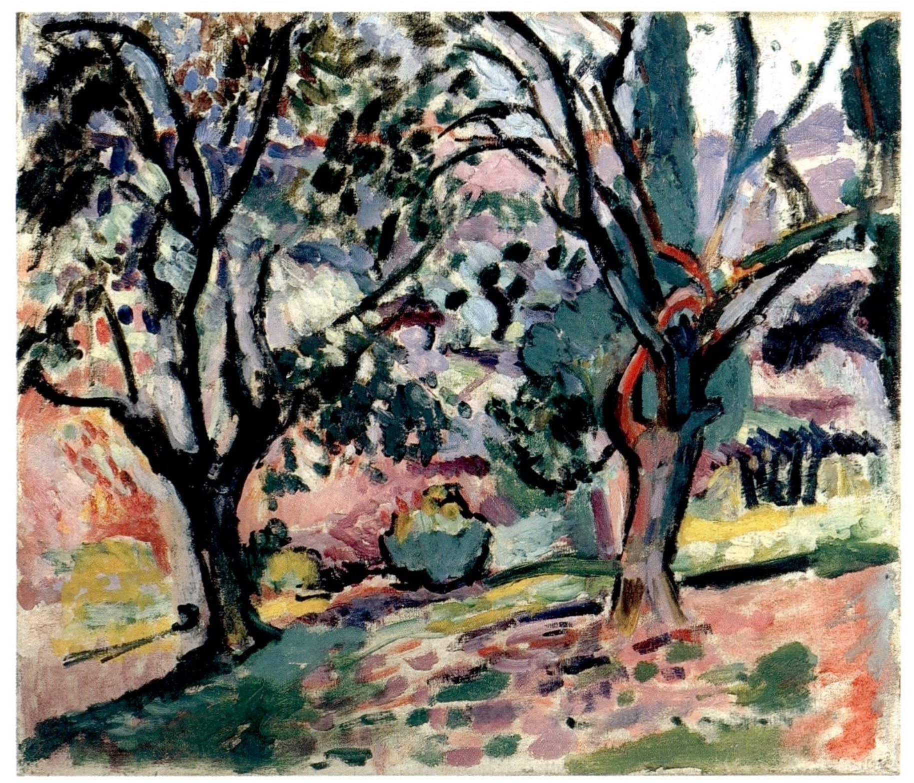

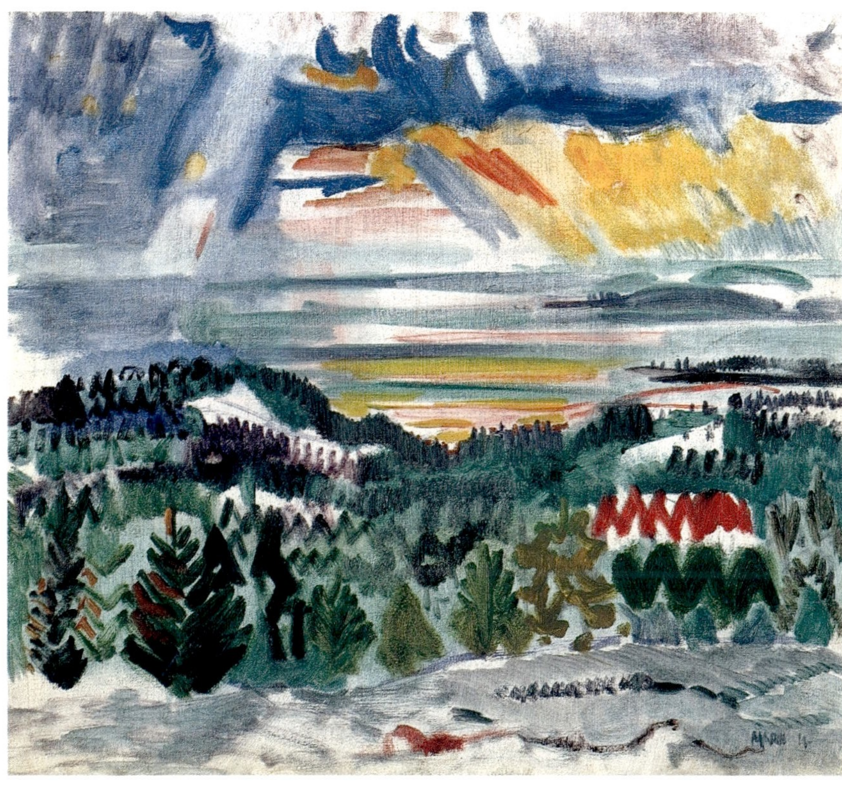

FIG. 17
HENRI MATISSE
Promenade among the Olive Trees, 1905
Oil on canvas. 17½ x 21¾ in.
The Metropolitan Museum of Art, New York,
Robert Lehman Collection, 1975

FIG. 17a
JOHN MARIN
Landscape, 1914
Oil on canvas. 22 x 25 in.
Private collection, New York

quently employing both hands.[13] He favored improvisation in collaboration with his materials but shunned self-indulgence: the wholeness of the painting and the nature of the subject almost always guided his hands. Through the twenties, a breathless joy in what and how he was painting pervades his work.

Another oil done in 1914 (a dated landscape, 22" x 25") contains calligraphic abbreviations that are similar to those that punctuate many of the watercolors of the next several years. Pine trees become zigzagged triangles; the sun's rays become parallel, diagonal, stroked lines that turn into horizontals when reflected on the water. The loose systematization of this linear shorthand resembled the written landscapes that began to appear in Chinese painting during the Yuan Dynasty (1271–1368). A similarly hectic and even more emphatic calligraphy would resurface in the late forties to play a major role in the final phase of Marin's development.

Marin's work, like that of so many of America's first modernists, was often prone to restlessness, but, like the paintings of Hartley and Dove, it seldom seemed eclectic. In 1915, his brush moved from specifically recognizable representations of the Maine coastline to a bracing economy and openness that verged on flat abstraction. And indeed abstraction was much in the air. Dove had been exhibiting with Stieglitz since 1912. Hartley returned to America in the winter of 1915 and soon thereafter showed his near-abstractly patterned *Military* paintings (1914–1915). Hartley's German sojourn had brought him in contact with Kandinsky and the Blaue Reiter group; their lessons were merged with his still-prevalent enthusiasm for Cézanne as well as his interest in Parisian Cubism. Kandinsky had been represented in the Armory Show by an abstract *Improvisation* (#27, 1912), which Stieglitz had purchased. By nature Stieglitz was more partial than Marin to Kandinsky's spiritualism, but the spontaneity of Kandinsky's nature-derived abstractions and the comparisons he made in his writing between music and painting are closely related to Marin's own concerns. The programmatic, conceptual restraints of the Synchronists Stanton Macdonald-Wright and Morgan Russell are far less likely to have elicited Marin's sympathy. Surviving evidence of Marin's opinions about Dove, Hartley, Kandinsky, and other peers is more than rare, nor is it easy to pin down specific influences. Nonetheless, the tendency of contemporary critics like Henry McBride and Charles Caffin to credit him with a wholly self-induced development invites skepticism.

Much of what does make Marin unique is his liberation of the individual strokes and their visible mediation between the observed subject and the flatness of the canvas plane. Dove's short, buzzing strokes and Kandinsky's more thinly painted and modulated swaths are subjugated to the forms they describe. Throughout their shifts from Ryder-inspired romanticism to Cézannesque constructiveness, Hartley's marks remain crustily sculptural. Marin's strokes proceed to revel in indecision as readily as in rhythm, and they simultaneously subvert and celebrate the configuration of the subject.

"Did you ever start to start and keep it up until some time to you there came the time when you didn't just start to start but started? The starts to start to start are the real ones though...."[14] Starts, false starts, doubts, and deliberations are all part of the evidence of the momentum of making that Marin deployed across the plane of the support. The equilibrium of the whole that he sought was based not on any preconceived pattern of finality, but on the balancing of flux. At times the conspiracy visually evident between Marin and his materials all but overpowered the forces of the subject being painted. Many of the more abstract watercolors done in the mid-teens are almost pure flights of paint. This is true too of the startling physicality that pulses through the majority of the some one hundred oil paintings that comprise the *Weehawken Sequence* executed around 1916.

With very little warning and almost no precedent, Marin suddenly pulled all the stops in oil painting's repertoire. The traces in oil of watercolor's washed transparency were here banished; the density, viscosity, and opacity of oil's own artillery were now deployed in serious play. The paint was hurled and hurried onto small panels (around 9″ x 12″). The finger-snapping speed was at least partially induced by the cold weather and the need to avoid numbness. All seem to have been started and stopped, outdoors, in late fall and/or early winter. The season accounts for the dominance of dark, wet earth tones and cold gray-blue, highlighted with orange. Painted from the Jersey side of the Hudson, some look across to Manhattan, some to the Weehawken warehouses, some to sparsely wooded nature. They range from minimally massed, vast vistas to dense, horizonless flatness. Except for the monogrammed squiggle of a bare tree or two, many are virtually abstract.

While watercolor soaks into and becomes one with the paper support, oil forms a filmy skin on top of the canvas support. The gummy elasticity of oil as it is pulled, scrubbed, and scumbled across the surface is seldom less than insistent in the *Weehawken Sequence*. The stubby marks in many of the paintings have an anarchic plasticity that looks forward to the abstract coagulations of paint Guston would produce in the fifties. Where long views across the Hudson were desired, the strokes gather in parallel bunches pushed into perspectival vectors. In the more abstract paintings, the strokes simply describe and become the real scale of the movements of the hands—the self-propelled dance of their making. Many of the paintings are more like purely improvisatory sketches than finished work. Often they seem to demand a larger format to fully resolve the fury of paint.

The clear unfurling of the process of painting and

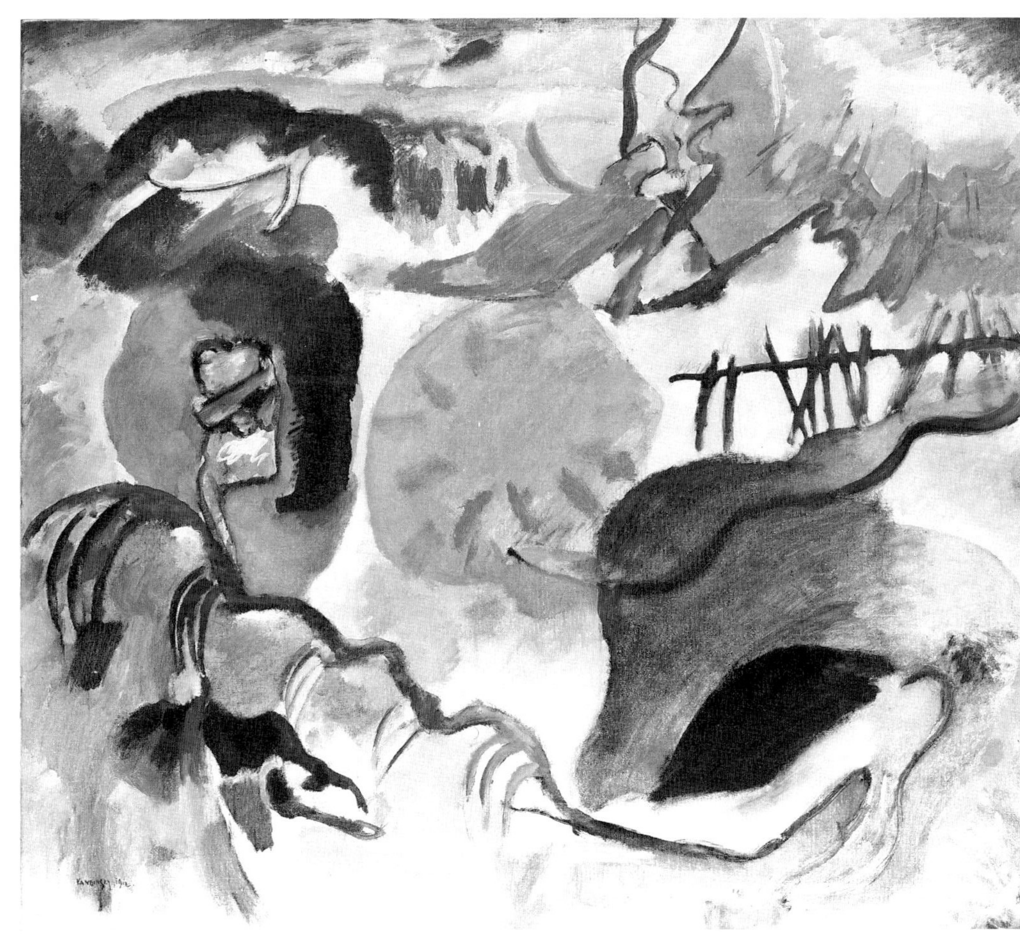

FIG. 18
WASSILY KANDINSKY
Improvisation No. 27, 1912
Oil on canvas. 47⅜ x 55¼ in.
The Metropolitan Museum of Art, New York,
The Alfred Stieglitz Collection, 1949

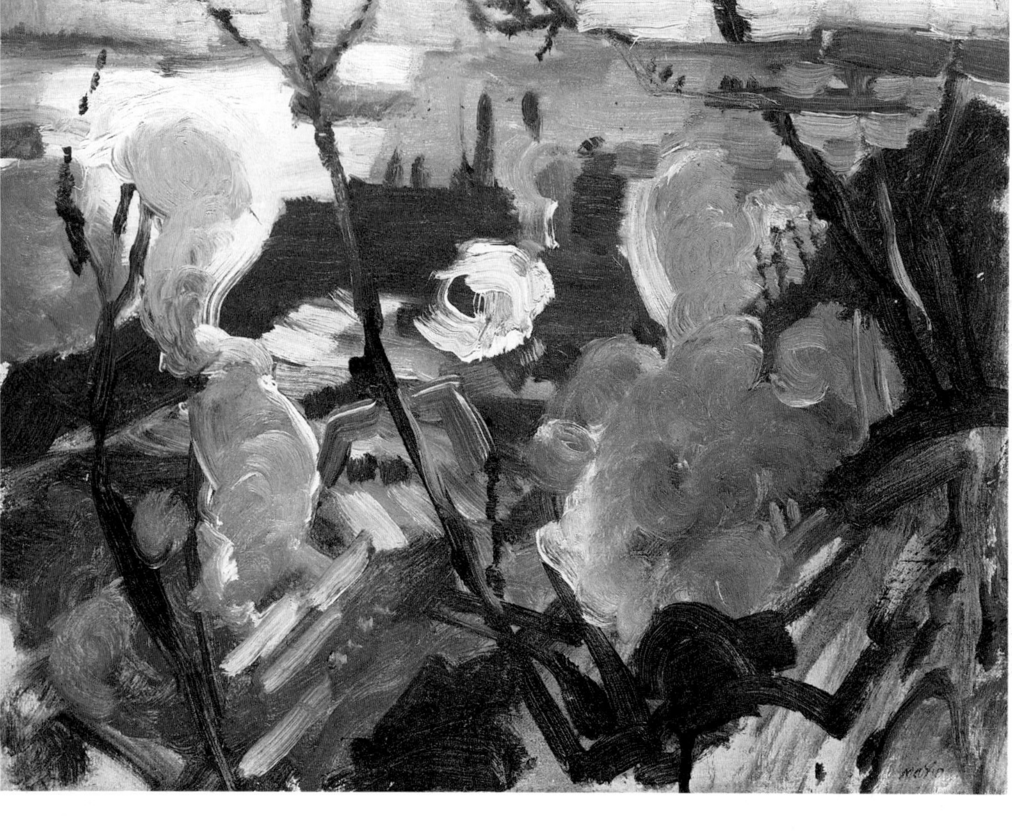

Fig. 19
JOHN MARIN
Weehawken Sequence (No. 68), 1916
Oil on canvas board. 9 x 12 in.
Collection Mr. and Mrs. William Janss, Sun Valley, Idaho

the dense, agitated physicality of these small panels extend the expressive painterliness of Derain's and Vlaminck's Fauvism toward the modernist abstraction that would fully fluoresce in New York in the late forties. In spite of their small size and their frequent, seeming incompletion, these paintings are singular in their opticality. Several years would elapse before Soutine would begin his related but more overtly expressionist, even tortured, landscapes.[15] Marin himself would wait until the 1930s before fully incorporating the experiments made in his laboratory of oil into the new body of his painting.

The *Weehawken Sequence* was not exhibited. The paintings passed out of history, into storage, until 1947, when the seventy-seven-year-old Marin and MacKinley Helm, who was working on a catalogue essay for a Marin retrospective, were going through the works (many undated) that Marin himself had stored. On the basis of Marin's memory of his whereabouts, the two arrived at 1903–1904 as a date for them.[16] But Weehawken was a frequent site for Marin and not a very reliable indicator of a firm date. The paintings bear no relationship to the pale washes of a Weehawken watercolor dated 1904, nor to any of the other paintings done at that time. Furthermore, the works in the sequence are unlikely to have been made prior to at least some familiarity with Van Gogh and the Fauves, and it is possible that Helm took conscious or unconscious advantage of Marin's memory lapse to support his own Francophobia. Based on stylistic analysis and the clear relationship to a larger oil painting of Weehawken dated 1916, Sheldon Reich has convincingly placed the *Weehawken Sequence* around this year.[17] This dating is also fully compatible with the schematic openness and the urge to abstraction typical of so many of the Marin watercolors (dated and exhibited) between 1915 and 1918.[18]

The *Weehawken Sequence* is part of a period of bold

experimentation, both for Marin and for many of his peers, and it was followed by the consolidation and/or retrenchment that so often succeeds upheaval. The aesthetic turmoil caused by Cubism was followed by the political turmoil and devastation of the First World War. The war both freed and isolated American artists from European influences. The establishment of Dada headquarters in New York by the émigré artists Duchamp and Picabia had little immediate effect; their investment in urban(e) irony would have to be held some forty years before paying dividends in Pop currency. Most American artists, especially those in the Stieglitz group, were still too forthright and too nature-bound to respond to Duchamp. The Surrealism of the twenties would have to wait until the forties before the Americans took from it what the French could not see. Many artists, in both Europe and America, returned to more recognizably figurative pursuits, as both Stanton Macdonald-Wright and Delaunay did in 1916. Derain and Vlaminck had already turned away from their Fauvist abstract flatness and chromatic cacophony toward subdued representational space and form. Hartley, after a series of flat grisaille Cubist abstrations done in 1916, turned in 1917 to figuration inspired by American folk art and American Indian art. Stieglitz, who had at first been a singular figure at the vanguard of America's internationalism, now focused more exclusively on his native American tribe—in spite of being torn by his pro-German sympathies. Severini would be the last European he would show. Georgia O'Keeffe's debut, three days before America's declaration of war, brought both 291 and a chapter in America's cultural history to a close. Until 1925 financial difficulties would force Stieglitz to operate as a dealer and guru without walls. Nevertheless, his relationship with most of his artists, especially with Marin, suffered little interruption.

The bemused consternation with the war that Marin expressed in his letters to Stieglitz was symptom-

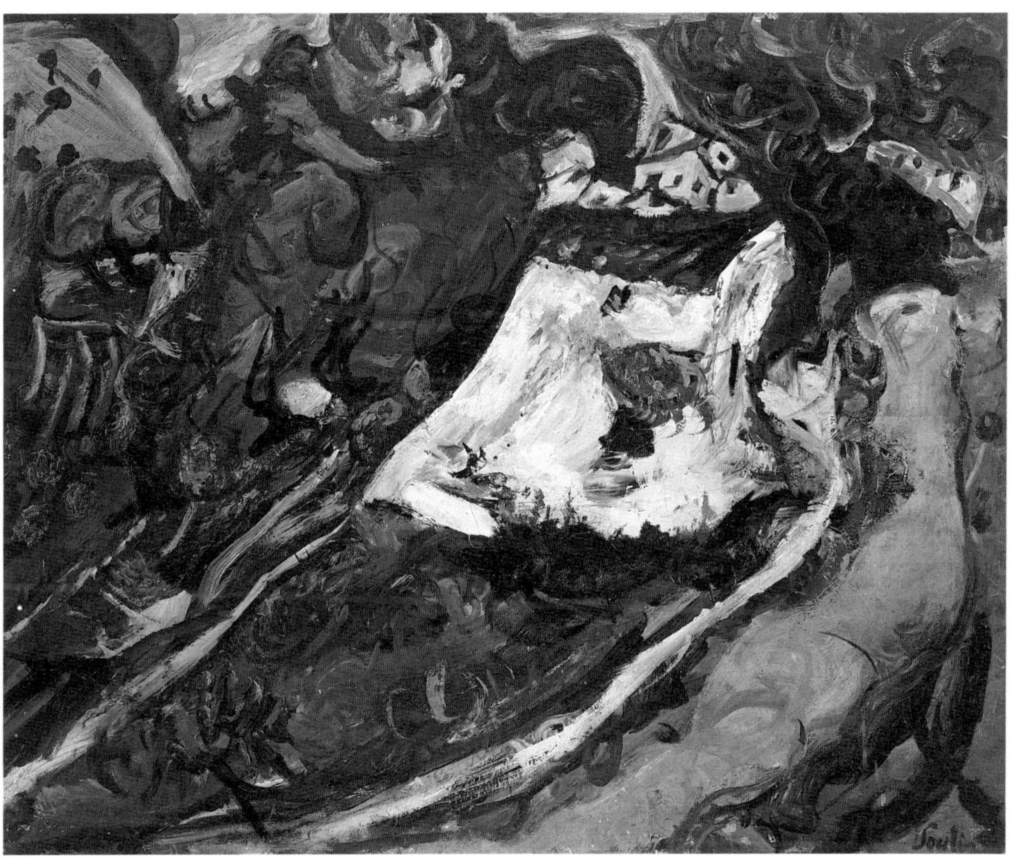

Fig. 20
CHAIM SOUTINE
The Old Mill, ca. 1922–23
Oil on canvas. 26⅛ x 32⅜ in.
The Museum of Modern Art, New York,
Vladimir Horowitz and Bernard Davis Funds

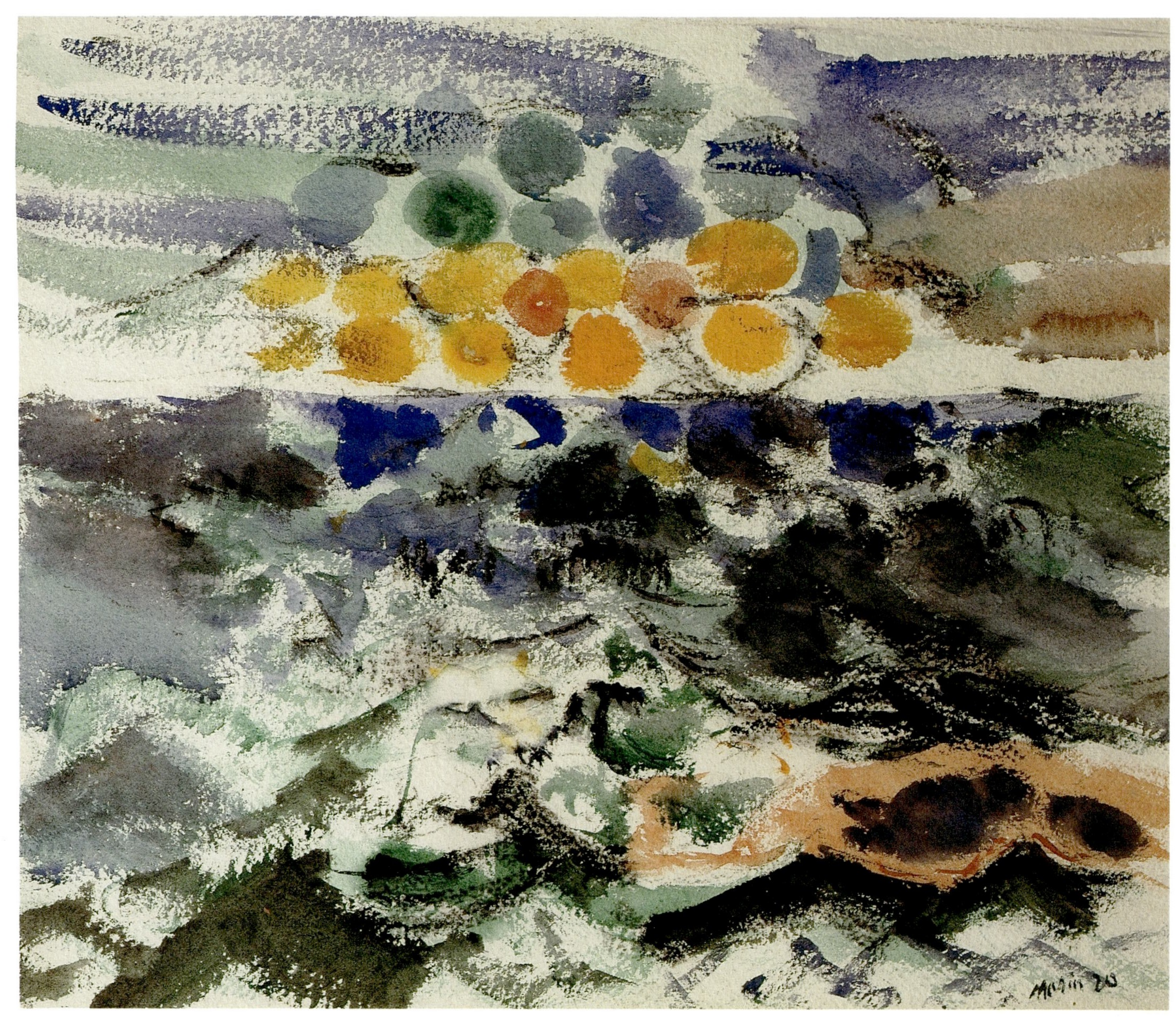

Fig. 21
JOHN MARIN
Sunspots, 1920
Watercolor on paper.
16⅜ x 19⅝ in.
The Metropolitan Museum of Art, New York,
The Alfred Stieglitz Collection, 1949

atic of the separateness America still felt from Europe, as was the government's reluctance to join a foreign war. Isolationism (and defensiveness) would increase before subsiding. Small Point, Maine, where Marin summered in 1917, could still seem equidistant between Europe and Mars, and here it was the forces of the sea that were claiming much of Marin's concentration.

After a brief experiment with flat, outright abstractions composed of overlapping, curvilinear planes similar to Hartley's more rectilinear paintings of 1916, Marin returned to his more inspired improvisations. He painted landscapes and seascapes with the cursory exuberance and near flatness that had emboldened his brush since 1915, but after 1917 he began more visibly to defer to the observation of his subjects. The high-voltage energy of emancipated strokes now regularly returned to its more representational responsibilities. Without compromising the flatness of the support, the horizon reclaimed its role.

"Chickens walk, they don't hop."[19] The subject's unique structure and characteristics must be respected, just as the structure of the painting's support and the nature of the medium must be respected. The subject is not imitated, but brushed and activated into flatness. "This is the prow of a ship. I draw abstractly."[20] The visible process of how specific observation becomes the painting preoccupied Marin in the twenties and the thirties. His *Sunspots* (1920) are not on the sun but on paper—sparkling retinal hallucinations triggered by the sun. The rising and setting sun, the beaming transparency that watercolor is capable of, and Marin's obsession with light are brushed fluidly into fusion in countless watercolors painted in the twenties. Indeed, the fleeting reflectiveness of the sun's light, so prominent in the work of the twenties, seems to have precluded for the moment the denser and more opaque desires of oil. Only two known oils were done in 1921, and none again until 1928.

In the twenties, the effusive spontaneity so visible in the watercolors and oils of the mid-teens was joined by Cubist architectonics—now more dramatically than in the paler Lower Manhattan scenes done between 1912 and 1914. Broader thrusting strokes fly into prismatic flux. The contours of buildings are overlaid with open and closed triangular planes that frame the skyscrapers with monumental vectors of energy. Emphatic black lines defining silhouettes or simply driven by their own concerns underscore a more vivid palette. Marin's Cubism has a wacky vicariousness; it veers and turns into irreverent configurations whose seemingly electrified calligraphy shows little respect for the cool clarity and regularity of most other Cubists' planes.

Marin no longer restricted Cubism to the city but brought it to the country as well. The skyscrapers' triangular auras now find a more representational place as sails on the boats that dominate the increasing number of seascapes. Deep wooded and mountainous vistas are seen through and dissolve into a shifting web of cracked, wet planes. The view into the distance is pulled back onto the flatness of the paper's plane. Cubist fracturing simultaneously undermines and makes possible a greater variety of representation. Sometimes Cubism is pushed to the edges to become a framing device that simply punctuates the rectangular boundaries of the support—like the dark blue, bleeding band at the top of so many Japanese woodblock landscapes that takes the sky out of nature and puts it back into the domain of the paper. These interior frames or enclosures become a Marin monogram in the twenties; they vary from a simple wreath of planar strokes to more complexly layered configurations that elaborate the entire painting. Of course, numerous paintings bear no visible trace of Cubism at all.

Although the variety of Marin's production in any given year invites disproof of generalizations, the pantheistic expressiveness of the early twenties tended to

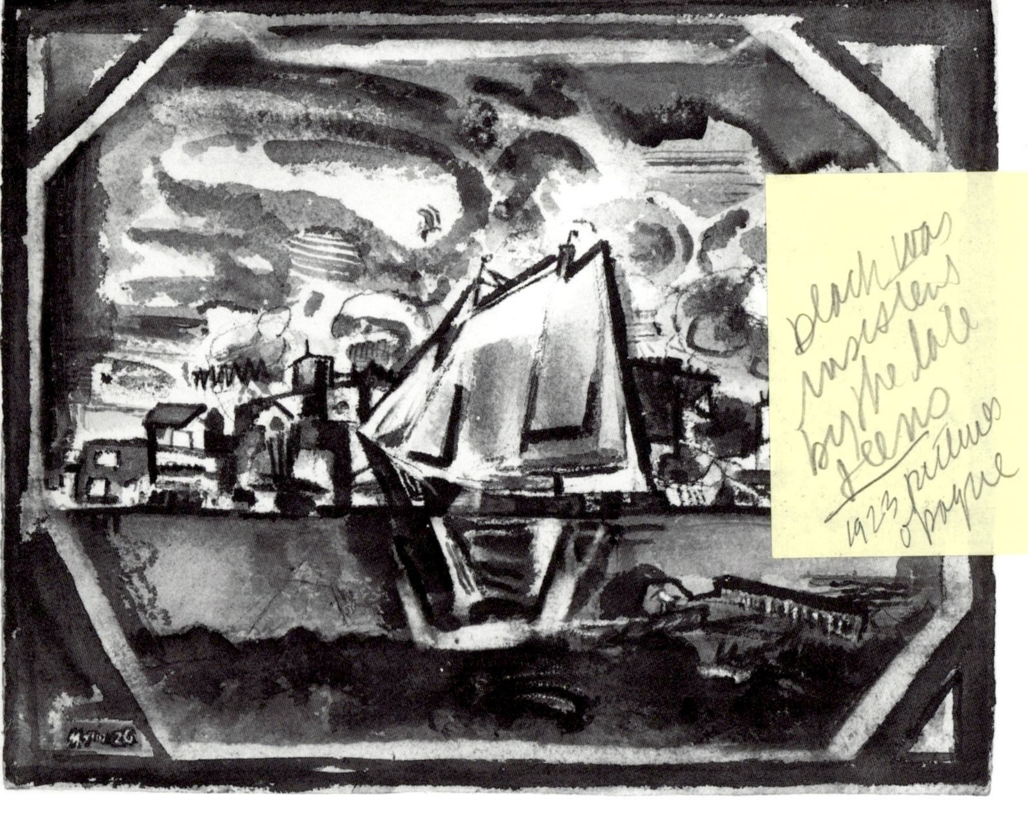

FIG. 22
JOHN MARIN
Pertaining to Stonington Harbor, Maine, No. 1, 1926
Watercolor on paper, 13 x 16¾ in.
Philadelphia Museum of Art,
The Alfred Stieglitz Collection

subside into calmer control in the mid-twenties—occasionally of a near-Oriental serenity, and occasionally risking postcard-view corniness. The greater compositional planning and control of many of the watercolors reflect the fact that they were completed in the studio, but working outdoors was still an urgent necessity. In spite of his sporadic attacks of lumbago and sciatica, it was still common to see Marin, encumbered by the tools of his trade, darting through the landscape to seek an often precarious perch.

The newly insistent black in the watercolors was, in the late twenties, often joined by a heavier blue (in the more agitated seascapes) and by near-opaque earth tones (generally in mountain views, especially some of those done in New Mexico in the summers of 1929 and 1930). This increased density and opacity, together with the more deliberated compositional control, signal a new restlessness in Marin. Watercolor was being pushed toward oil (earlier the reverse had obviously been true). And in 1928 Marin returned to oil; by 1930 he would make oil his primary concern and would be almost prepared to take full advantage of the lessons of his earlier *Weehawken Sequence.*

Two of the six oil paintings of 1928 extend the drama of the skewed Cubist city views in the watercolors of the early twenties. While still thinly painted and enlivened by large sections of bare canvas, both *Related to Brooklyn Bridge* and *Related to St. Paul's* employ blunter, darker tones that are more akin to the downtown area's cavernous jumble of planes than are the more limpid tones of watercolor. The weightier drama of the oil, however, has yet to compensate fully for the absence of the buoyant brilliance of watercolor. A third urban oil portrays two standing figures framed in an abstract shuffle of rectangles. These puppetlike characters, invented in the studio and first seen in the watercolors of the early twenties, would assume greater prominence in subsequent oils done when Marin finally established a permanent winter studio in his new home in Cliffside, New Jersey.

The three landscapes of 1928 reach deeper into the viscosity of oil and the bleaker side of its tonalities. In the two *Region of Sparkill, New York* paintings, an opaque skin of muted earth tones is pulled across the canvas, and Cubism gives way to the organic wholeness of the hills. *Movement in Brown with Sun* is a studio fabrication that unfolds in a contrapuntal play moving from bare canvas to thin washes to dense matteness. A rambling, multipeaked glyph, possibly mountains, possibly sea, topped by sun and thick white clouds, floats in a polygon of bare canvas; a frame of deepest black-brown, lightened by a thin scribble of white, fills the rest of the canvas. This nature-derived abstraction anticipates the thinner, calligraphic conflagration and Cubist, planar play of the late forties. But in the thirties Cubism's dialogue with nature was to be less visible.

Marin's turn to oil came at a time when his reputation as a watercolorist had reached all but epic proportions. In 1925 Stieglitz started a new enterprise, The Intimate Gallery, with Marin and O'Keeffe as his major stars (he had married O'Keeffe in 1924, with Marin as witness). It was not mere hyperbole when, in an introduction to the catalogue for his artist's 1927 exhibition, Stieglitz referred to "Marin's established and ever increasing prestige as probably the world's foremost watercolorist." The energy Stieglitz had invested in Marin was devoted almost entirely to his abilities as a watercolorist and would largely continue to be so. But while Stieglitz's charisma remained compelling, his own development was now virtually complete, while Marin's unceasing intensity would push his brush into the unknown until his death. His scarce public appearances made Stieglitz his surrogate, while he, like most of Stieglitz's artists, became shrouded in mysterious seclusion and self-containment. No one stepped forward to champion the oil paintings, and Marin's reputation as a vanguard modernist, as a great American artist, as a watercolorist, and as a painter in oil were often seen by critics to be in conflict.

The twenties witnessed the formation of a new, modernist-dominated art establishment: the Phillips Memorial Collection opened in Washington, D.C., in 1921; the Barnes Foundation was chartered in 1922; and the Museum of Modern Art in New York was inaugurated in 1929 with an exhibition of Cézanne, Gauguin, Seurat, and Van Gogh. At the same time the need to define a specifically American art was becoming increasingly acute, not only in conservative circles, but in liberal ones as well. This goal frequently entailed denying, ignoring, or vilifying the manifestations of modernism in American artists. Abetted by Stieglitz and by Marin himself, many critics who admired Marin ignored the contribution Fauvism and Cubism had made to his work. Enthusiasts such as Waldo Frank, Lewis Mumford, the German art historian Julius Meier-Graefe, and Paul Rosenfeld all sidestepped Paris and tended to focus on Marin as the foremost practitioner of the peculiarly American medium of watercolor.[21] Thomas Craven, beginning in 1924 a retrenchment from modernism that would become shrilly racist in the thirties, bemoaned both Marin's new expressiveness and "intellectual design." He praised the earlier work, which he claimed had emanated from Cézanne, when Marin had, Craven said, "quite simply abandoned himself to nature."[22]

Stieglitz's artists had little to unite them but some of their common roots and a general commitment to modernism. America's search for identity in the twenties was exacerbated by the fact that no monolithic style or group could claim the spotlight. Marin did indeed stand alone, as did so many others, yet he did not emerge from a cocoon of his own creation. He was

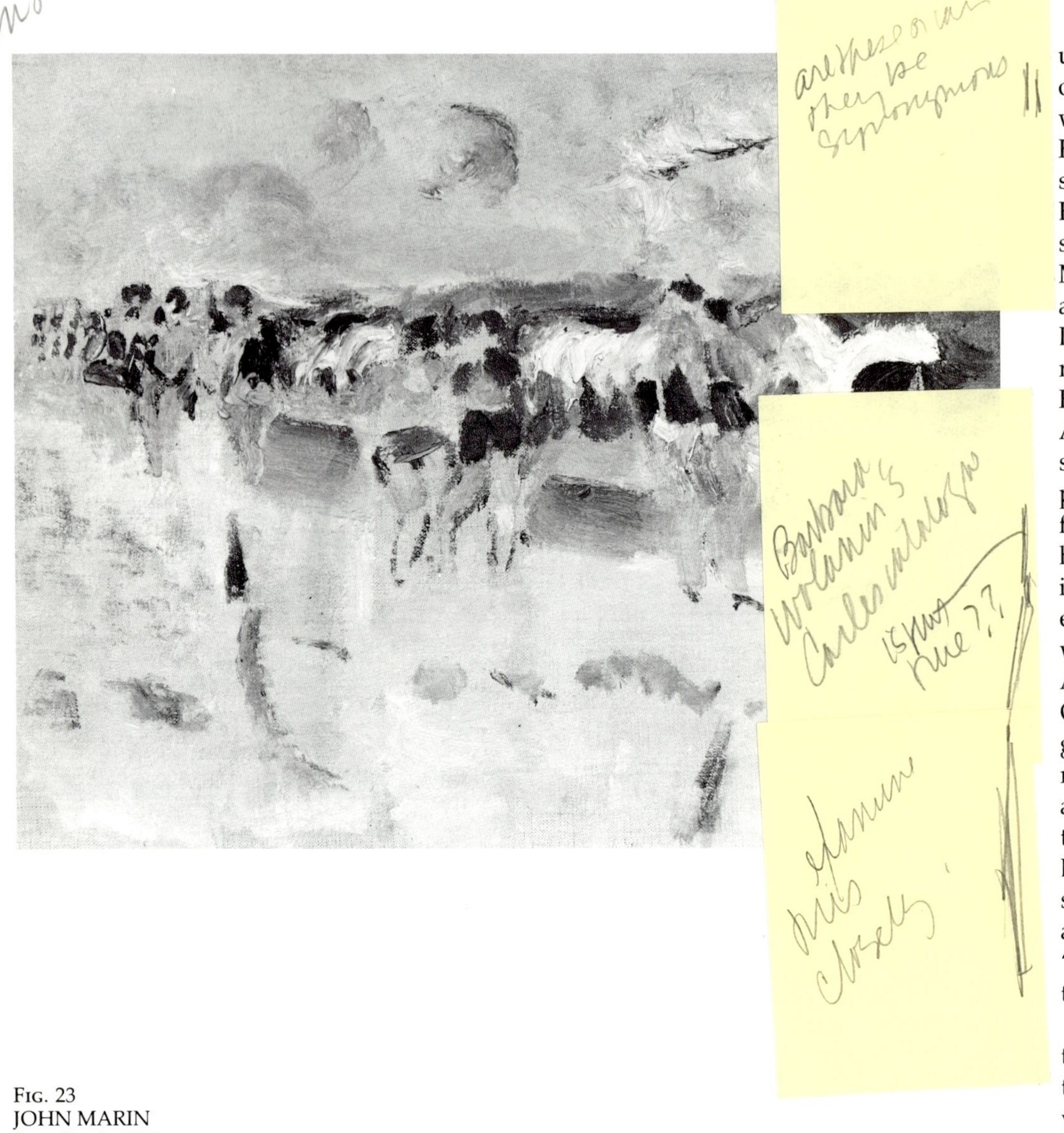

Fig. 23
JOHN MARIN
Jones Beach, 1931
Oil on canvas. 14 x 18 in.
Collection Dr. and Mrs. William Lannik,
Lido Beach, New York

unique in his ability to merge Cubism not only with the organic irregularities of the rhythms of nature but also with the organic irregularities of the rhythms of paint. From the mid-teens through the twenties, when Cubism spread out from still life back into landscape, both in Europe and America, it generally took a crystalline sculptural form—the stained-glass Gothic Cubism of Macke, Feininger, and, occasionally, Klee; the cylindrical and tubular constructions and construction workers of Léger; the steely staccato of the Futurists; the slide-ruled regularity of Le Corbusier's and Ozenfant's Purism, in France, and Sheeler's and Demuth's Precisionism in America. Marin's more internally impulsive liquidity separated him from hard-line Cubism, but his painterliness also had little in common with that of his friends Hartley and Carles. He was alone, in America, in his strong commitment to the revelation of the painting's making. He had little influence on fellow artists except as role model (especially for practitioners of watercolor, such as Demuth). What *was* peculiarly American, and what Marin did share with Hartley, O'Keeffe, Sheeler, Demuth, and others, was a need to ground painting in specific observation—the sites of European paintings were usually more generalized and abstracted—and the merging of this empirical observation with the more romantic realm of intuition. Unlike Dove, Hartley, and O'Keeffe, Marin eschewed overtly spiritual symbolism. His openness, intuitive directness, and refusal of the programmatic—all could be labeled "American," but all had gained much of their momentum and vocabulary from Europe.

The issue of Americanism escalated into rancor in the thirties, spurred on by the political confusion and the economic disasters caused by the Depression. Many viewed with deepest suspicion anyone deprived of Anglo-Saxon heritage or appearance. On the art front, bitter battles would be fought between modernists, on the one hand, and Social Realists and Regionalists, between abstractionists and representationalists. Marin, in spite of his French-Spanish name, would increasingly be referred to as a Yankee, apple-pie American. His reputation continued to grow, but largely on the basis of his watercolors. Although an empathic look back to American nineteenth-century painting was highly visible in many of his oils, they were largely viewed with circumspection or negativity.

Stieglitz could insulate Marin from the deprivation of the Depression, but apparently he had neither the energy nor the desire to wage the kind of battle for Marin's oils that he had mounted for the watercolors. Plagued by his own financial woes, he closed The Intimate Gallery in 1929, but quickly rebounded to open what would become his final venture. With the help of the photographer Paul Strand and the aspiring photographer Dorothy Norman—who became not only his most devoted financial backer but also his Boswell—Stieglitz opened the all-too-aptly named An American Place in 1930. To inaugurate The Place, as it came to be known, Stieglitz presented first a group show, and then a Marin watercolor exhibition.

Meanwhile, Marin himself inaugurated the decade with a revival of the vitality of the *Weehawken Sequence*. Of the nine oils he painted in 1930, eight comprised a series of small (ca. 14" x 18" or 18" x 14") landscapes moving from fall through winter (*Fall* nos. 1–5, *Winter* nos. 6–8). *Fall of 1930, No. 1, No. 2,* and *No. 3* are virtual curtains of crackling color that spread over all or almost all of the flat, horizonless surface. Differing lengths of choppy strokes thrust up and down in the irregular clotted verticality of the wooded, hilly landscape. The strokes move from virtual independence to coagulating bunches, from dryly pulled thinness to fuller-bodied wetness, from scumble to shrublike clusters. Ochre, orange, bright yellow and red, and greens moving from yellow to blue hum the acid harmonies of fall. Chronologically and stylistically, these paintings are

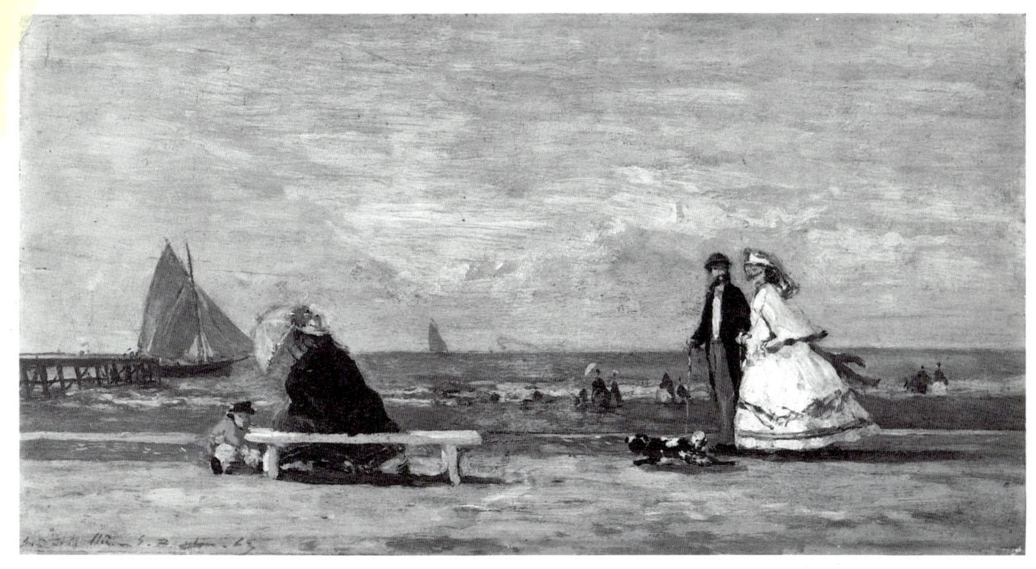

Fig. 24
EUGENE-LOUIS BOUDIN
Beach at Trouville, 1863
Oil on wood panel. 7¼ x 13¾ in.
The Phillips Collection, Washington, D.C.

situated between the frenetic energies of Derain's and Vlaminck's Fauvism and the harsh, crusty monumentality of Clyfford Still's autumnal abstractions of the late forties.

The last two *Fall* paintings encourage the paint to breathe in more representational space; also more representational are all three of the *Winter* paintings, suffused with the season's chalky muteness. The last oil painting done in 1930 is of the sea. The grayed blues and broad, relatively modulated stillness of stroke, as well as the horizontal bands of outcropping rocks and an island barely squeezed between the high horizon and the top edge of the canvas, are combined in a muffled, reductive composition reminiscent of Whistler's soft-voiced seascapes. The firmer strokes and the high horizon are pure Marin. The seascape was a quiet beginning, in oil, of a relationship that would grow in depth and intensity to become responsible for some of Marin's most compelling paintings.

In the thirties, Marin would unite the medium of oil with the subject of the ocean to create deeply moving medleys of paint. The rhythmically charged flatness and openness, the willed surrender to paint's liquidity, and the entrancement with the workings of nature so crucial to Marin become totally compatible and congruent with the movements of the ocean. Its incalculable repertoire of flux, flow, and reflectiveness moving into and out of flatness would bring Marin into full mastery of his newly favored medium. The weight and lustrous density of oil are a better match for the ocean than is the thinner-bodied translucence of watercolor. With notable exceptions (such as the four *Off York Island, Maine* works of 1922), most of Marin's watercolors of the sea from the twenties are stabilized and centralized by sailboats or dominated by the rocky shore. Often they were motivated by the movement of light and the currents of air rather than by the more palpable currents of the ocean itself. In oil, Marin immersed himself not in its ambiances but in the nature of the ocean itself.

In 1931 the ocean configured more than half of the some twenty oil paintings Marin completed in Small Point, Maine. Generally, an uneven diagonal of irregularly corruscated strokes anchors the painting on a rocky shorefront and counterpoints the insistent, overall horizontality of the rumbling sheet of sea that rises (more than it recedes) almost to overflow the thin strand of sky at the top of the canvas. Occasionally Cubism rises to the surface, but more often it is dissolved in more organic configurations. Here a pine moves out of natural shape to rise up in a pointed stack of thickly painted planes; there an island or rock outcropping becomes a band or zigzag that reflects the canvas rectangle more than the subject. In one painting of *Small Point Harbor,* with a lower than customary skyline, densely painted floating bars and rectangles bring the sky back into unity with the surface plane and seek their reflections on the sea—ambassadors of flatness perhaps more Oriental than Cubist.

"In painting water, make the hand move the way the water moves."[23] Marin set about making his brush simultaneously seaworthy and paintworthy, synchronizing the ocean's surface with that of the canvas. The strokes vary with the tide and weather. Choppy strokes react to the wind wrinkling the surface; more smoothly modulated strokes mirror placid clarity; strokes of rolling regularity follow the tide; bundles of pointed strokes are pushed into each other as they bounce off rocks that have been pressured into shapes by thinner, scratchier marks. Marin's pleasure in the rich viscosity of oil now brought the churning physicality of paint into greater tension with the canvas support and urged the flow of oil into a compositional clarity that had frequently been lacking in the more experimental Weehawken paintings. He now had good reason to write about "the paint job which is a lusty thing."[24] By the end of 1931, he had established the painterly principles that would guide his hands into the next decade.

In 1933, Marin rented the house on Cape Split in

Addison, Maine, that he would buy the following year and paint in, during the warmer months, for the rest of his life. Here his new power in oil reached its apogee. In *Off Cape Split, No. 1* (1934, 22⅛" x 28"), the daring diversity and boldness that mark the boulders in the foreground play against the greater regularity of the glistening green and blue of the ocean. The monumental simplicity of the boulder shapes grants vastness to the painted sea that covers but a tiny piece of canvas. *The Ladle* (1934, 22" x 28") beams and revels in more intimate pleasures of paint. A low, splashed rectangle of sea is topped by a slathered scoop of paint that is the island named in the title. The island rides the sea with porpoiselike playfulness and plasticity.

Marin's Maine is not a hospitable bather's resort. (The politer side of the ocean's shore is visible in the soft-sand-and-froth-filled painting done at Jones Beach in 1931, where Marin seems to have paid his respects to Boudin, whom he openly admired.) The Maine coast invited drama more than dalliance. The rugged, often brooding pine- and rock-bound shoreline is reflected in Marin's dark palette: deep blues and greens that are offset by a limited range of earth tones. Black takes on a breadth as color and shape that it had seldom been permitted in the more purely linear role it played in the watercolors of the twenties.

The forcefulness of oil's density and the highly activated accumulation of strokes into the great massing of the seascape rock formations are pushed into a more orderly urgency in the new oils of New York City. In New York, the boulders become Cubist canyons; once more, Cubism holds sway in the city. The watercolor-dependent linearity of the 1928 cityscapes gains in weight and planar tension. The dark tones glide and collide in density rather than thinness. Light is no longer so exclusively derived from the whiteness of bare canvas, but shines through and is derived from the paint itself. A nocturnal, lunar clarity most often pervades the urban scenes, but a garish yellow sun can also be called in to a daytime play. Marin's increasing compositional complexity and sureness is more than visible in the packed, pulsing stacking of planes and shapes in *Lower Manhattan from the Tip End* (1931). The almost chaotic escalation of Cubist checks and balances moves into and out of spatial depth in oppositions that are clearly calibrated to come to rest in the canvas's flatness. In *Study, New York* (1934), the more open and decoratively flat lateral dynamics are decelerated by a broad, fretted interior frame that mimes Art Deco skyscraper detailing.

Marin was now obviously becoming more reliant on finishing some work in his Cliffside studio. And most of the paintings of human figures that he was producing were now not only finished in the studio, but started there. The figure, which had first reappeared in a 1920 watercolor, and then among the oils of 1928, began to make increasing appearances in oil after 1931. At first it evinces none of the gusto so evident in Marin's other subjects; the figures are part of a peculiarly American race that is naively simple and stiff and seldom embodies any sensual or psychological pleasure or pain, yet still resists a purely formal abstractness. They are literally and figuratively a race suspended in animation. Members of this race also populate the paintings of Prendergast, Eilshemius, and Avery, among others. Many of Marin's figures of the thirties seem to be unintended victims, rather than motivators, of the transient, urban planes that surround them—subways, waiting rooms, restaurants, and so on. The four participants in *Figures, Street Movement* (1935) are among the few that Marin successfully integrated into the city's space and paint. The clattering of transparent rectangles from which the figures barely emerge makes a giddy hieroglyph out of the uneasy anonymity of the urban pedestrian. More at home on the plane are the figures at the sea: first, more and perhaps most successful in their planar integration, the mundane bathers at Jones Beach in 1931; then, starting in 1932, nude bathers that become increasingly acrobatic in the late thirties and finally ram-

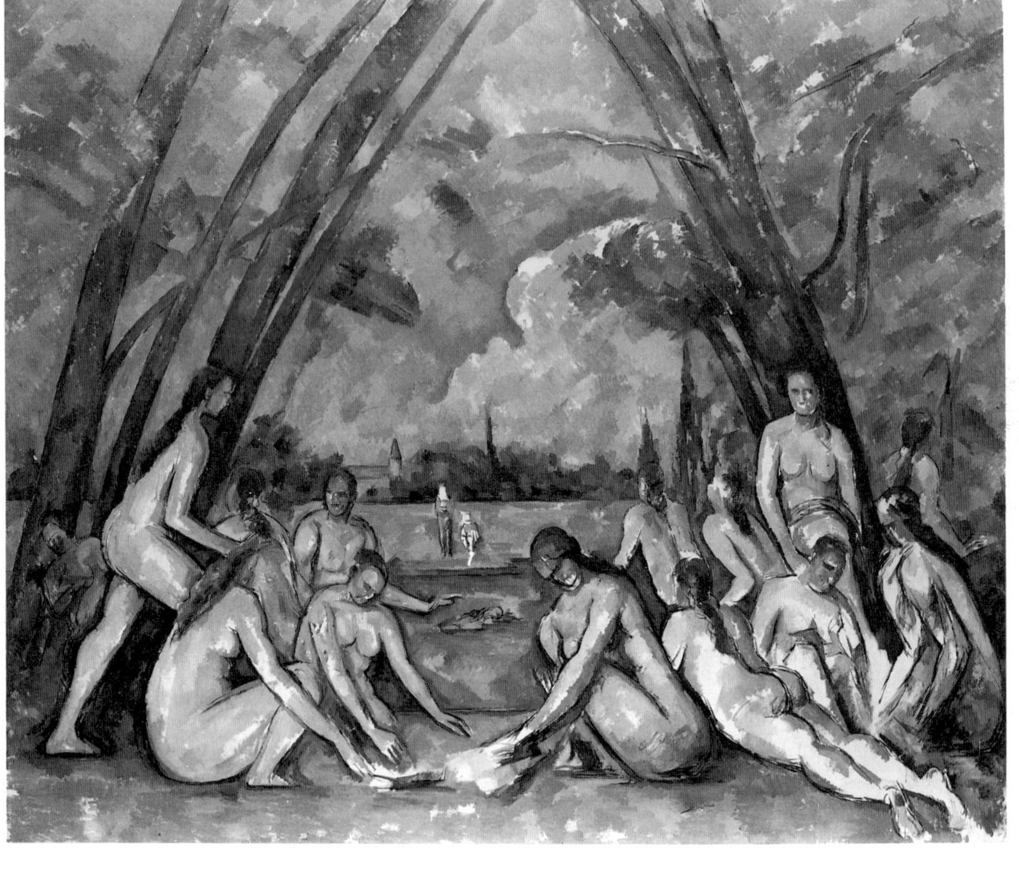

Fig. 25
PAUL CEZANNE
The Large Bathers, 1906
Oil on canvas. 82 x 99 in.
Philadelphia Museum of Art,
Purchase, W.P. Wilstach Collection

bunctiously ethereal in the forties and early fifties. These arcadian New England naiads, at least in their later manifestations, may well be one of Marin's few direct debts to Cézanne—specifically to his *Bathers* (1906), which Marin saw around 1941 for the first time and is reported to have admired.[25] Nevertheless, even the figures' openness to the ocean does not always prevent them from seeming like an afterthought; at best, their presence appears to be a happy coincidence.

Almost without question, Marin's strongest achievements in the thirties were at the ocean. Since until quite recently the subject has been relegated to mothballs or to the tourist trade, to claim that Marin is one of the greatest seascapists, if not *the* greatest one, of the twentieth century seems rather faint praise. But excluding Mondrian's radically reductive, sea-inspired abstractions of the early teens, only the more brooding and sculptured beauty of Hartley's Ryderesque late-thirties seascapes can vie with Marin.

Marin's and Hartley's devotion to the sea as subject reveals the still-strong roots their painting had in nineteenth-century American landcape—Ryder for Hartley, and Whistler and Homer for Marin. While Ryder was a direct influence on Hartley, as Whistler was on Marin, Marin's relationship to Homer is mostly one of parallels and affinities. The generous fluidity of Homer's watercolors may have had some influence on him, but more likely, they simply and importantly set a precedent for the credibility of the medium. Homer bemoaned the public's preference for his oils to his watercolors; Marin bemoaned the reverse. Homer, too, loved the drama of the sea, Maine, and paint, but his thinner application of paint and more representational space find no reflection in Marin's impassioned flatness. Marin's ocean paintings of the thirties are related to Homer in the heroic ruggedness of their sites and mood—a mood that, for many, made each a pioneer of one of America's last frontiers. At the moment when nent winter studio in his new home in Cliffside, New Jersey.

The three landscapes of 1928 reach deeper into the viscosity of oil and the bleaker side of its tonalities. In the two *Region of Sparkill, New York* paintings, an opaque skin of muted earth tones is pulled across the canvas, and Cubism gives way to the organic wholeness of the hills. *Movement in Brown with Sun* is a studio fabrication that unfolds in a contrapuntal play moving from bare canvas to thin washes to dense matteness. A rambling, multipeaked glyph, possibly mountains, possibly sea, topped by sun and thick white clouds, floats in a polygon of bare canvas; a frame of deepest black-brown, lightened by a thin scribble of white, fills the rest of the canvas. This nature-derived abstraction anticipates the thinner, calligraphic conflagration and Cubist, planar play of the late forties. But in the thirties Cubism's dialogue with nature was to be less visible.

Marin's turn to oil came at a time when his reputation as a watercolorist had reached all but epic proportions. In 1925 Stieglitz started a new enterprise, The Intimate Gallery, with Marin and O'Keeffe as his major stars (he had married O'Keeffe in 1924, with Marin as witness). It was not mere hyperbole when, in an introduction to the catalogue for his artist's 1927 exhibition, Stieglitz referred to "Marin's established and ever increasing prestige as probably the world's foremost watercolorist." The energy Stieglitz had invested in Marin was devoted almost entirely to his abilities as a watercolorist and would largely continue to be so. But while Stieglitz's charisma remained compelling, his own development was now virtually complete, while Marin's unceasing intensity would push his brush into the unknown until his death. His scarce public appearances made Stieglitz his surrogate, while he, like most of Stieglitz's artists, became shrouded in mysterious seclusion and self-containment. No one stepped forward to champion the oil paintings, and Marin's reputation as a vanguard modernist, as a great American artist, as a watercolorist, and as a painter in oil were often seen by critics to be in conflict.

The twenties witnessed the formation of a new, modernist-dominated art establishment: the Phillips Memorial Collection opened in Washington, D.C., in 1921; the Barnes Foundation was chartered in 1922; and the Museum of Modern Art in New York was inaugurated in 1929 with an exhibition of Cézanne, Gauguin, Seurat, and Van Gogh. At the same time the need to define a specifically American art was becoming increasingly acute, not only in conservative circles, but in liberal ones as well. This goal frequently entailed denying, ignoring, or vilifying the manifestations of modernism in American artists. Abetted by Stieglitz and by Marin himself, many critics who admired Marin ignored the contribution Fauvism and Cubism had made to his work. Enthusiasts such as Waldo Frank, Lewis Mumford, the German art historian Julius Meier-Graefe, and Paul Rosenfeld all sidestepped Paris and tended to focus on Marin as the foremost practitioner of the peculiarly American medium of watercolor.[21] Thomas Craven, beginning in 1924 a retrenchment from modernism that would become shrilly racist in the thirties, bemoaned both Marin's new expressiveness and "intellectual design." He praised the earlier work, which he claimed had emanated from Cézanne, when Marin had, Craven said, "quite simply abandoned himself to nature."[22]

Stieglitz's artists had little to unite them but some of their common roots and a general commitment to modernism. America's search for identity in the twenties was exacerbated by the fact that no monolithic style or group could claim the spotlight. Marin did indeed stand alone, as did so many others, yet he did not emerge from a cocoon of his own creation. He was

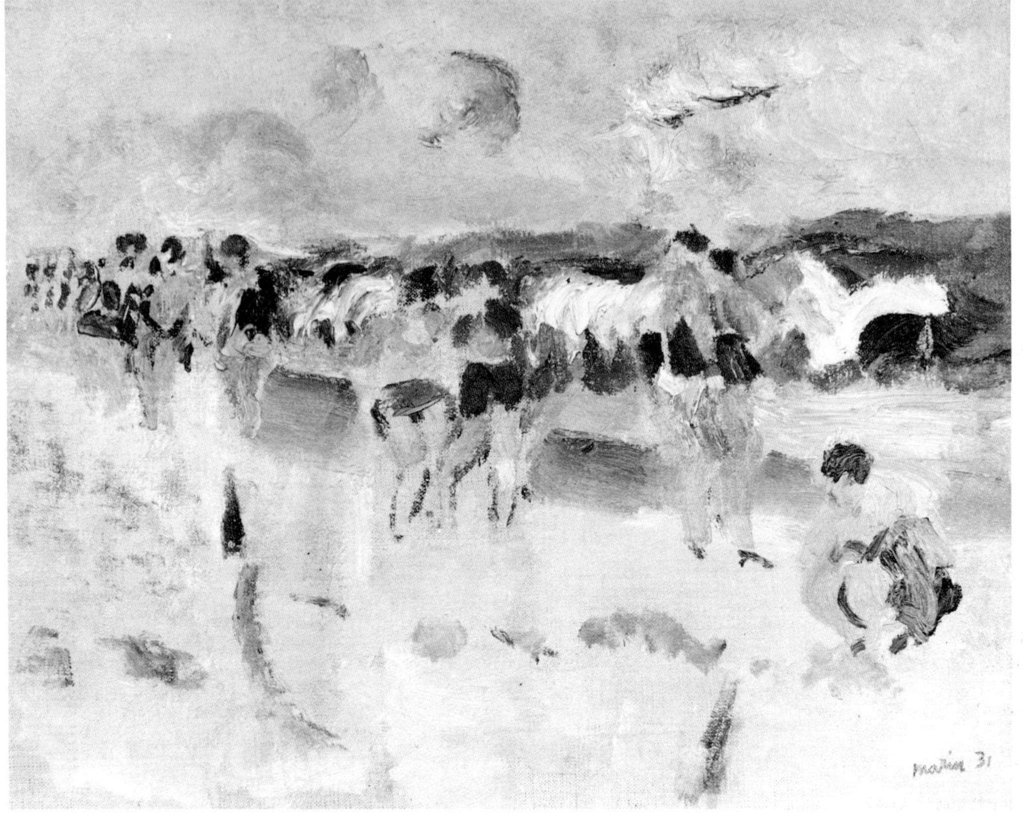

Fig. 23
JOHN MARIN
Jones Beach, 1931
Oil on canvas. 14 x 18 in.
Collection Dr. and Mrs. William Lannik, Lido Beach, New York

unique in his ability to merge Cubism not only with the organic irregularities of the rhythms of nature but also with the organic irregularities of the rhythms of paint. From the mid-teens through the twenties, when Cubism spread out from still life back into landscape, both in Europe and America, it generally took a crystalline sculptural form—the stained-glass Gothic Cubism of Macke, Feininger, and, occasionally, Klee; the cylindrical and tubular constructions and construction workers of Léger; the steely staccato of the Futurists; the slide-ruled regularity of Le Corbusier's and Ozenfant's Purism, in France, and Sheeler's and Demuth's Precisionism in America. Marin's more internally impulsive liquidity separated him from hard-line Cubism, but his painterliness also had little in common with that of his friends Hartley and Carles. He was alone, in America, in his strong commitment to the revelation of the painting's making. He had little influence on fellow artists except as role model (especially for practitioners of watercolor, such as Demuth). What *was* peculiarly American, and what Marin did share with Hartley, O'Keeffe, Sheeler, Demuth, and others, was a need to ground painting in specific observation—the sites of European paintings were usually more generalized and abstracted—and the merging of this empirical observation with the more romantic realm of intuition. Unlike Dove, Hartley, and O'Keeffe, Marin eschewed overtly spiritual symbolism. His openness, intuitive directness, and refusal of the programmatic—all could be labeled "American," but all had gained much of their momentum and vocabulary from Europe.

The issue of Americanism escalated into rancor in the thirties, spurred on by the political confusion and the economic disasters caused by the Depression. Many viewed with deepest suspicion anyone deprived of Anglo-Saxon heritage or appearance. On the art front, bitter battles would be fought between modernists, on the one hand, and Social Realists and Regionalists,

Cubism was shattering previous notions about painting, Homer, in his old age and traditional technique, was generally considered the most important painter in America. And at the moment when Abstract Expressionism would again shatter previous notions about painting, Marin, in his old age, would generally be considered the most important painter in America.

In the thirties, modernism was besieged as never before since its first introduction to American art. The right as well as the left accused it with excluding meaningful subject matter. The right sought a populist comprehensibility and looked to the farm belt for art's salvation, while the left sought to replace aesthetic radicalness with political radicalness, reviling the formal elitism that failed to protest visually the poverty at home and the terrifying rise of totalitarianism abroad. The decline in Hartley's reputation that began in the late twenties was, at least partially, caused by the suspicions aroused by his continuing trips to France and to Germany; the very titles (locations) of his landscapes offered his detractors evidence enough. Yet Marin's reputation continued to grow. His supporters searched their closets to find yet another American flag to drape him in; even his harshest critics bowed to his skills (generally in watercolor).

The Regionalists, with Thomas Hart Benton the most prominent among them and Thomas Craven their evangelist, sought to atone for the sins of European excess committed by the modernists. Benton, who had been to France (1908–1911) and had absorbed Cézanne, Neo-Impressionism, and Fauvism, rejected modernism in the twenties in favor of trying to transplant El Greco to his native Missouri soil. Craven celebrated the prodigal son's return to "strong representation and clearly defined meanings which may be shared and verified by large groups of people."[26] Stieglitz he labeled a "Hoboken Jew... hardly equipped for the leadership of a genuine American expression."[27] Marin he still credited with

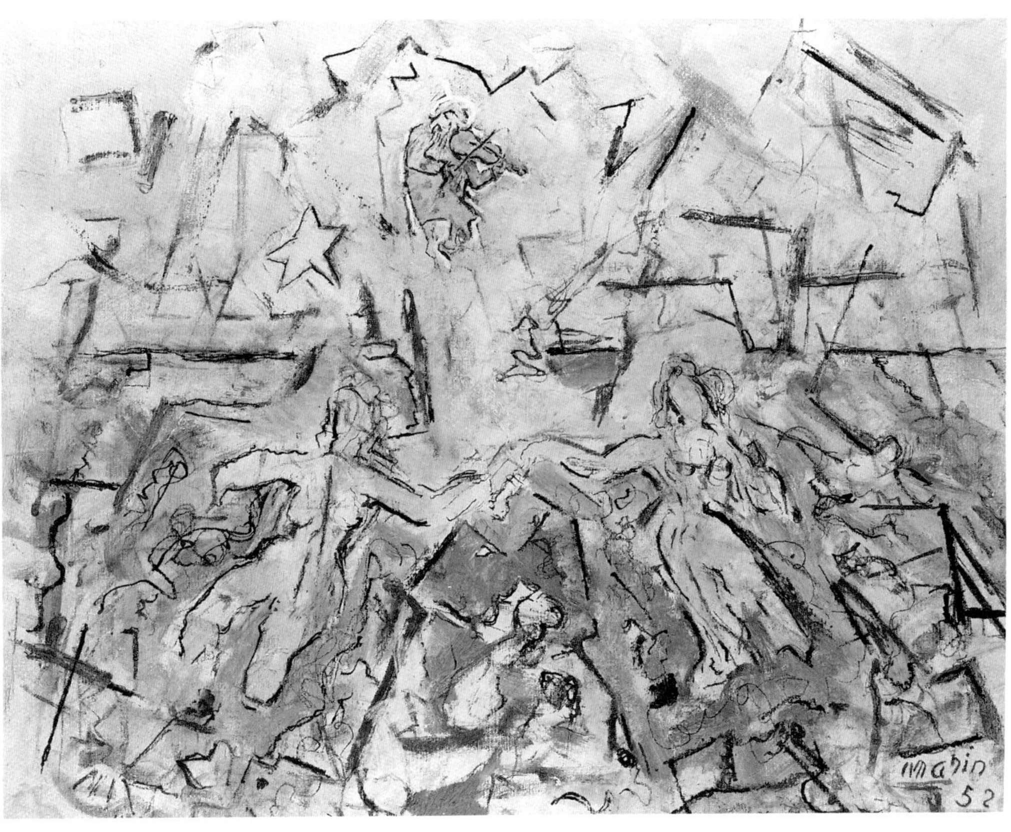

FIG. 26
JOHN MARIN
Sea Fantasy, 1952
Oil on canvas. 22 x 28 in.
Courtesy Kennedy Galleries, Inc., New York

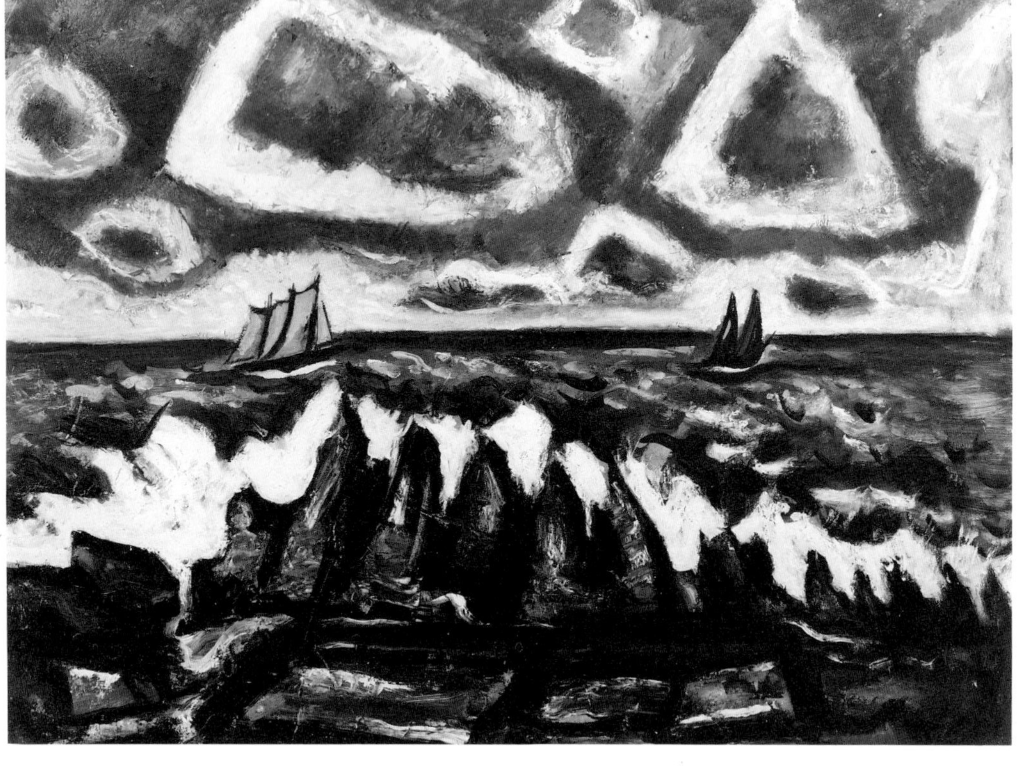

FIG. 27
MARSDEN HARTLEY
Northern Seascape, Off the Banks, 1936–37
Oil on cardboard. $18\frac{3}{16}$ x 24 in.
Milwaukee Art Museum,
Bequest, Max E. Friedmann

"poetic insight" and "talent," but he decried Marin's inability to escape from Stieglitz's permissiveness.[28] Craven found that Grosz, Rivera, and Orozco, together with Benton, were returning art to the people and declaring the tenets of modernism dead.[29] Neither Craven nor anyone else could guess at the radical American modernism that would burst forth in the following decade, with one of Benton's most avid students in its vanguard.

If the Regionalists and the Social Realists (largely led by The Eight) were vying for credit in the purging of French influences from American art, the beleaguered supporters of modernism were only slightly less anxious in their denials of France. Marin's rising reputation was confirmed in 1935 by the first monograph to be published on him, by E. M. Benson. With Marin's collusion, Benson went out of his way to insist that "Marin's plastic solutions are generally the result of being catapulted into them by the sharp impact of an experience with nature."[30] After condescending to Cézanne, Benson continues his often sensitive descriptions of Marin's development without a single mention of Fauvism or Cubism; the framing devices of the twenties are simply referred to as "cloud enclosures." Benson's book set the basic mold for most of the succeeding efforts of Marin supporters—a mold formed almost entirely by nature, America, and watercolor. The oils, especially throughout the thirties, would be greeted with ambivalence at best.

In 1936 Marin was honored with a large retrospective at the Museum of Modern Art; the show included 160 watercolors, 32 etchings, and 21 oils, the last all done between 1931 and 1935. Stieglitz, who had difficulty with all institutions other than himself, was made director of the exhibition, and catalogue essays were contributed by Henry McBride, Hartley, and Benson. Any retrospective at this time would perforce have to reflect watercolor's majority in Marin's output, but neither McBride's short, chatty essay nor the deep warmth of Hartley's words touched on the oils. Benson acknowledged their new importance to Marin, but assigned any cogent judgment of them to the future. Again Fauvism and Cubism were bypassed, and Marin was proclaimed "an isolated figure in American art."[31] Marin was indeed now quite isolated, but he was hardly building on a foundation composed solely of Whistler and nature. As his friendship with Hartley and Carles continued, so too did his dialogue with modernism.

If Marin himself had any doubts about his oils, they were not visible in the paintings. In the late thirties, oil continued to gather in force and physicality; the increasingly turbulent ocean fumes and foams across some of his most successful paintings. In *Wave on Rock* (1937), the entire canvas is swamped by short, peaked, muscular strokes that lap and layer as they gather in on the central spume of frothy white. Such paintings as *Sea After Hurricane* (1938) and *Heavy Sea* (1938) continue this tumultuous overallness and rejoice in the drama of the power of paint to turn the emptiness of canvas into a vast polyphony of rhythmically coherent mark-making. "As for message—as for story—The very doing—the very way it is done—the very what is being done by—they the parts—lead to this message—to this story—in fact is the message—is the story."[32]

Marin's work and his words bear strong connections with the Abstract Expressionism of the late forties and fifties, but his vastness remained contained within the confines of easel painting. Until the end 22″ x 30″ would remain the almost standard size of his oil paintings. The compositional checks and balances retained but radically flattened by the Fauves and the Cubists would always stay a part of his vocabulary. Even in his most frantic paintings of the ocean, the strokes surrender some surge to the rectangle, whether in a narrow band of horizon, or in their sporadic flattening out in confirmation with the rectangular edges of the canvas. "Order" and "boundaries" are as important to Marin's vocabulary as "movement," "forces," and "disorder." In *Lobster Boat, Cape Split, Maine* (1938), the short, choppy strokes of the ocean and the thinner, longer flurry of strokes of the sky are driven leftward with gale force. But the clouds gather to a near halt in the upper left corner, and the overscaled triangle of the lobster boat prow is firmly anchored in flatness to the bottom edge of the canvas.

The frames Marin frequently carved and painted, from 1930 on, for his oil paintings—rarely for the watercolors—simultaneously reinforce the view inside and its resolution into objectness. The conventional frame's task of punctuating and isolating the view into the canvas is subverted with colors and configurations that relate to the painting and help pull it back into flatness. The frames often extend interior framing devices to the exterior edges of the canvas. They were carved and painted with a simple directness—something like a restrained folk art rococo. The panoramic objectness that dominated painting from the late forties until quite recently renounced all frames and resulted in making Marin's quite difficult to accept. The recent revival of more pictorial space has brought frames back into play and now offers a better climate for Marin's harmonic intentions. When they are not troubled by a certain artiness, the frames do indeed add an extra dimension to the tension of the painting plane. Conceptually they are closer to early Cubist devices and to the occasional frames Hartley had made as early as 1914 than they are to the more traditional window-view framing made by Whistler in the nineteenth century.

Marin's dialogue with flatness, a dialogue that would again become more specifically Cubist in the forties, relates him (as well as Carles) to a whole new group of modernists who were coming to the fore in the thirties. European modernism was once more gathering momentum. The American Abstract Artists Association, including such artists as Josef Albers, Burgoyne Diller, and George McNeil, banded together under the umbrella of abstraction that had been formed by the influences of Picasso, Matisse, and Mondrian. Stuart Davis's jazzy rearrangements of mundane Americana were breathing new life into synthetic Cubism, and two émigrés from Europe, Arshile Gorky and Willem de Kooning, met and began an exchange with each other and with both Picasso's and the Surrealists' work of the twenties. Gorky, first with his brazen 1920s pastiches of Cézanne and then those of Picasso done in the 1930s, was the earliest to embody the new and more willful confrontation with European modernism that would lead into the great American abstraction of the late forties. In spite of Marin's professed wariness of the French, until well into the forties he was regarded by many artists living in New York as America's major carrier of the torch of modernism. It is unlikely that he had any direct influence on the younger generation, but he was certainly strongly admired by them, especially by de Kooning.[33]

Marin's increasing prominence notwithstanding, the painter in oil remained an embattled figure. The Stieglitz group grumbled about the oils and Stieglitz himself showed little of the fervor he continued to evince for the watercolors. (At his death, Stieglitz owned some 200 Marin watercolors, but barely a handful of the oils.) It has been reported and denied that Stieglitz, who had started exhibiting the oils together with the watercolors in 1931, tried in 1938 to dissuade Marin from the darkness of his pursuits in oil.[34] Marin responded to the many criticisms of his oils with a rather hilariously defensive introduction to his 1938 exhibition. Addressing his "Oil Kids," he concludes by observing that "there be those who have said—may still say—You should never have been born—Give them not a thought."[35] The critic Jerome Mellquist, who had already favorably reviewed the oils included in the 1936 Museum of Modern Art retrospective, was one of the few to praise the oils in 1938.[36]

If Marin's impasto was not as wild and thick in its viscosity as that of Soutine's paintings, his painterly physicality was nonetheless quite singular in America. Perhaps only Edwin Dickinson's wispy Whistlerian seascapes and figure studies of the thirties can match Marin's ardor in exposing painting in the making. But the trenchant physicality and somber tonalities of his oils evoked negative reviews from the critics of the day, whose orientation was more closely geared to the smooth gyrations of his watercolors. (Many of the watercolors of the thirties actually followed oil's lead into brooding gravity.) Not until the paint began to thin and the colors to brighten would Marin's oils be met with favor.

Marin's role as precursor and precedent maker for the budding new modernism would become increasingly distanced by differing intentions, but many striking parallels would continue. He had preceded the younger artists in his liquid enlivening and loosening-up of the Cubist grid, but he would continue, to varying degrees, to be dependent on his observation of nature. Many of the future Abstract Expressionists were becoming more and more engaged with the aleatory procedures of Surrealism and the *Urwelt* of the unconscious. In addition, the Mexican muralists, whom Craven had praised for their popular subject matter, were now instead being studied for the possibilities they held out for modernism to achieve a new, heroic scale. This interest in scale was reinforced by the work on murals done by many of the artists who joined the WPA to survive the Depression (both Pollock, who had studied with Benton at the Art Students League, and de Kooning joined the WPA in 1935).

Marin's 1936 retrospective took place in the same year as "Cubism and Abstract Art," but that same year the Modern also staged "Fantastic Art: Dada and Surrealism." Surrealism was renewing and modifying the modernist dialogue with Primitivism and spurring a new American interest in myth. These concerns were reflected and influenced by some of the Modern's other exhibitions: for example, "American Sources of Modern Art" (including Aztec, Mayan, and Incan art) in 1933; "Prehistoric Rock Pictures in Europe and Africa" in 1937; "Twenty Centuries of Mexican Art" in 1940; and "Indian Art of the United States" in 1941 (the same year that a Miró exhibition was presented). The new abstraction being partially catalyzed by these exhibitions drew further encouragement from the large selection of Kandinsky's work available in New York with the opening of The Museum of Non-Objective Painting (now the Guggenheim) in 1939.

Marin's love for the observation of nature would, in the mid-forties, give way increasingly to studio conceptualization and the memory of nature rather than its direct experience, but until his last breath he disavowed abstraction. In 1939 he still turned to nature directly to breathe life into his paint: he looked again at the wooded landscape and mountains that had previously activated his brushes. In thirteen small (12″ x 16″) paintings of *Spring*, each a different view of mountains and foliage, a lightening of touch and brightening of palette began to set in. The lower horizon line of many of the paintings challenges the flatness of the canvas, and the predominant overallness of the ocean paintings is interrupted with the more independently isolated configurations of the woods. The strokes bristle and stipple rather than speed; turbulence subsides into sunnier joy.

This renewed interest in mountains hardly spelled the end of the ocean for Marin. His rushing brush would never stop seeking synchrony with the organic excitement of the sea. Gales and hurricanes continued to race across his canvases; but here too, dark drama began to ease more and more into evanescence. *My Hell Raising Sea* (1941) was painted with much of the party rowdiness implied by the title. The festiveness is underscored by the increasing appearance of playful nudes by

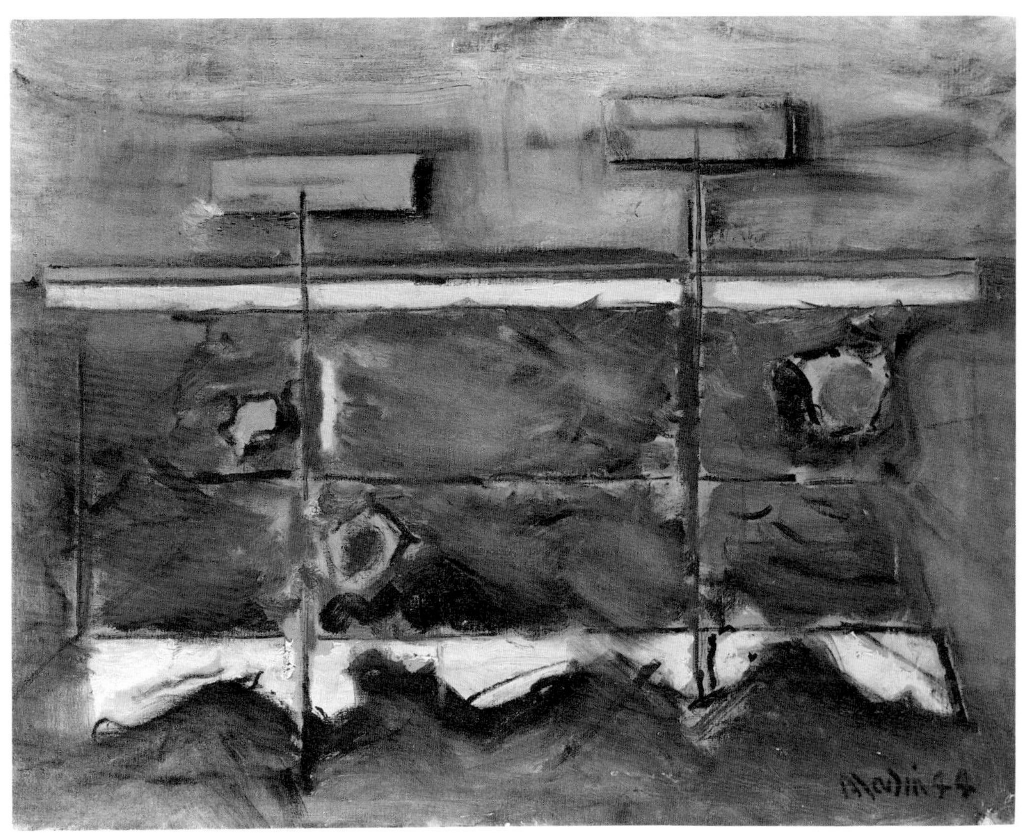

FIG. 28
JOHN MARIN
Related to Hurricane, 1944
Oil on canvas. 22 x 28 in.
Courtesy Kennedy Galleries, Inc., New York

the sea, as well as by a new interest in circus performers, both human and animal, which had made their first appearances in the thirties. The boats, so frequent in the watercolors, now begin to move more regularly through oil, and they, like the nymphs and the frequently included islands, make shapes that counterbalance the surge of the sea.

After 1937 the frequent move of the watercolors toward the opacity of oil was arrested, and the medium's inherent transparencies were fully restored. Some of this transparency began to seep into the oils of the forties. Marin began to show more concern with the reflection and refraction of light. The oil was thinned, but hardly to watercolor consistency; hues grew more lucid or were lightened with white. The layering of wet strokes created a more complex modulation of light. The sea's and the canvas's surface, as a mirror of light, became more pronounced; the dense, dark blues and greens surrendered to a greater variety of not only hue and tone but also thick and thin paint. Bare canvas returned, but now to achieve a greater dynamism than in the earlier watercolor-dependent oils. In *Maine Sea with Island* (1940), the heavy black marks begin to thin and fade and the frantic strokes to subside; light and color are invited in to play a more significant role: green shimmering with white bobs up and down on the ocean's blue. In *Pink Rocks and Green Sea,* painted in the same year and at the same site, the surface is bleached and thinned by mist-shrouded sunlight. By 1944 the impasto had moved into a new collusion, with lilting immateriality. Only the insistence of the broken green horizon line and the schools of wriggling and rippling blue-green strokes separate the striated sky from its reflections on the ocean surface in an untitled seascape of 1944. The clarity of counter-pointing strokes, light, and space assume a blissful ease.

The passage of Marin's oils into energized grace found more favor with his critics, but the oils were still often overlooked. The *New Yorker* profile of Marin by Matthew Josephson, published in 1942, gives evidence of his increasing fame, but makes not one reference to the oils.[37] Jerome Mellquist, however, continued to praise the oils and made Marin the final chapter ("The Master of Equilibrium") of his book on American modernism, which he began with Whistler.[38]

The continuing attempts by Mellquist and his generation to isolate the Americanism in modernism is in marked contrast to the new internationalism that was growing in New York in the forties—a new Americanism that was openly assimilating European modernism and pitting itself directly against it. The monstrousness of Hitler's war caused few disturbances on American shores (the pain suffered by the loss of loved ones notwithstanding); indeed, the disastrous dislocations taking place in Europe were a major ingredient in establishing New York as the new capital of the Western world. The arrival of artists like Breton, Ernst, Masson, Matta, and Mondrian heightened the cosmopolitan tension and augmented the experimentation and the growing confidence of a younger generation. The year 1942, when both Mellquist's book and Marin's profile in *The New Yorker* were published, also marked the inauguration of Peggy Guggenheim's gallery Art of This Century. Advised by the likes of her husband at the time, Max Ernst, and Breton, Duchamp, and Alfred Barr, she had put together a major collection of Surrealism, and the gallery became a magnet for younger American painters. Jackson Pollock, who had been so influenced by Ryder before turning to Picasso and Surrealism, had his first exhibition at Art of This Century in 1943. Stieglitz's American Place now depended solely on Marin, O'Keeffe, and Dove for its exhibitions; Hartley, who died in 1943, had previously severed his relations with Stieglitz. Stieglitz's extraordinary enterprise was going into eclipse, and his death in 1946, as well as Dove's the same year, put a virtual end to The Place. The gallery itself continued until 1950, when its remaining functions were assumed by Edith Gregor Halpert's Downtown Gallery.

Marin, who had already suffered the loss of his wife in 1945, was now quite alone. He was stricken with a heart attack in 1946, but with the encouragement of Paul Strand, and later of his son, John, Jr., he continued to work. The figurative isolation that had been thrust upon him for so long was now literal. His reputation continued to grow, but as an institution more than as a living force. Yet the vitality of his continuing development belied the stasis so often assumed with fame.

Starting in 1944, the hovering planes and fractures of Cubism took on a revived importance that would continue for the rest of Marin's career. These final paintings first preceded by several years and then were concurrent with various proto–Abstract Expressionist attempts to relieve the rigidity of the Cubist grid and blend it with a fluid physicality. Picasso himself had already moved beyond his earlier strictures, and for Matisse and the younger Miró, Cubism hardly mattered anymore. The Cubist framing devices Marin introduced in the twenties literally become a window in *Related to Hurricane* (1944); the storm is seen on the window's plane rather than through it. The suspension of planes in a transparent liquid solution continued in such subsequent paintings as *Boat with Blue* (1945), where one rectangle frames the boat and two rectangles in the sky are reflected on the water and bend the surface in vacillating flatness. So, too, do many of Rothko's 1946–1948 watercolors and oil paintings move, though more abstractly than those of Marin, out of landscape into a painterly, aerated rectangularity that respects the boundaries of the support.[39]

In *Tunk Mountains, Maine* (1945), the planes and angularity are integrated into the subject to create a flowing, crystallized landscape. One year after that work, painting the same subject, Marin thinned the oil to near-watercolor consistency and took generous advantage of the bare canvas without relinquishing oil's more emphatic materiality and resilience. The viscosity of the medium is fully exploited as the brushes push the paint from the immateriality of sky to the stippling of shrubs. The merging of Cubism with the more organic forces of paint and nature that had so frequently preoccupied Marin are similar in intent to the irregular, curvilinear planes of abstracted body parts with which de Kooning began to layer his canvases in 1945. Although by 1948 de Kooning would have moved to a more insistent and homogeneous abstract overallness than Marin would accept, he has retained to this day a loosely folding and unfolding structure beholden to Cubism. Like Marin, de Kooning has always eschewed the programmatic.

Movement—Sea and Sky (1946) dances in and out of Cubist planar distillations, but in *Movement in Greys and Yellows* (1946), Marin felt free to return to a quasi-representational solution: all is ruled by wondrous wetness. The sunset's shifting radiance oozes through broad strokes of clouds, and the grayed sea is awash in rolling and rollicking whitecaps that scatter the sun's reflection. The "movement" of the titles calls back to Whistler and marks Marin's increasing reliance on the more abstracted acts of memory and imagination that were taking place in his studio. By 1947 the similar dynamics of linear angularity in the sea and the mountains could make the subjects all but indistinguishable from one another, and Marin could justifiably title a painting *Movement: Sea or Mountain As You Will* (1947).

"I'm calling my pictures this year 'Movements in Paint' and not movements of boat, sea or sky, because in these new paintings, although I use objects, I am representing paint first of all and not the motif primarily,"[40] he wrote in 1946. But Marin stopped short of abstraction, which he continued to consider self-indulgent; he was as critical of Mondrian as he was of the new abstraction taking hold in New York. Not only did "motif" remain important to him, but also the boundaries of the canvas.

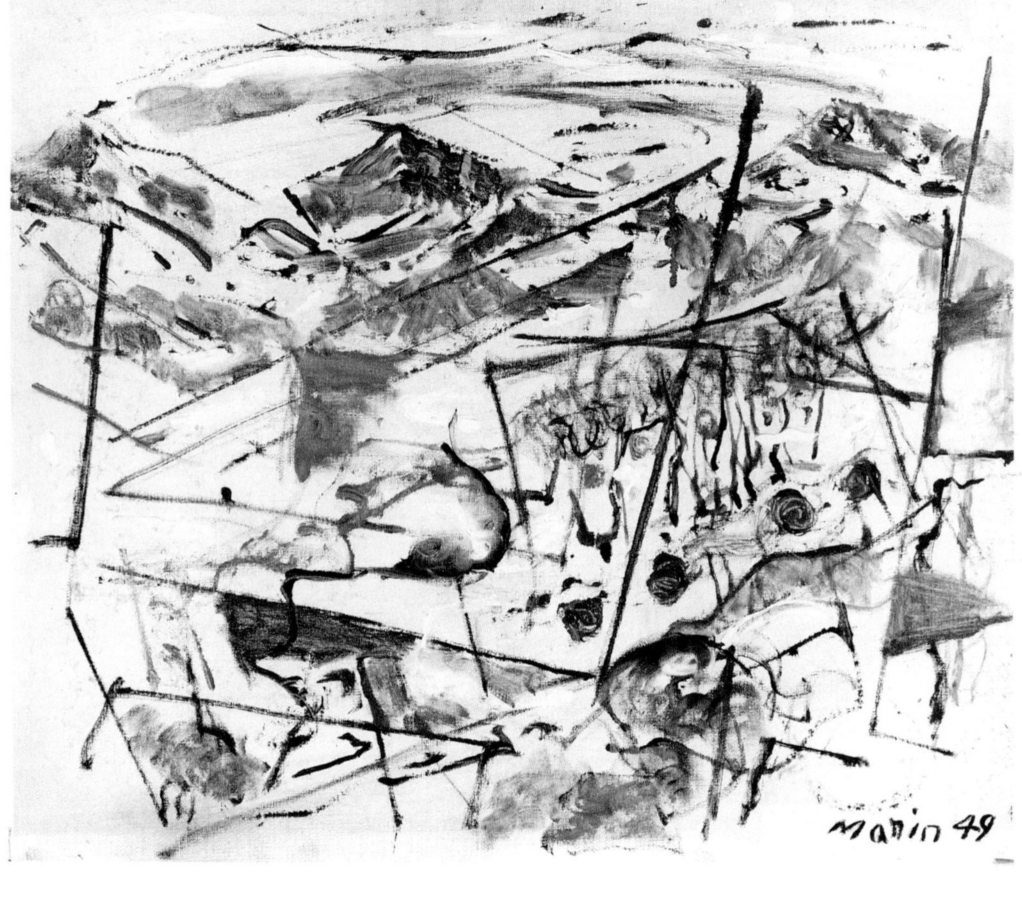

Fig. 29
JOHN MARIN
Jersey Hills, 1949
Oil on canvas. 24 x 29 in.
Collection Norma Boom Marin, New York

He always retained the small easel format of the early Fauves that still favored the subject as a view, although the view was made more and more to coincide with and conform to the flatness and the contour of the canvas. By 1947 Pollock, Newman, and Still had all, to varying degrees, achieved a new, self-consciously heroic abstraction that broke the boundaries of Cubism with a seamless painterly homogeneity. The sheer size of many of their works aspired to wallness and engaged peripheral vision. They replaced the rectilinear regulation of Cubism with an open and palpable vastness. Now it was not the view that was vast, but the actual painting. Pollock did not represent nature; instead, in an existential leap, he *became* nature. The luminous flatness of late Monet paintings, the flowing openness of Matisse, and the boundlessness of Miró's automatism all played a role in this new modernist abstraction that rendered "old" the solutions of Marin and many of his peers. In modernism's continuing round of revolutions, Pollock would challenge Marin's leadership.

In 1947, Marin's work was celebrated with a second retrospective, at Boston's Institute of Modern Art. (It traveled to the Phillips Collection in Washington, D.C., and the Walker Art Center in Minneapolis.) The exhibition was drawn from Marin's own reserve that had been selected by Stieglitz. The proportion of oils (19) to watercolors (45) was now more equitable, but one of the catalogue's essayists, Frederick Wight, credited the watercolors with more charm.[41] The other essayist, MacKinley Helm, found more favor in the oils but continued to extend the image of Marin as a billiard-playing loner, "as purely American as Buffalo Bill."[42] This image was more elaborately perpetuated in Helm's book on Marin, published the following year (it was here that the *Weehawken Sequence* was mentioned in print for the first time).[43]

Marin's awareness of the Abstract Expressionists is made clear in his foreword to Helm's book. In one of his more peevish utterances, he refers to "the so-called non-objective approach" as "quite too often a disease approach."[44] This defensiveness, so similar to that expressed earlier toward French painters, certainly was not grounded in any current lack of attention for his own work. In a 1948 survey of art critics and curators conducted by *Look* magazine, Marin was voted America's number-one artist, leading a group that included Max Weber, Stuart Davis, and Edward Hopper, among others (none of the younger Americans was included).[45] Clement Greenberg, the major champion of the emerging Abstract Expressionists, found reason in 1948 to praise Marin's oils over his watercolors: "His oils, however, tend to be stronger, ampler, even more temperamental than even the best of his watercolors."[46] In the same year, Greenberg pitted Pollock against Marin, "with whom Pollock will in time be able to compete for recognition as the greatest American painter of the twentieth century."[47] Indeed, the global ambition of Pollock and the Abstract Expressionists would shortly overshadow the more modest, epigrammatic modernism of Marin. When Alfred Barr was asked to choose three of the six artists to accompany Marin's retrospective of watercolors and oils at the 1950 Venice Biennale, he selected Gorky, Pollock, and de Kooning: all would soon reverse places with Marin.

Perhaps Marin's return after 1947 to the writerliness he first enlisted in the mid-teens was hastened by an interest in Oriental calligraphy and possibly even by a reaction to Pollock's new work. Line activates and agitates the lyric delirium of thinly painted planes that spreads across his final works in a synthesis of drawing, watercolor, and paint. The sweep of line and plane in paintings such as *Full Moon over the City No. 1* (1949) is at once thinner and more daringly free and spatial than in previous cityscapes. The calligraphic shorthand of the watercolors and oils of 1914 takes on a breathless speed and assurance in *Movement in Red, Blue,*

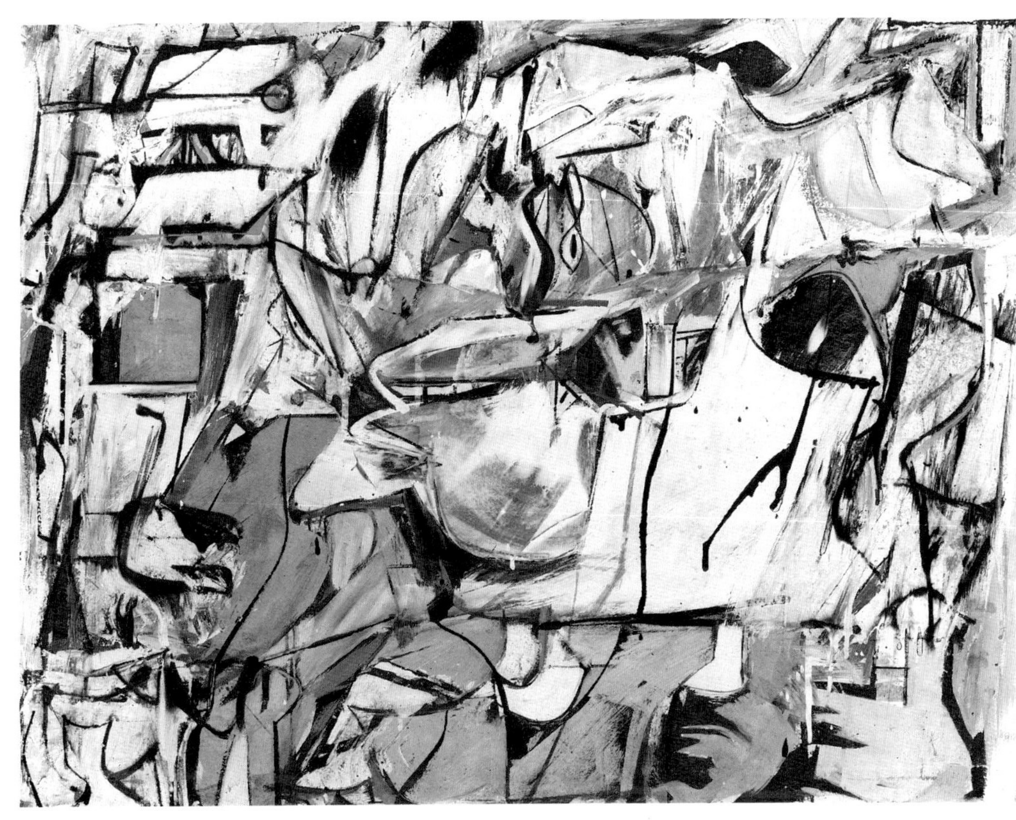

FIG. 30
WILLEM DE KOONING
Asheville, 1949
Oil on board. 25⅝ x 31⅞ in.
The Phillips Collection, Washington, D.C.

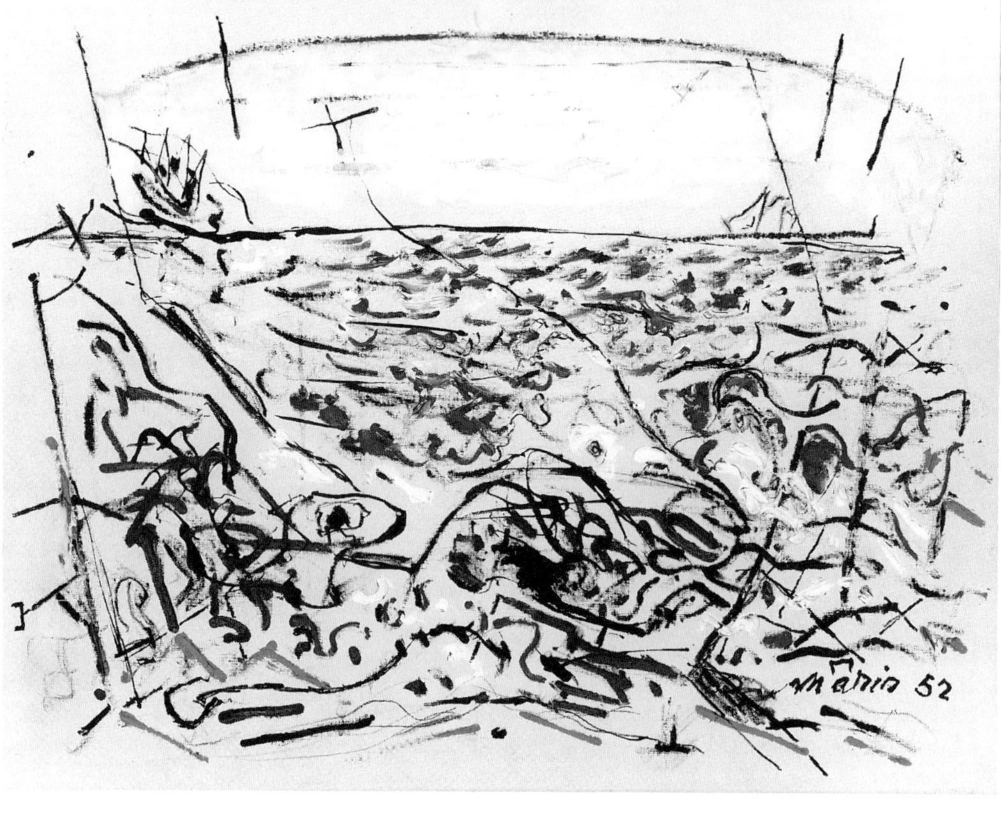

FIG. 31
JOHN MARIN
The Written Sea, 1952
Oil on canvas. 22 x 28 in.
Collection Norma Boom Marin, New York

and Umber (1950). The black that was so prominent in the thirties, and that began to be thinned in the early forties, is now further pared down and limbered up as it moves through multiple changes of direction, density, and configuration. To give his lines a more liquid urgency, Marin frequently applied thinned black paint with a syringe.[48] The line moving in and out of plane and contour turns *Turk Mountains* (1951) into a breezy imbroglio. The same line transforms the transparent rectangles that so frequently hung over or on the sea into an exquisite haiku, awash in pale gray and a few patches of blue in *Movement, Grey and Blue* (1952); Whistler, the Orient, and Cubism dissolve in a Marin solution. *The Written Sea* (1952) is just that—all is line, now spelling rocks, now spelling boats, now simply taking pleasure turning in and around on itself.

In its intimacy, its single color, its sheer joy in movement and rhythmic vitality, and its variations of line traveling in and out of conformity with a configuration, *The Written Sea* is strongly related to Chinese and Japanese calligraphy. Although one can be quite certain that Marin was familiar with Oriental landscape painting,[49] his awareness of the lesser-known calligraphy cannot be so readily posited.[50] Nonetheless, the resemblances are striking and obvious; and Marin was included with Tobey and Graves, both of whom had studied in the Orient, in a 1956 exhibition entitled "Contemporary Calligraphers."[51] Marin's calligraphy is freer and more energetic than Tobey's "white writing," although both remained mindful of Cubism.

Marin and Tobey were hardly alone in their strong preference for line. The paintings of Pollock, Kline, Tomlin, and early de Kooning are all grounded in the activation of line into paint and painting. If Marin's line was still partially ruled by conforming to the configurations of subject and canvas, its organic spontaneity and speed bear strong resemblance to contemporaneous Pollocks—especially to some of Pollock's intimate drawings of the fifties. Nonetheless, Pollock's more insistently programmatic engagement of chance in his "drip" paintings and the almost total immersion of his body movements in his paintings remain at a far remove in intentionality from Marin's use of both hands and a syringe. Marin's intentions are closer to those of such painters as de Kooning and especially Tomlin, who did not altogether disavow Cubism. The off-white planes shot through with a web of whiplash black lines in de Kooning's *Attic* (1949), though they are more intense and implacably frontal, are akin to the rustling linear planes snapped in and out of flatness in such Marins as *Sea Fantasy* (1952).

Bradley Walker Tomlin was much the gentlest of the Abstract Expressionists and perhaps the one whose work was closest to Marin's. With the encouragement of Motherwell, the early Cubist compositions he painted from 1939 to 1945 gave way first to Surrealist-derived automatism and cryptic symbolism and then to a purer, more painterly calligraphy (around 1948). Like Tobey (and occasionally Marin), Tomlin often referred to his paintings as being written, and he may well have been aware of Chinese calligraphy. The glyphlike meanderings of his line are more controlled and far less volatile than the movements of Pollock's line; their lyric intimacy and implicit reliance on the interior push and pull of the Cubist grid, although again more abstract, are closely related to Marin's paintings of the late forties in both composition and mood. The calligraphic dynamism and rawness of Kline's driven swaths of black paint have the heroic toughness and bigness so often associated with Abstract Expressionism, a toughness quite alien to the intimate mode of Tomlin and Marin.

Marin's final paintings are euphoric concertos of consciousness. Their lucidity and seeming modesty are grounded in the complex sophistication of his lifelong commitment to the workings of paint and nature. The vigorous grace of *Spring* (nos. 1 and 2, 1953) narrows

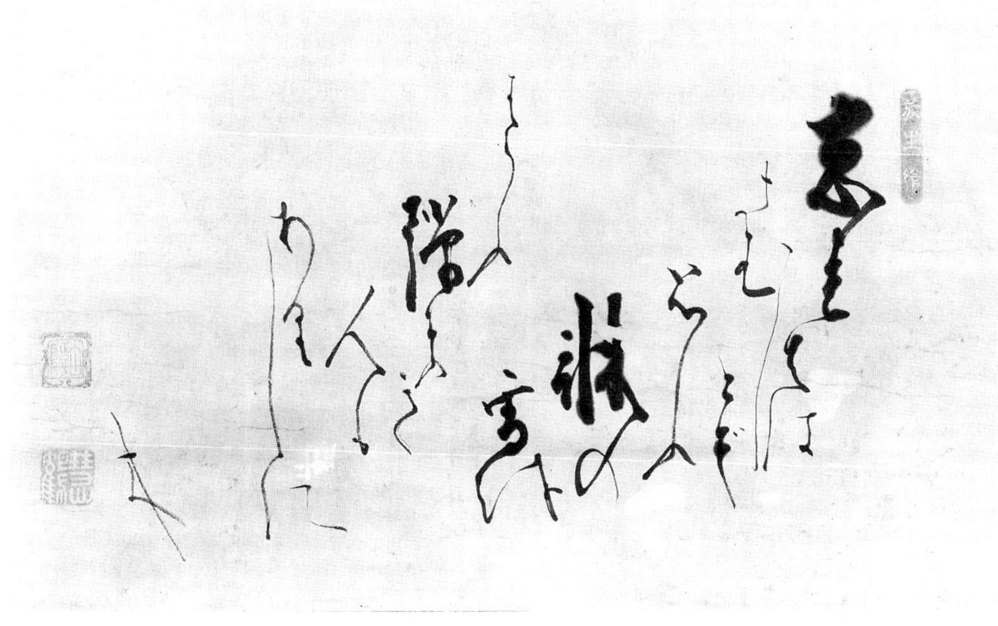

FIG. 32
HAIKUIN EKAKU
Poem about Snow
Japanese, Edo period
Ink on paper. 11½ x 18 in.
Fogg Art Museum, Harvard University, Cambridge, Massachusetts, Anonymous Purchase Fund

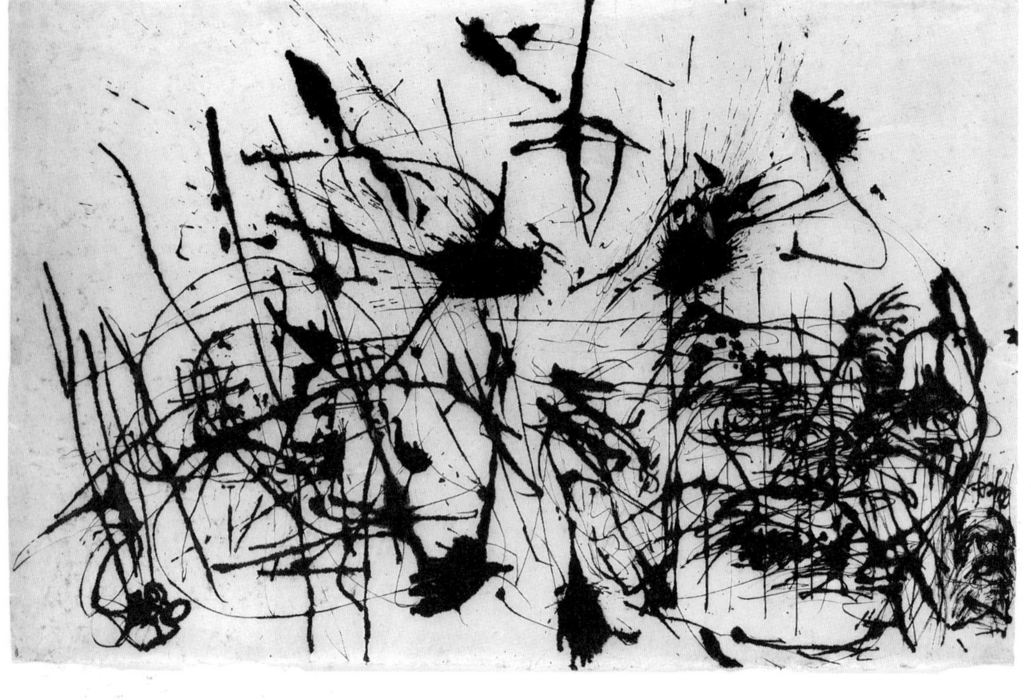

Fig. 33
JACKSON POLLOCK
Untitled, ca. 1951
Black ink on rice paper. 25 x 38¾ in.
Private Collection

paint down to its primal mark-making functions—marks as units of space, plane, color, and contour, paint as paint as nature. The movement from pasty opacity to thinnest transparency; from whispering, febrile straightness to more spontaneous, organic irregularity; from emphatic red to muted washes of gray to bare canvas—all are redolent of a life well remembered. In the blond grisaille of *Circus* (1953), mark making is freed of almost all its duties so that it may parade in a glyphic panoply of pleasure in itself.

Marin died in 1953, at a time when the Abstract Expressionist hegemony had already been fully consolidated and passed on to a younger generation. Regardless of the existential heroics and emotiveness that would shortly be subjected to modernist ironies and subversion, the Abstract Expressionists' variants of painterly overallness and frontality dominated many of the vital intentions of painting through the 1960s. Marin and peers such as Hartley and Dove became virtually obsolete for succeeding generations. His name was seldom mentioned outside of art schools or in the conversations of older critics and collectors (Fairfield Porter was among the few artists to praise and seek encouragement in Marin's version of painterliness). Marin's watercolors and oils, seen regularly through the thirties and forties by the developing Abstract Expressionists, were seldom credited as precursors or possible influences. Perhaps Marin became the victim of the same defensiveness he and many of his fellow artists (and critics) evinced toward the French modernists. For just as the need for an independent American art had seemed to require discrediting the importance of the Fauves and the Cubists, so later did the need for a more international Americanism seem to require the dismissal of the allegedly provincial earlier American modernists. The more willful self-consciousness and the frequent grandiosity—some of it indeed real—that became part of American painting with Abstract Expressionism would make the more modest forthrightness of a Marin or a Dove seem minor.

Since the late 1960s, increasing numbers of artists and critics have come to question modernism's relentless revolutions, upheavals that have been instigated by the quest for an ever-greater self-referential abstractness. While it is still often guided by modernist strategies, painting has once again embraced representation and referentiality. Early American modernism has been reviewed and revived and has even become an influence on a new generation of artists. Besides Ryder, Hartley and Dove have made noticeable contributions to Bill Jensen's development, for example. Malcolm Morley has come to admire Marin, and the agitated expressiveness of his paintings has much in common with some of Marin's paintings of the thirties. New retrospectives and catalogues raisonnés have helped restore the role of the early modernists. Sheldon Reich's excellent catalogue raisonné (published in 1971 and currently being revised) and his accompanying stylistic analysis have done much to see through the obfuscations that so frequently clouded the Stieglitz circle. Much remains to be done: Dove's paintings must be seen with Kandinsky's; Hartley's extraordinary late figure paintings must be viewed with and compared to those of Rouault and Soutine. The larger context eschewed by many of the early modernists themselves must now be attempted. Marin's oil paintings, so scantly praised during his lifetime, deserve far greater prominence in the story of his own development and in the broader history of twentieth-century painting. If not the equal of Matisse, Picasso, Pollock, or de Kooning, his forceful vision in oil paint is nevertheless that of a major artist. He was equally blessed and cursed by the modesty of his format, but the ambition that strives for masterpieces was not part of Marin's constitution. Of his peers, only Weber had the will (but not the way) to challenge and emulate Parisian leadership directly. But the singular clarity of

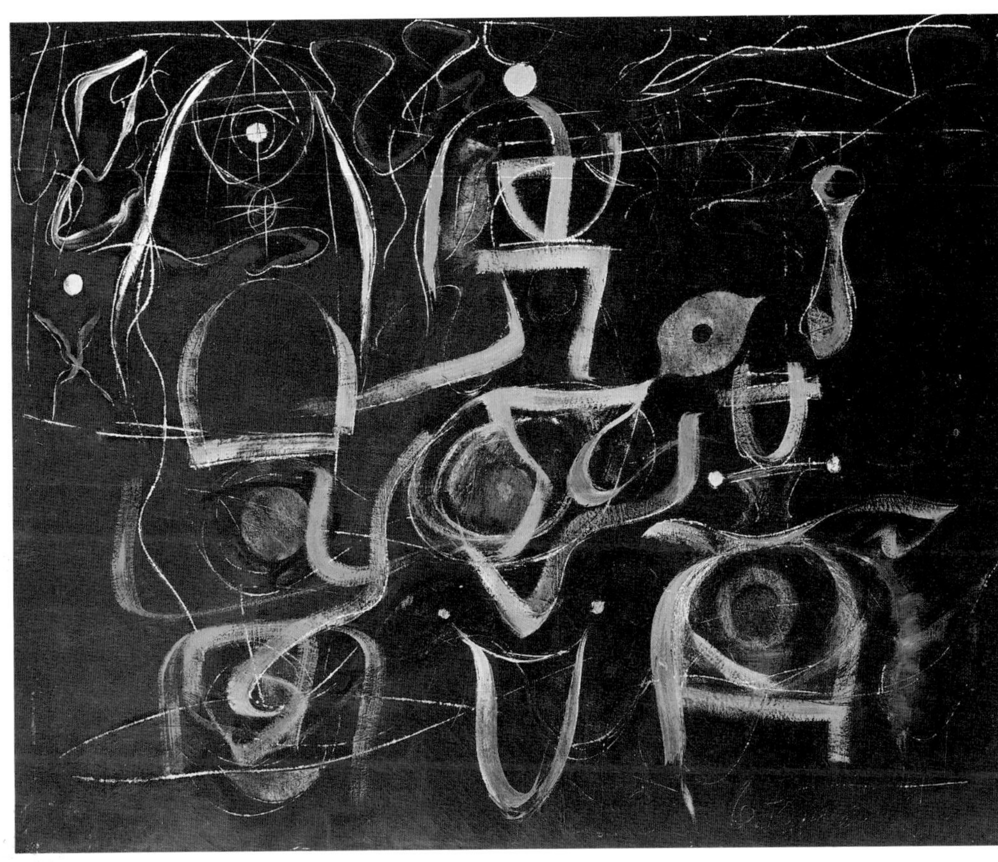

FIG. 34
BRADLEY WALKER TOMLIN
Number 3, 1948
Oil on canvas. 40 x 50⅛ in.
The Museum of Modern Art, New York,
Fractional gift of John E. Hutchins in
memory of Frances E. Marder Hutchins.

Marin's intentions often assumes a sweeping authority that belies his unassuming side. The smallness of his lyric mode is quite capable of bigness. His oil paintings need more time and exposure to find their proper place. It is hoped that this essay and exhibition will help to restore and reveal the painted pleasure and intelligence Marin hoped for himself when he wrote of that "artist—releasing the different folds of his seeings at periods of his many livings—He—be he working on a flat surface reforms his seeings on this surface to a seeing of his own choosing so that which he chooses shall live of its own right on this flat—"[52]

Notes

1. Sheldon Reich's thorough study of Marin (*John Marin: Part I, A Stylistic Analysis*, and *Part II, Catalogue Raisonné*, Tucson, University of Arizona Press, 1970; currently being revised) has already gone a long way toward placing Marin's work in a larger context. Reich's work is the major source for any serious study of Marin and has been invaluable to both this exhibition and this essay.

2. Matthew Josephson, "Leprechaun on the Palisades," *The New Yorker*, March 14, 1942, p. 27.

3. E. M. Benson, *John Marin: The Man and His Work*, Washington, D.C., The American Federation of Arts, 1935, p. 19.

4. Marin, in conversation with E. M. Benson in *John Marin*, p. 16: " 'When in this country I saw Cézanne I said to myself there's a painter not much else. . . . You and others have given Cézanne too much space, helped on by those Frenchmen.' "

5. This was reconfirmed in conversation with John Marin, Jr., on May 15, 1986.

6. Among his many activities, Fenellosa established and conducted the Department of Chinese and Japanese Art at Boston's Museum of Fine Arts in the 1890s; encouraged Charles Freer in his Whistler and Oriental acquisitions; lectured widely; and wrote a major book on Chinese and Japanese art which was published posthumously in 1912.

7. It would be exhibited in its entirety in 1914 with a catalogue by John Ferguson.

8. Marsden Hartley, "As to John Marin and His Ideas," *John Marin*, New York, The Museum of Modern Art, 1936.

9. MacKinley Helm, "Conclusions to a Biography," *John Marin Memorial Exhibition*, Los Angeles, Art Galleries, University of California, 1955, unpaginated. Discounting Cézanne and calling Marin "the greater constructor of landscape," Helm quotes a conversation vis-à-vis Cézanne in which he stated his preference for Sung Dynasty landscape. Marin is quoted as responding, "Ah, you have it . . . . Those old fellows knew how to make pictures."

10. *Camera Work*, no. 42–43 (April–July 1913), p. 4.

11. *Camera Work*, p. 4.

12. The Futurist Manifesto was published in the United States in *The New York Sun*, February 25, 1912.

13. MacKinley Helm, *John Marin*, Boston, Pellegrini & Cudahy, in association with the Institute of Contemporary Art, 1948, p. 33.

14. In a 1913 letter from Marin to Stieglitz, quoted in Dorothy Norman, ed., *The Selected Writings of John Marin*, New York, Pellegrini & Cudahy, 1949, p. 5.

15. Soutine worked almost exclusively in Ceret, in the French Pyrenees, from 1919 to 1922. There the lessons learned since his arrival in Paris from Lithuania in 1911 helped his paintings acquire their extraordinary turbulence.

16. Helm, *John Marin,* p. 9.

17. Reich, *John Marin, Part I,* pp. 89–97.

18. There is, as well, a related series of dated etchings (1915–1917) of Weehawken views (mainly of a grain elevator), the earliest ones done with hurricane gusts of lines, and the later ones turning to a startlingly reduced minimum of Cubist, planar notation.

19. In a 1919 letter from Marin to Stieglitz, quoted in Norman, *Selected Writings,* p. 52.

20. Norman, *Selected Writings,* p. 52.

21. Waldo Frank, "The American Art of John Marin," *McCall's,* June 1927, p. 37; Lewis Mumford, "Brancusi and Marin," *The New Republic,* vol. 48 (December 15, 1926), pp. 112–113; Julius Meier-Graefe, "A Few Conclusions on American Art," *Vanity Fair,* vol. 31 (November 1928), pp. 83ff; Paul Rosenfeld, "An Essay on Marin," *The Nation,* vol. 134 (January 27, 1932), pp. 122–124.

22. Thomas Craven, "John Marin," *The Nation,* vol. 118 (March 19, 1924), p. 321.

23. In a 1932 letter from Marin to Stieglitz, quoted in Norman, *Selected Writings,* p. 149.

24. In a 1931 letter from Marin to Stieglitz, quoted in Norman, *Selected Writings,* p. 139.

25. Helm, *John Marin,* p. 88.

26. Thomas Craven, *Modern Art: The Men, the Movements, the Meaning,* New York, Simon & Schuster, 1934, p. 313.

27. Craven, *Modern Art,* p. 312.

28. Craven, *Modern Art,* p. 326.

29. At the time Craven's book was published, Rivera, having refused to remove the depiction of Lenin from his Rockefeller Center murals, had to suffer their destruction.

30. Benson, *John Marin,* p. 20.

31. E. M. Benson, "John Marin—'and Pertaining Thereto,' " *John Marin,* New York, The Museum of Modern Art, 1936, p. 19.

32. John Marin, "A Few Notes," *Twice a Year,* Spring–Summer 1939, reprinted in Norman, *Selected Writings,* p. 185.

33. This was confirmed in a conversation of July 8, 1986, with Elaine Fried de Kooning, who first met her husband in 1938 and shared, as she continues to do, a painterly dialogue with him.

34. Sue Davidson Lowe, *Stieglitz: A Memoir/Biography,* New York, Farrar, Straus & Giroux, 1983, p. 353. Dorothy Norman, in a conversation of December 12, 1985, vigorously denied any interference by Stieglitz in Marin's work.

35. John Marin, "To My Paint Children," in the catalogue for his American Place exhibition that opened February 14, 1938; reprinted in Norman, *Selected Writings,* p. 179.

36. Jerome Mellquist, "Marin and His Oils," *The Nation,* vol. 146 (March 12, 1938), pp. 308–309. Mellquist proclaimed 1938 as "the year of Marin's oils" and concluded, "Marin is richer than he was before, and so are we."

37. Josephson, "Leprechaun," p. 27.

38. Jerome Mellquist, *The Emergence of an American Art,* New York, Charles Scribner's Sons, 1942.

39. According to John Marin, Jr., in a conversation on May 15, 1986, Rothko found much to admire in *Related to Hurricane* when he saw it, around 1966.

40. Marin being quoted in 1947 in Helm, *John Marin,* p. 101.

41. F. S. Wight, "Pertaining to Marin's Style," *John Marin, a Retrospective Exhibition,* Boston, Institute of Contemporary Art, 1947, p. 32.

42. MacKinley Helm, "John Marin: A Portrait," *John Marin, a Retrospective Exhibition,* Boston, Institute of Contemporary Art, 1947, p. 14.

43. Helm, *John Marin,* p. 33.

44. Helm, *John Marin,* Foreword.

45. "Are These Men the Best Painters in America Today?" *Look,* vol. 12 (February 3, 1948), pp. 44ff.

46. Clement Greenberg, "John Marin," 1948 article reprinted in *Art and Culture,* Boston, Beacon Press, 1965, p. 182.

47. Clement Greenberg, "Jackson Pollock," *The Nation,* January 24, 1948, p. 108.

48. " 'I fill up a glass ear syringe with diluted oil paint, usually black paint, and while I press on the plunger I draw.' " Quoted in Helm, *John Marin,* p. 72.

49. In one of the many references made by various writers to Marin's Oriental influences, Mellquist, describing the work of the mid-teens, writes of Marin as "not forgetful of the ancient Chinese whom he came more and more to appreciate." Mellquist, *The Emergence of an American Art,* p. 397.

50. In my conversation with him on May 15, 1986, John Marin, Jr., remembered his father purchasing a book on calligraphy, but to this date he has been unable to locate it.

51. The exhibition was held at the Contemporary Arts Museum, Houston, Texas. In his catalogue essay, Frederick S. Wight gives no documentation of any direct involvement Marin may have had with Oriental calligraphy.

52. John Marin, "Marin Writes," *John Marin, a Retrospective Exhibition,* Boston, Institute of Contemporary Art, 1947, p. 10.

PLATES

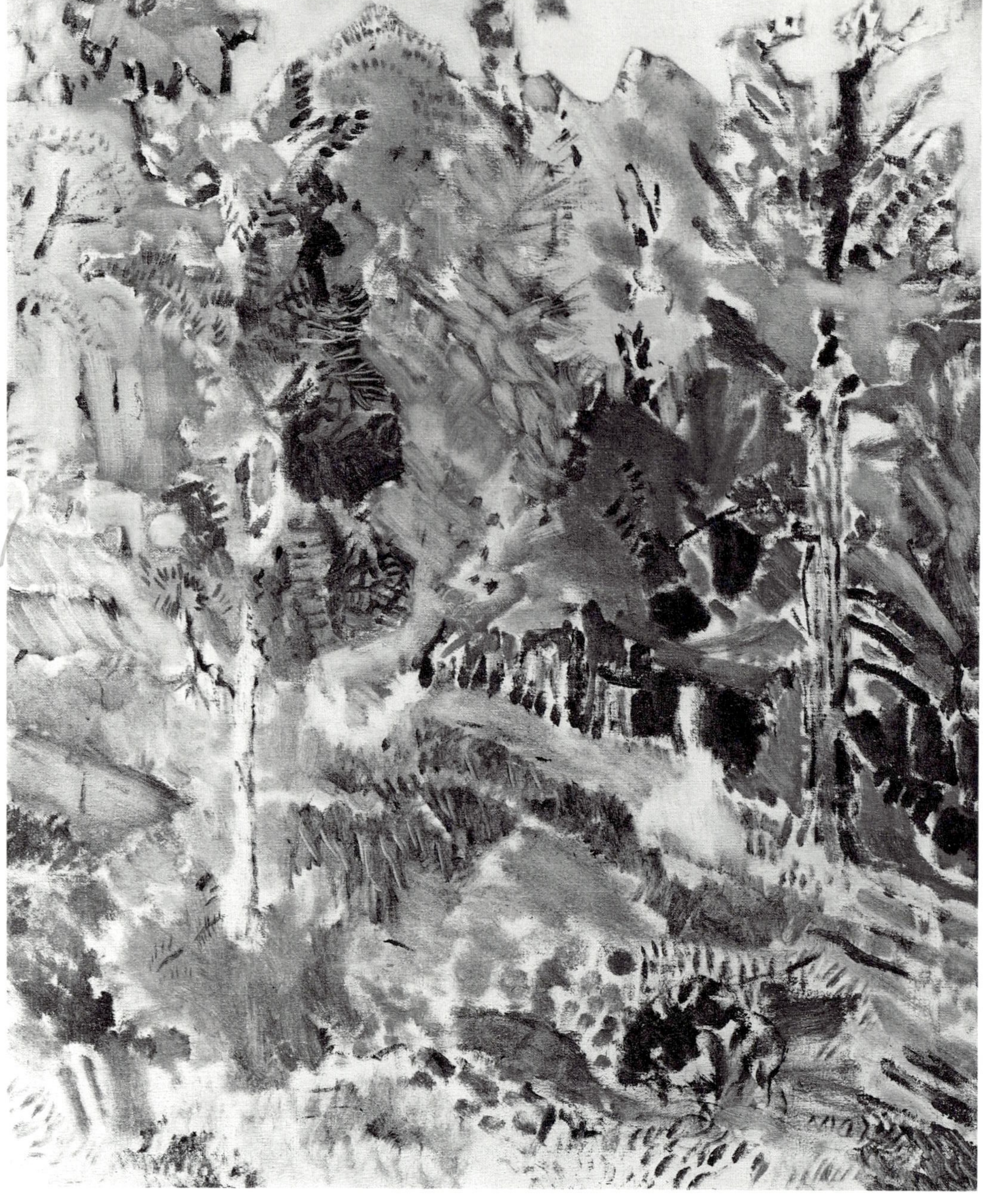

1. *Autumn, Castorland, New York*, 1913

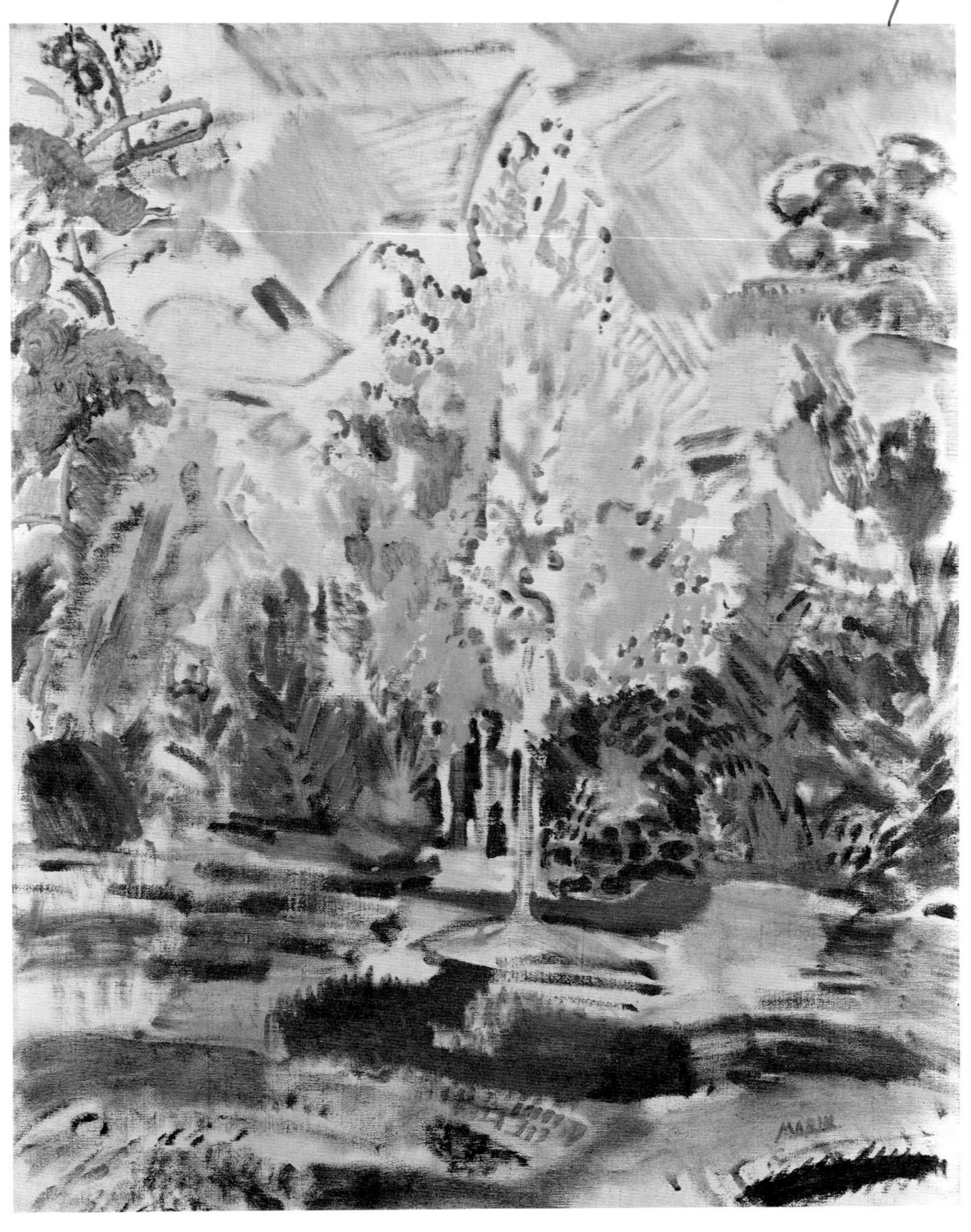

2. *The Little Maple Tree, Castorland, New York,* 1913

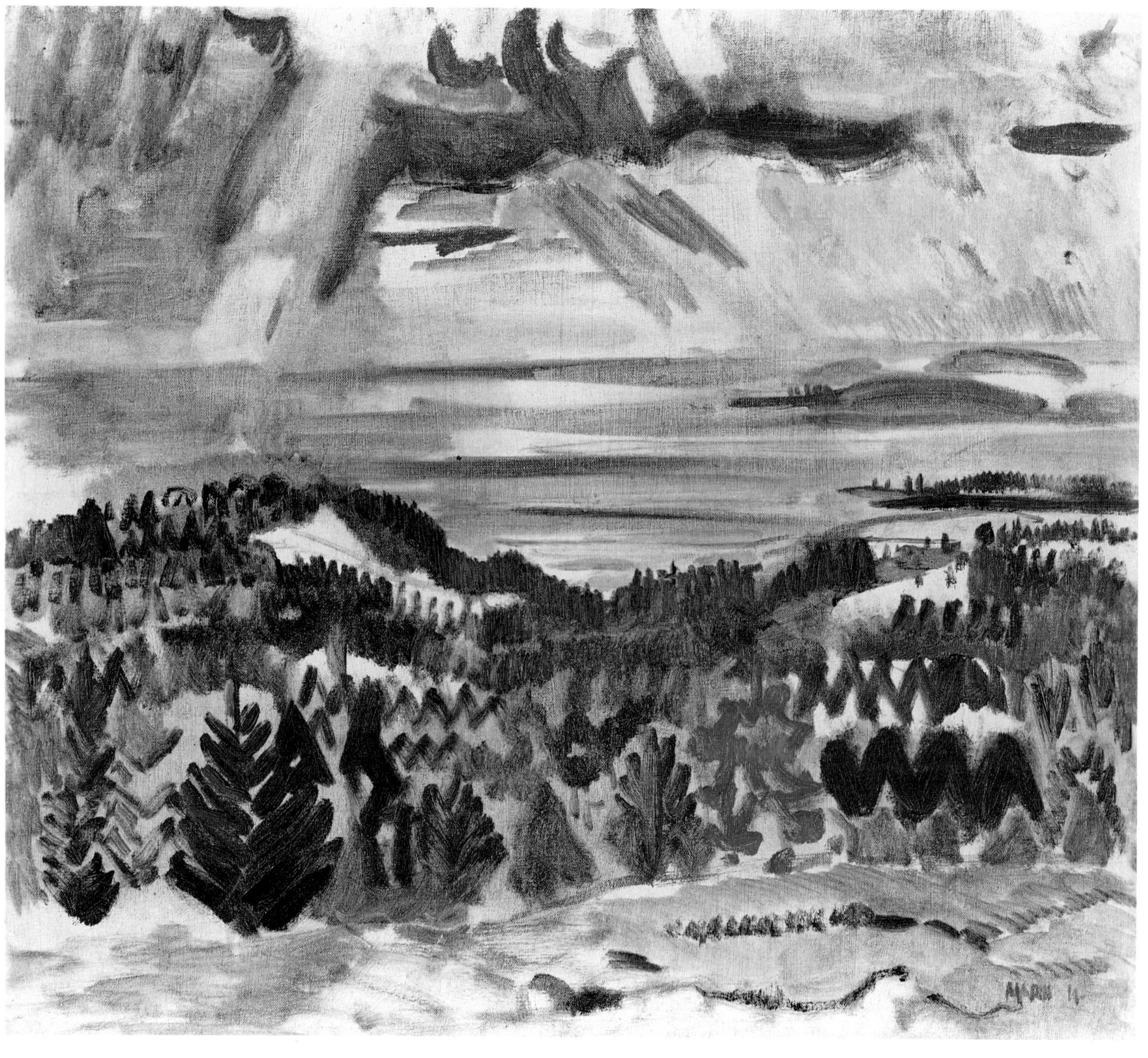

3. *Landscape,* 1914

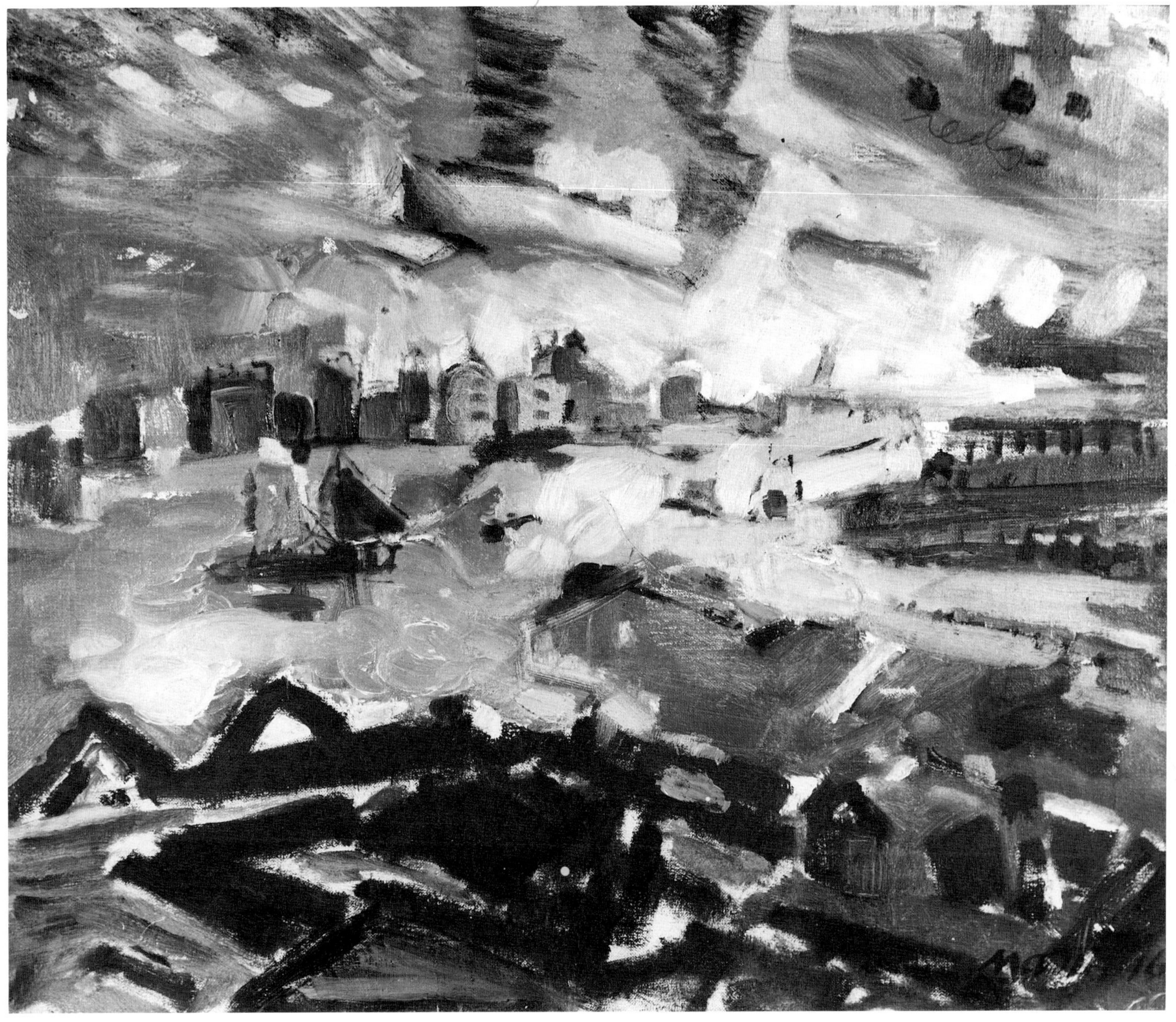

4. *River Scene from Weehawken, New Jersey*, 1916

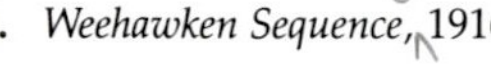

5. *Weehawken Sequence,* 1916

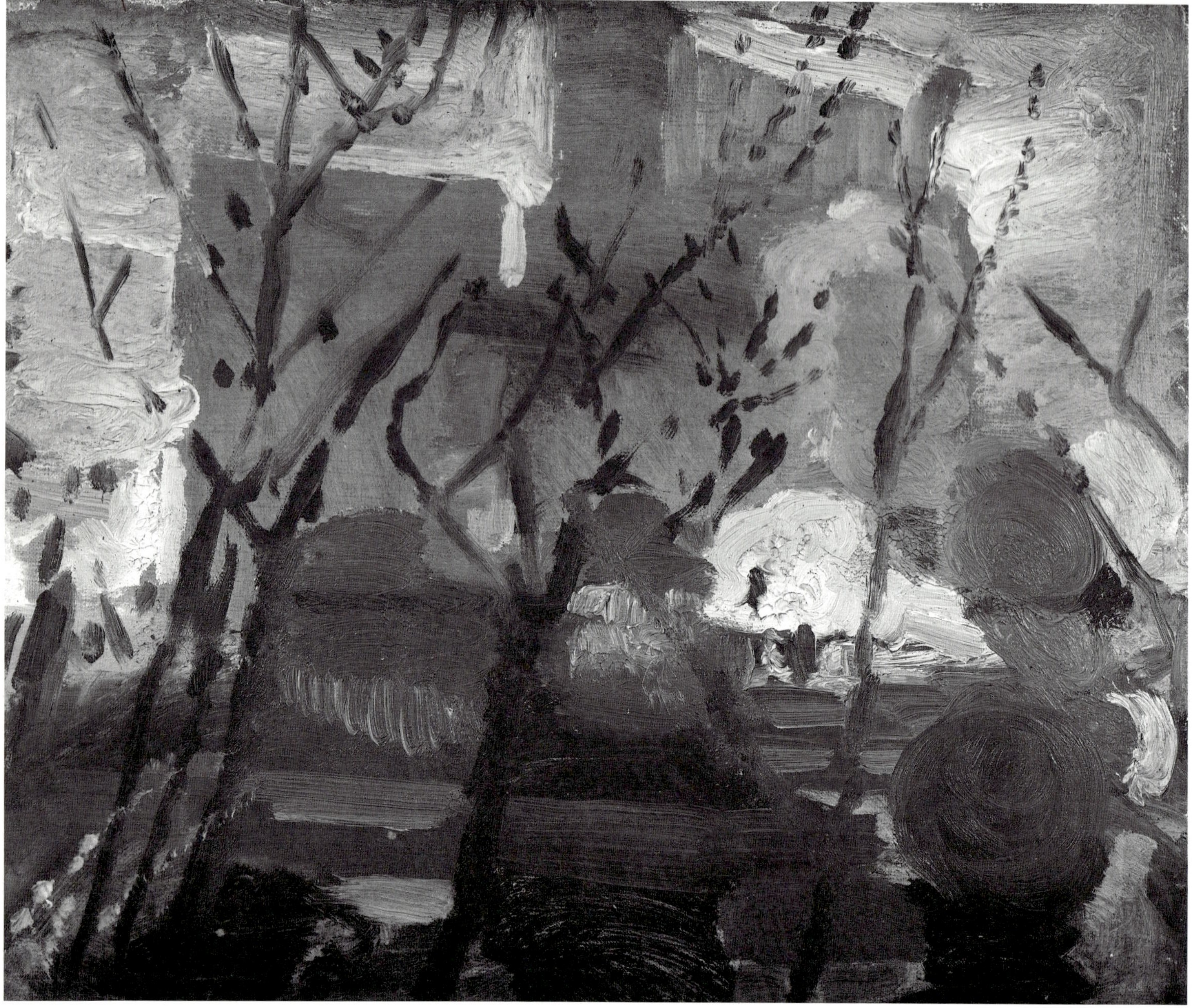

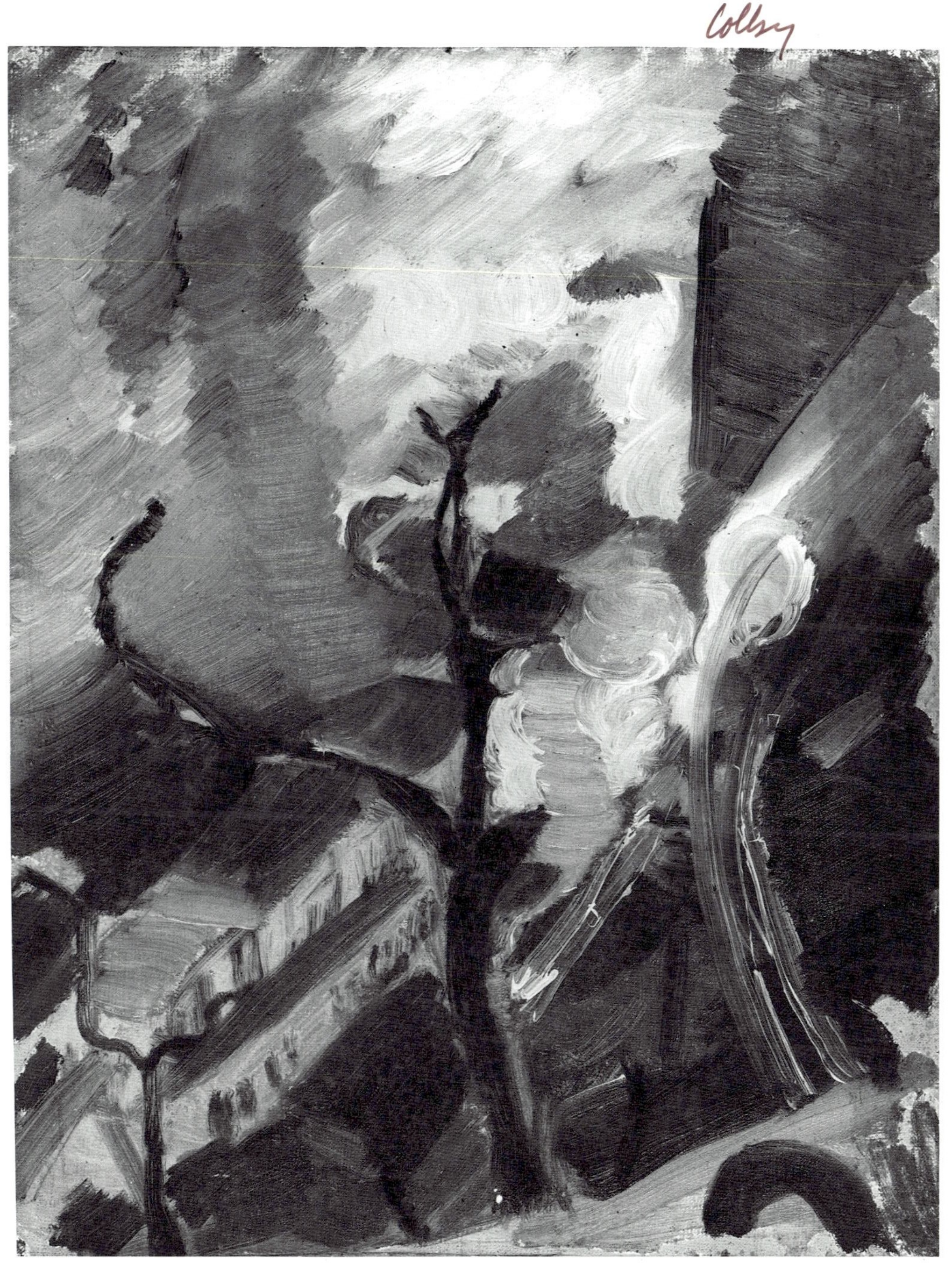

6. *Weehawken Sequence #65*, 1916

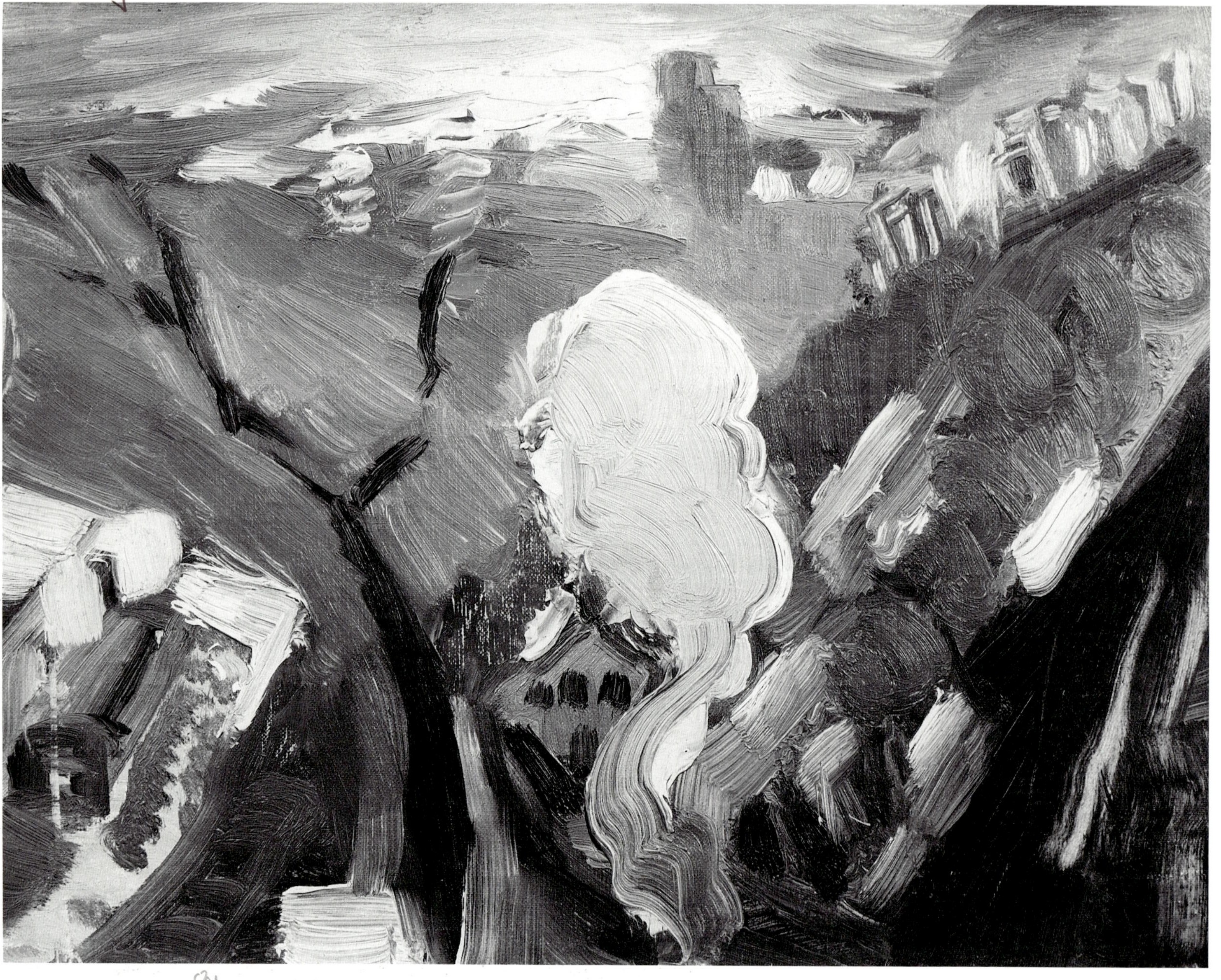

7. *Weehawken Sequence (No. 5),* 1916

Machias

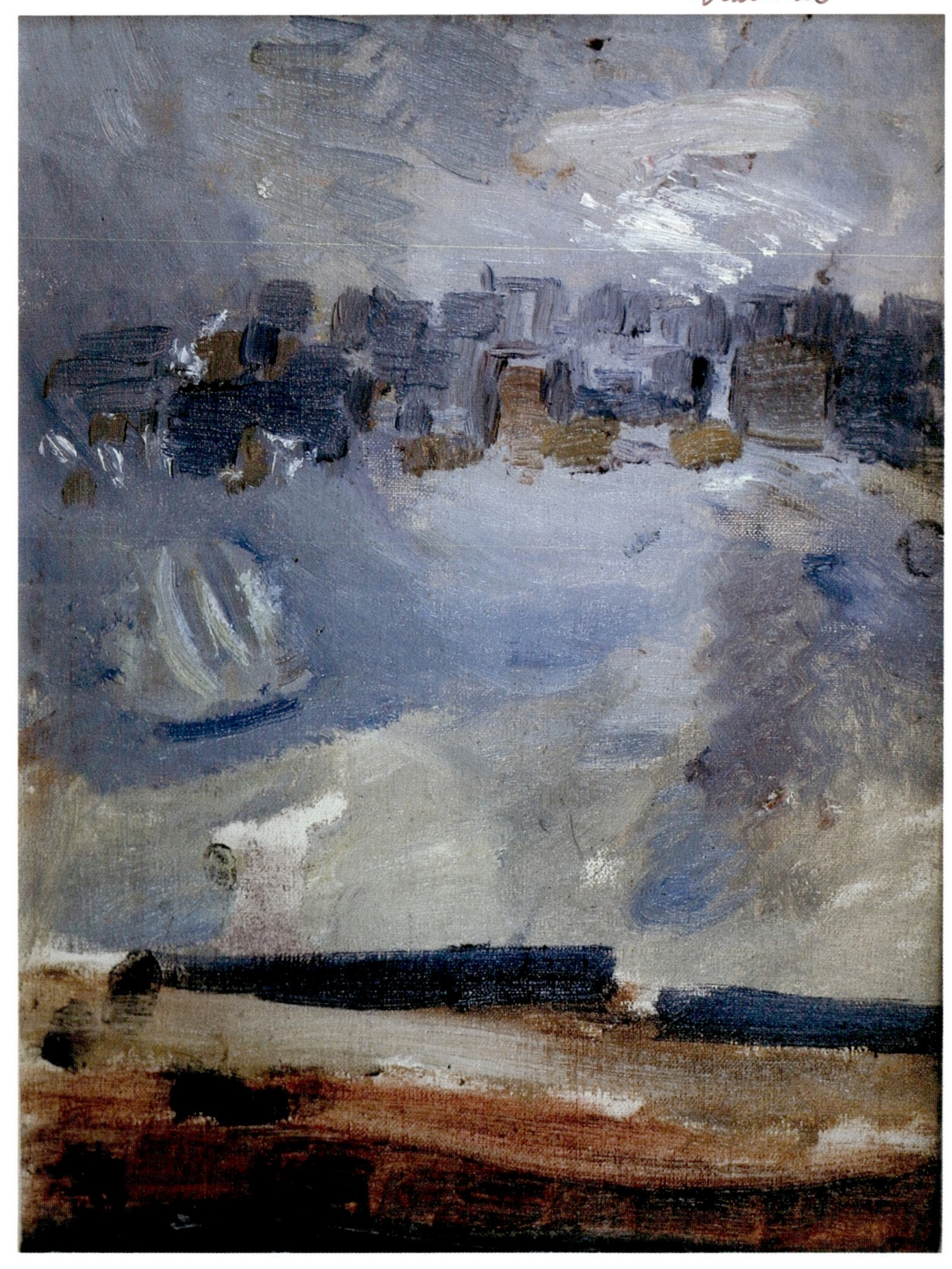

8. *Weehawken Sequence #80*, ca. 1916

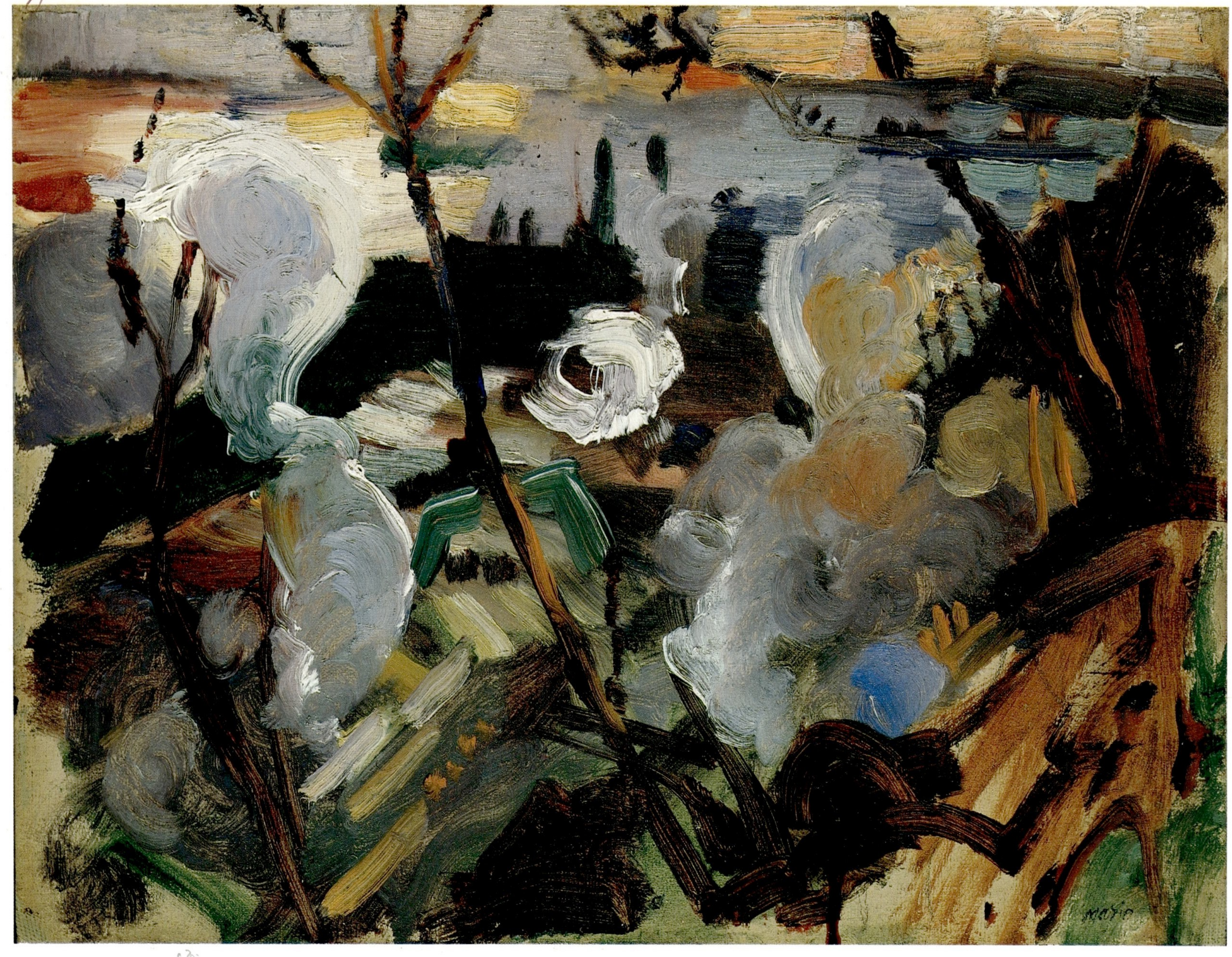

9. *Weehawken Sequence #68*, 1916

Kennedy

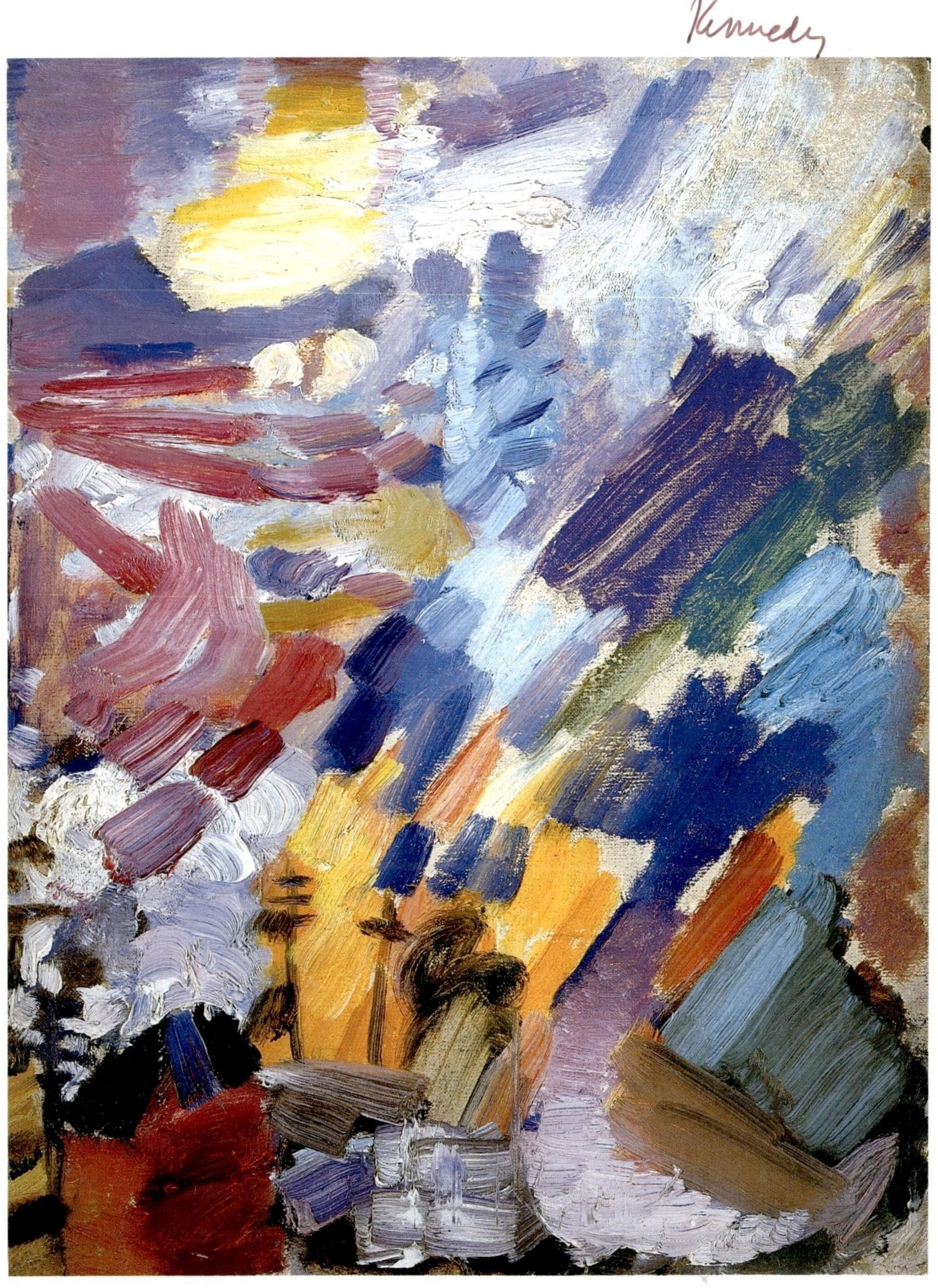

10. *Weehawken Sequence*, ca. 1916

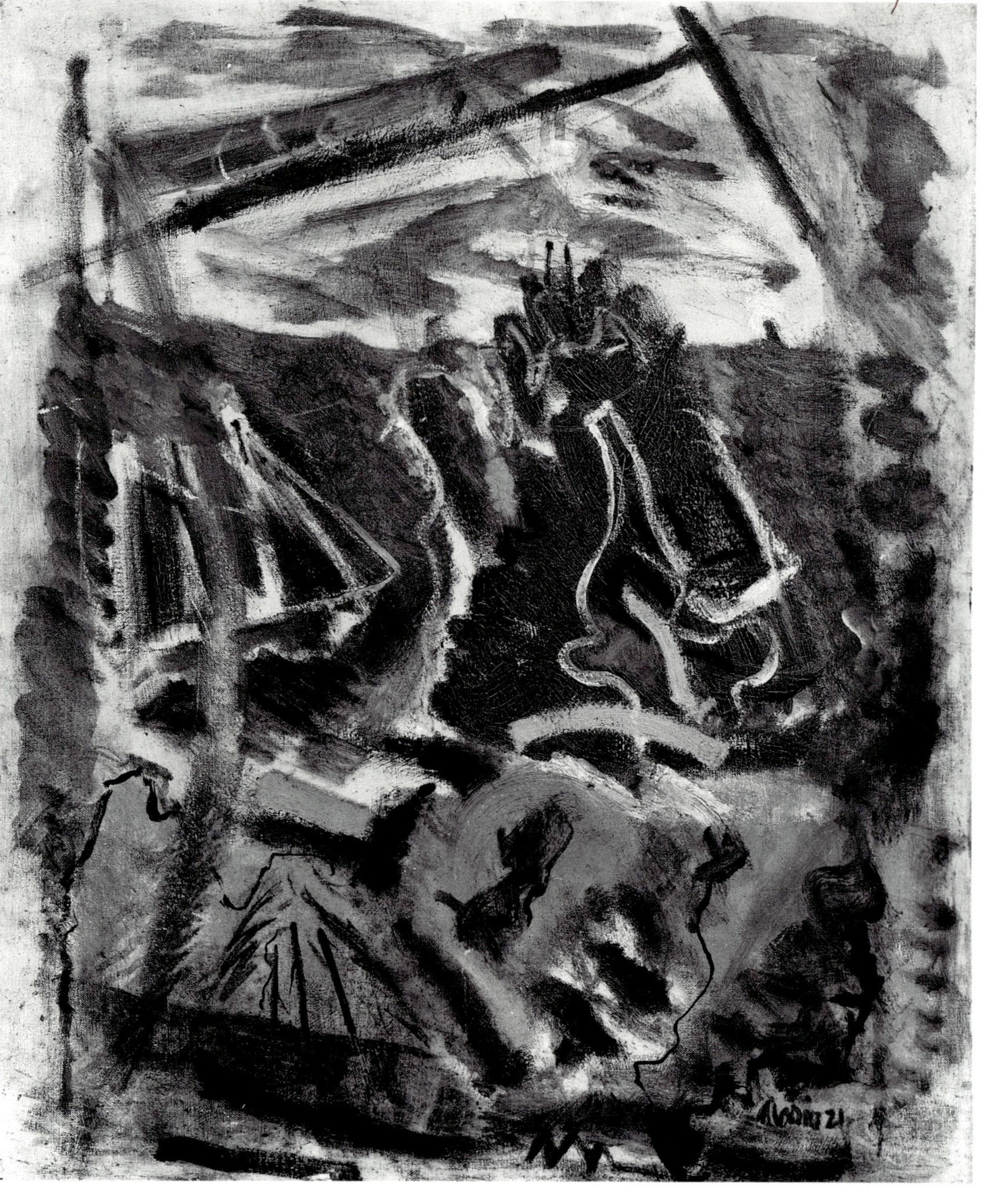

11. *Sea, Tree, and Boat*, 1921

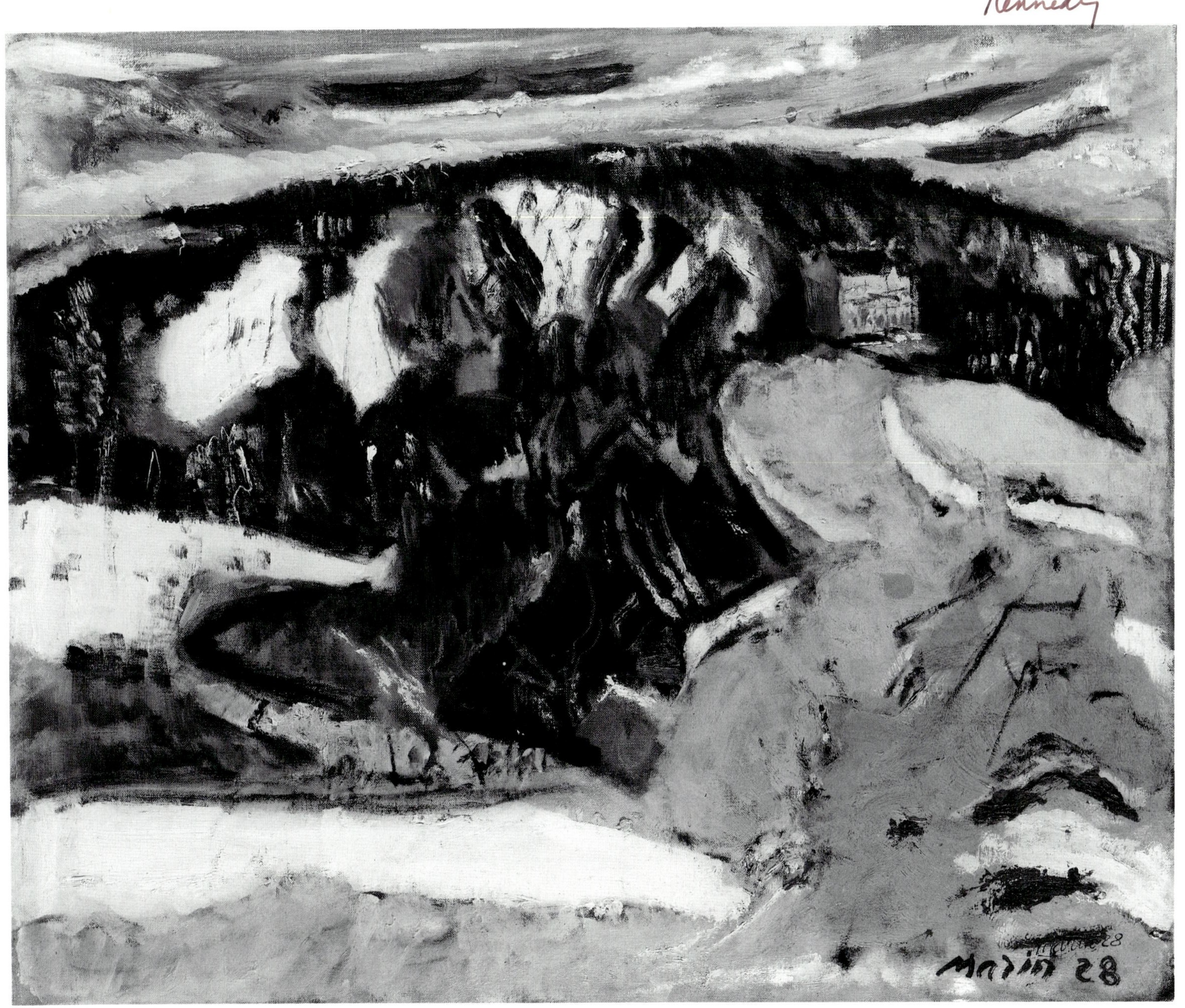

12. *Region of Sparkill, New York No. 2*, 1928

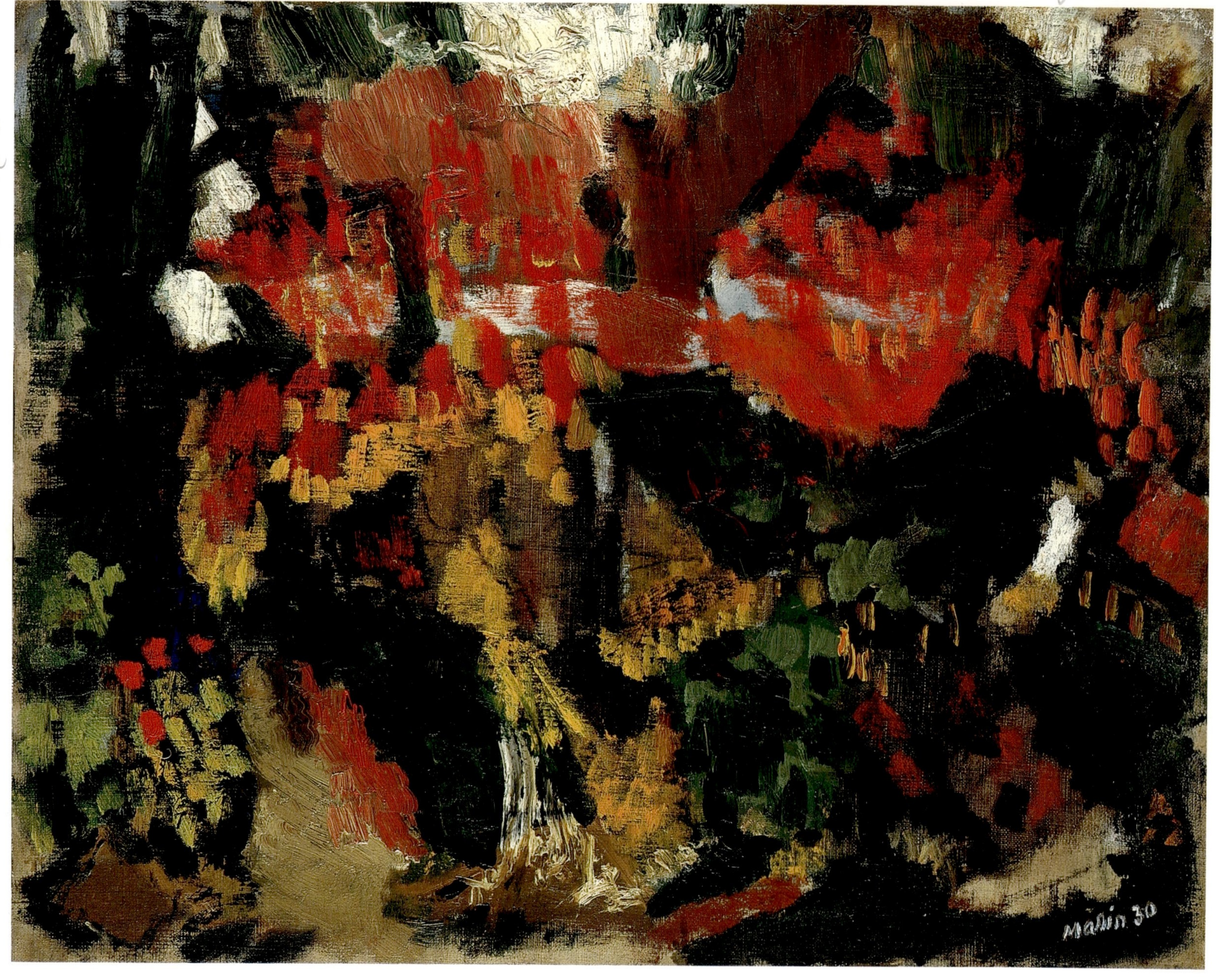

13. *No. 1, Fall of 1930*

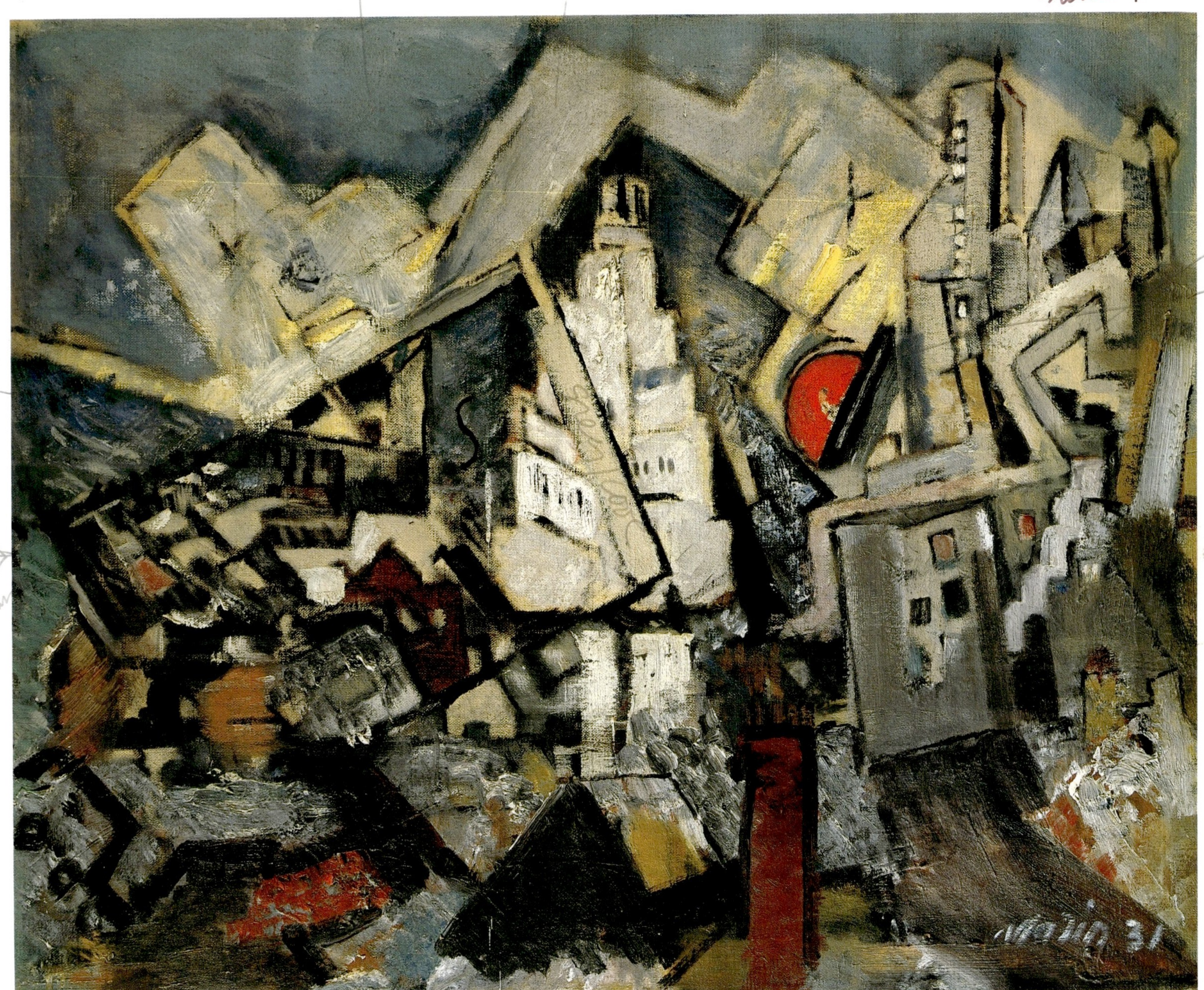

14. *Lower Manhattan from the Tip End*, 1931

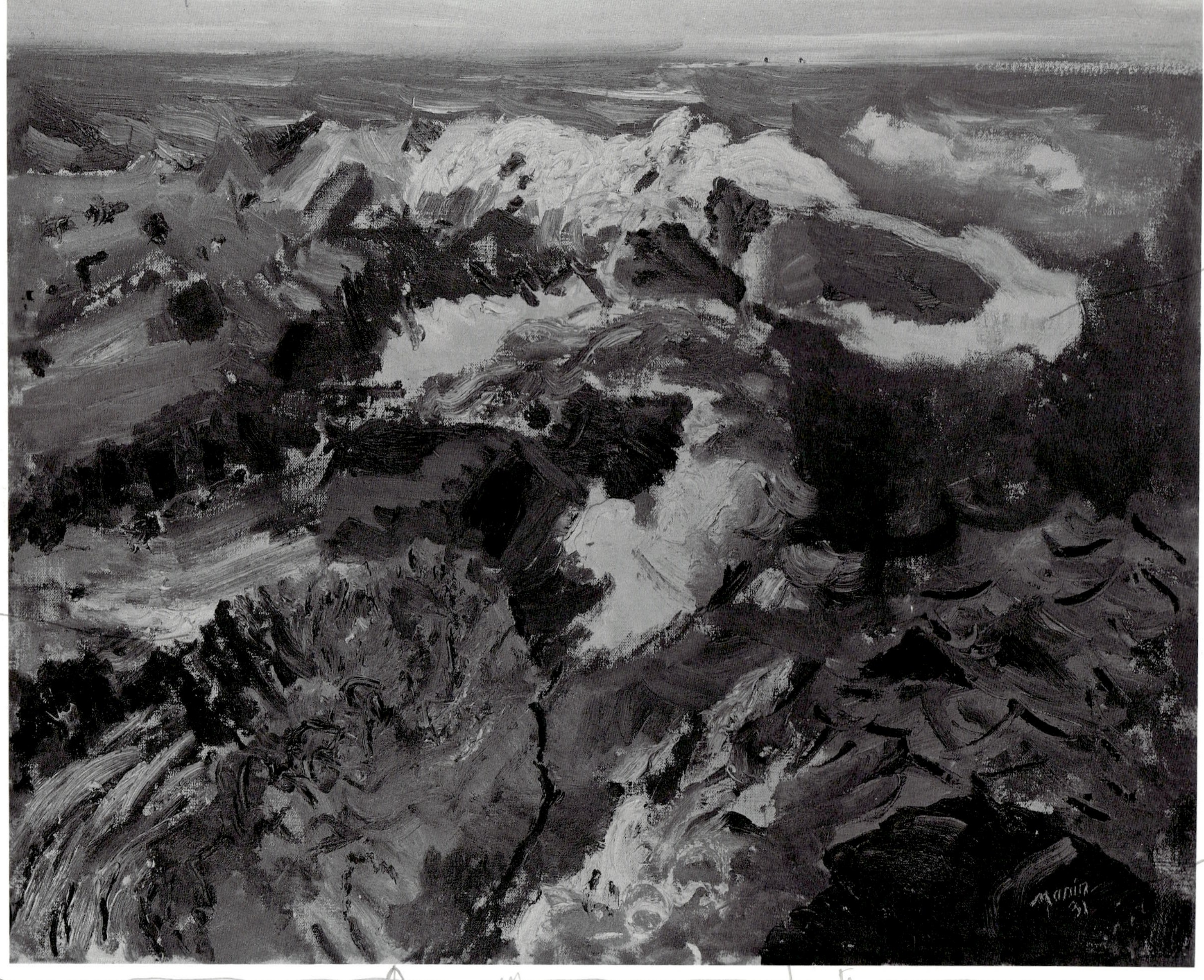

15. *Rocks and Sea, Small Point, Maine*, 1931

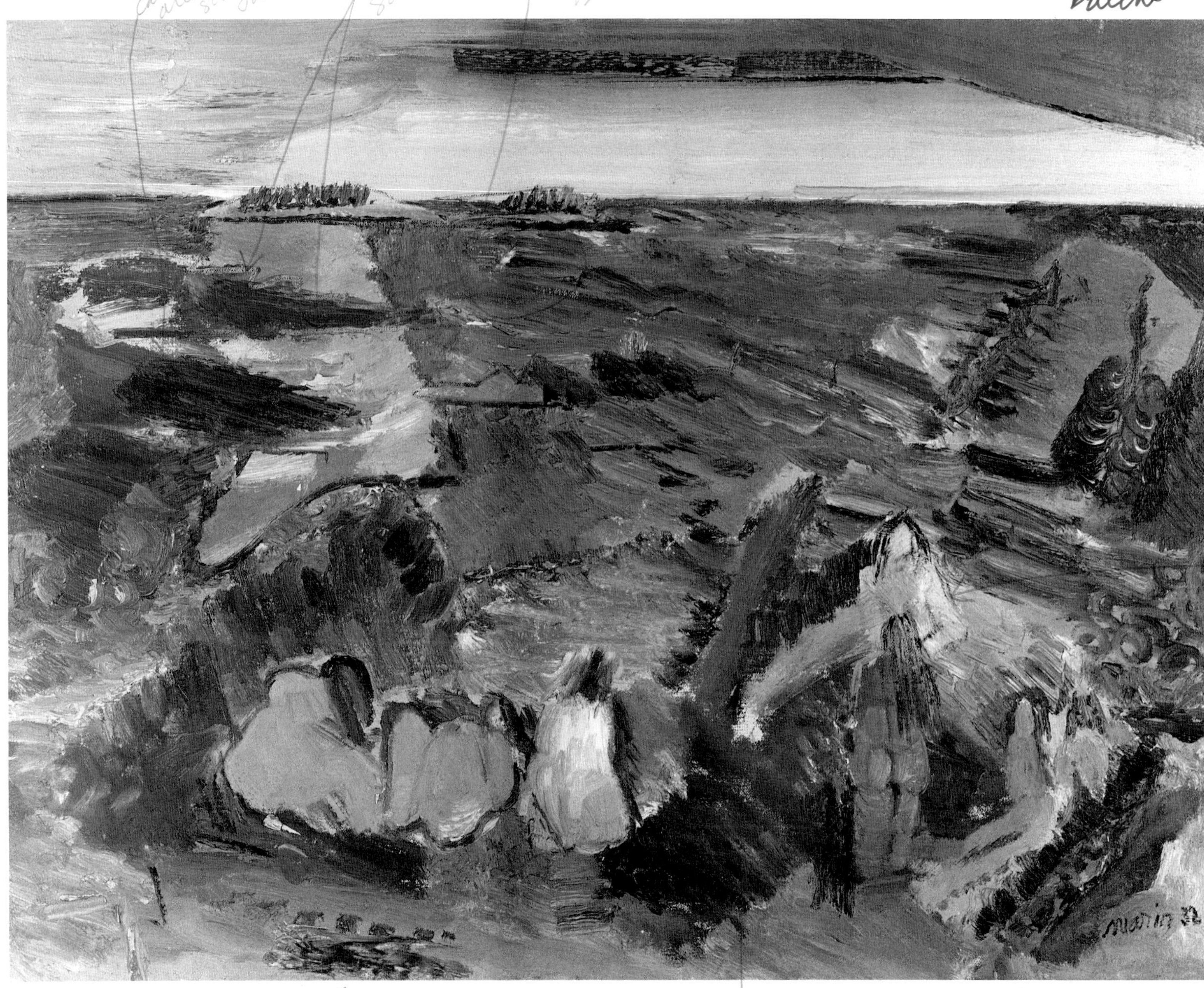

16. *Bathers,* 1932

17. *Looking Up Fifth Avenue from Thirtieth Street*, 1932

18. *Composition, Cape Split, Maine No. 1, 1933*

Santa Barbara : a real loss

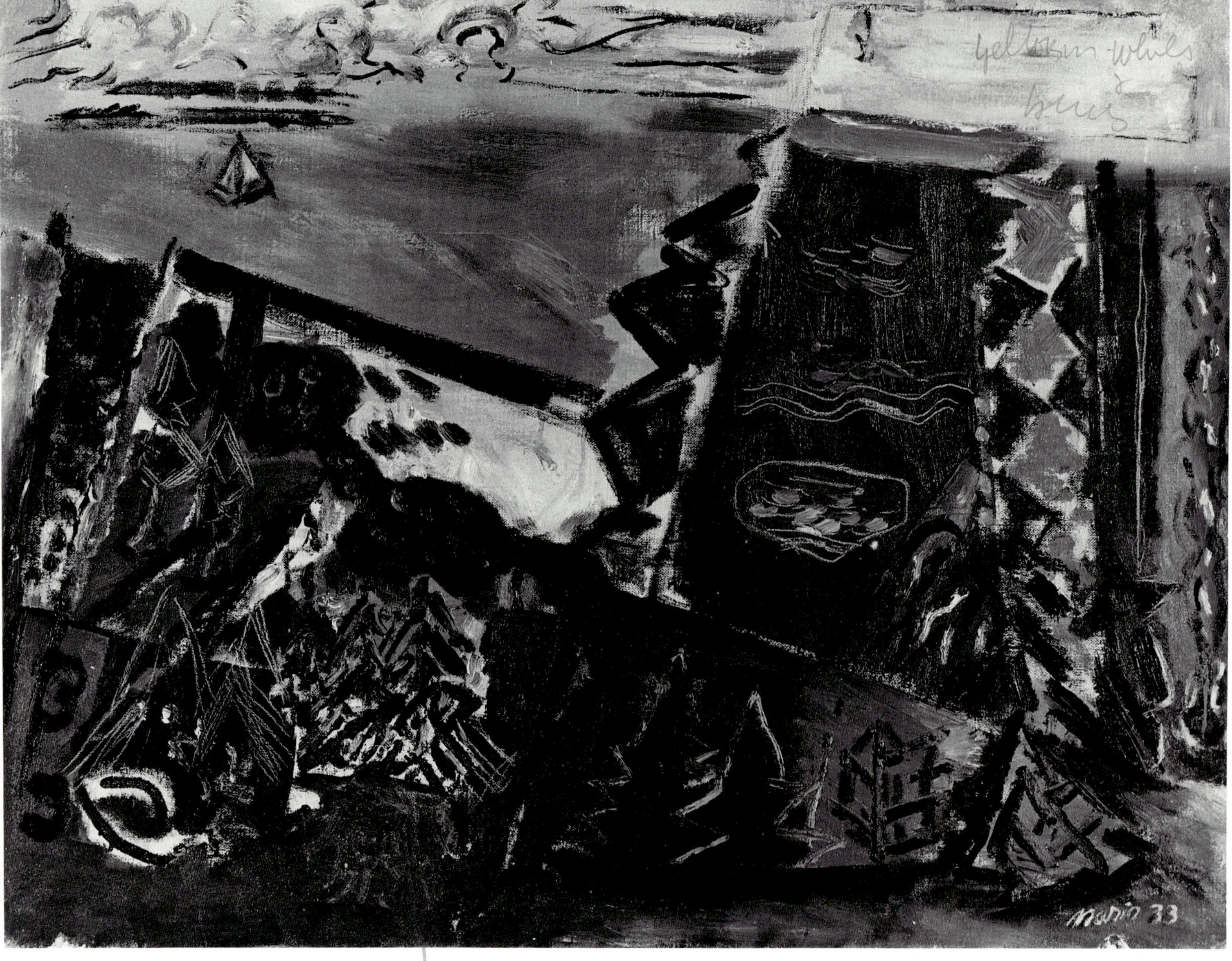

19. *Composition, Cape Split, Maine No. 3*, 1933

thick & multi-colored

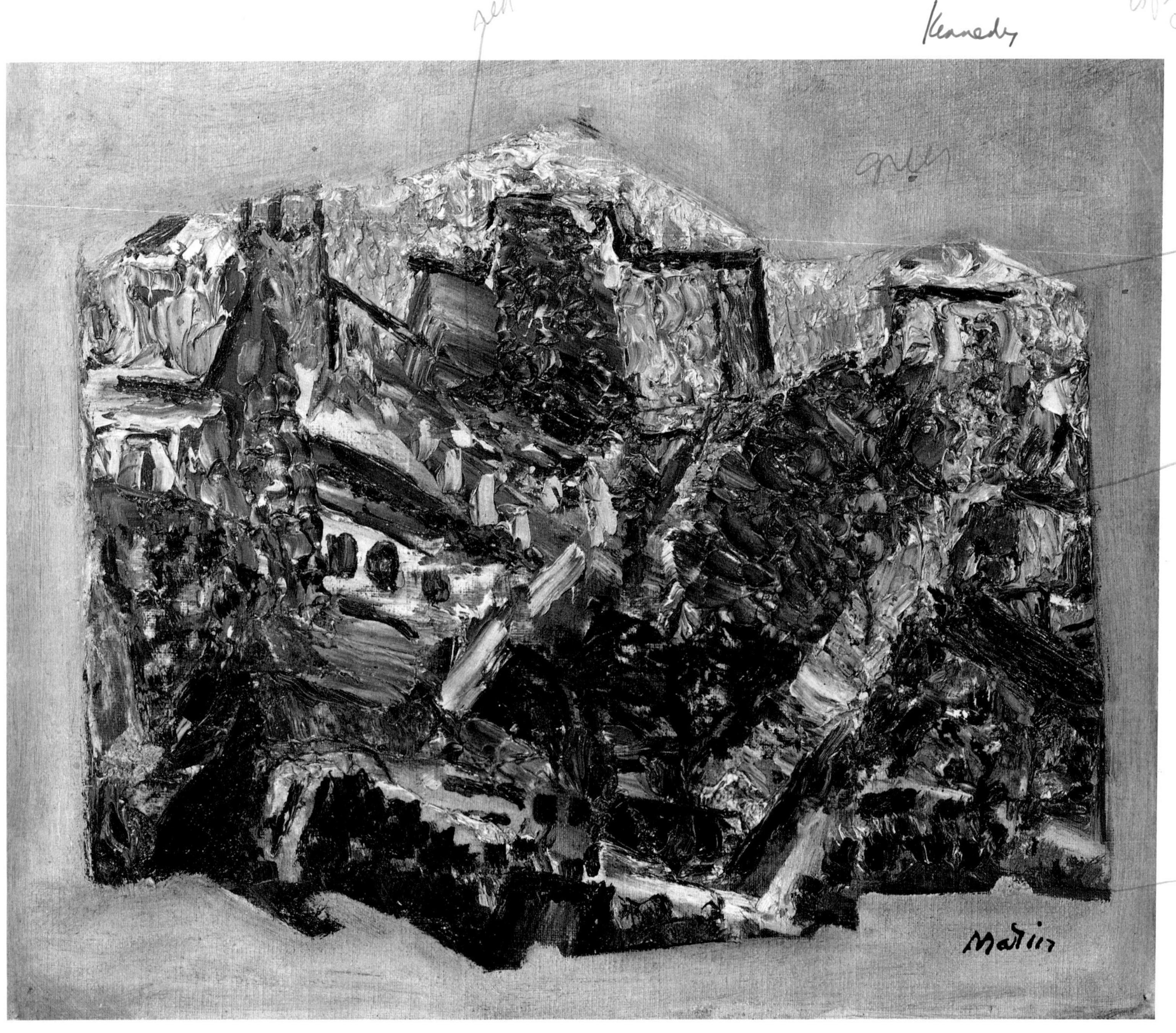

20. *New York,* ca. 1934

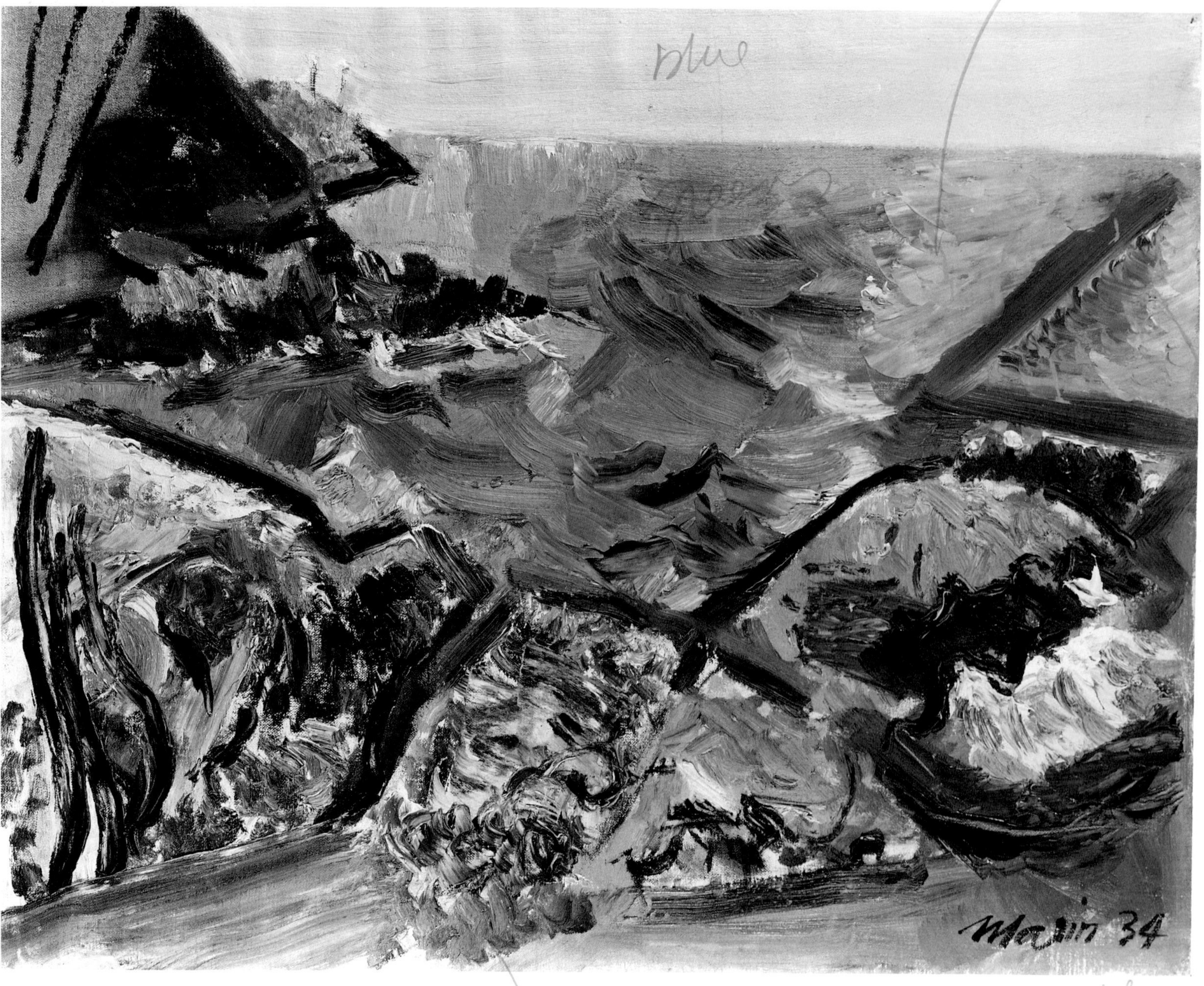

21. *Off Cape Split, Maine 1*, 1934

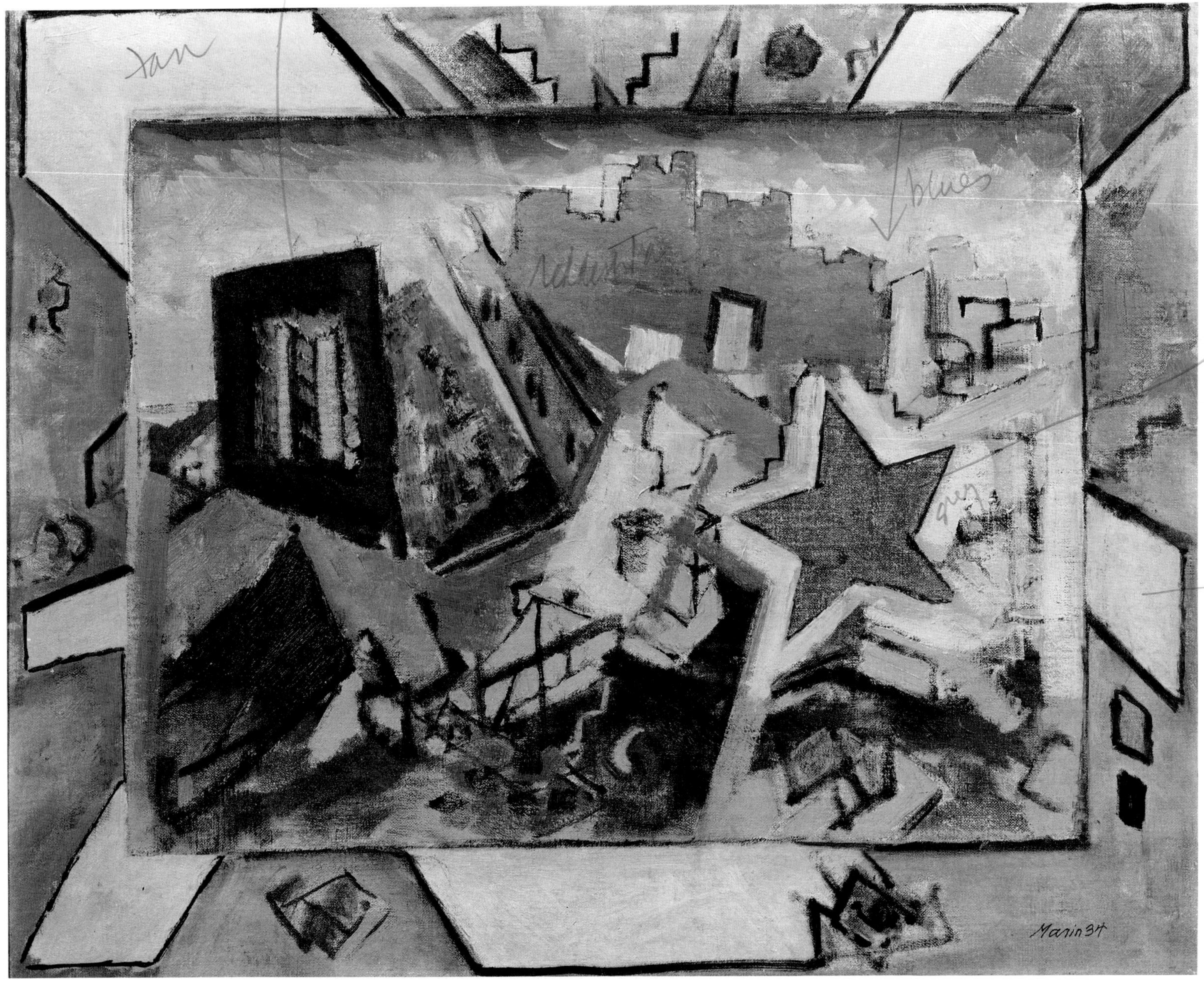

22. *Study, New York*, ca. 1934

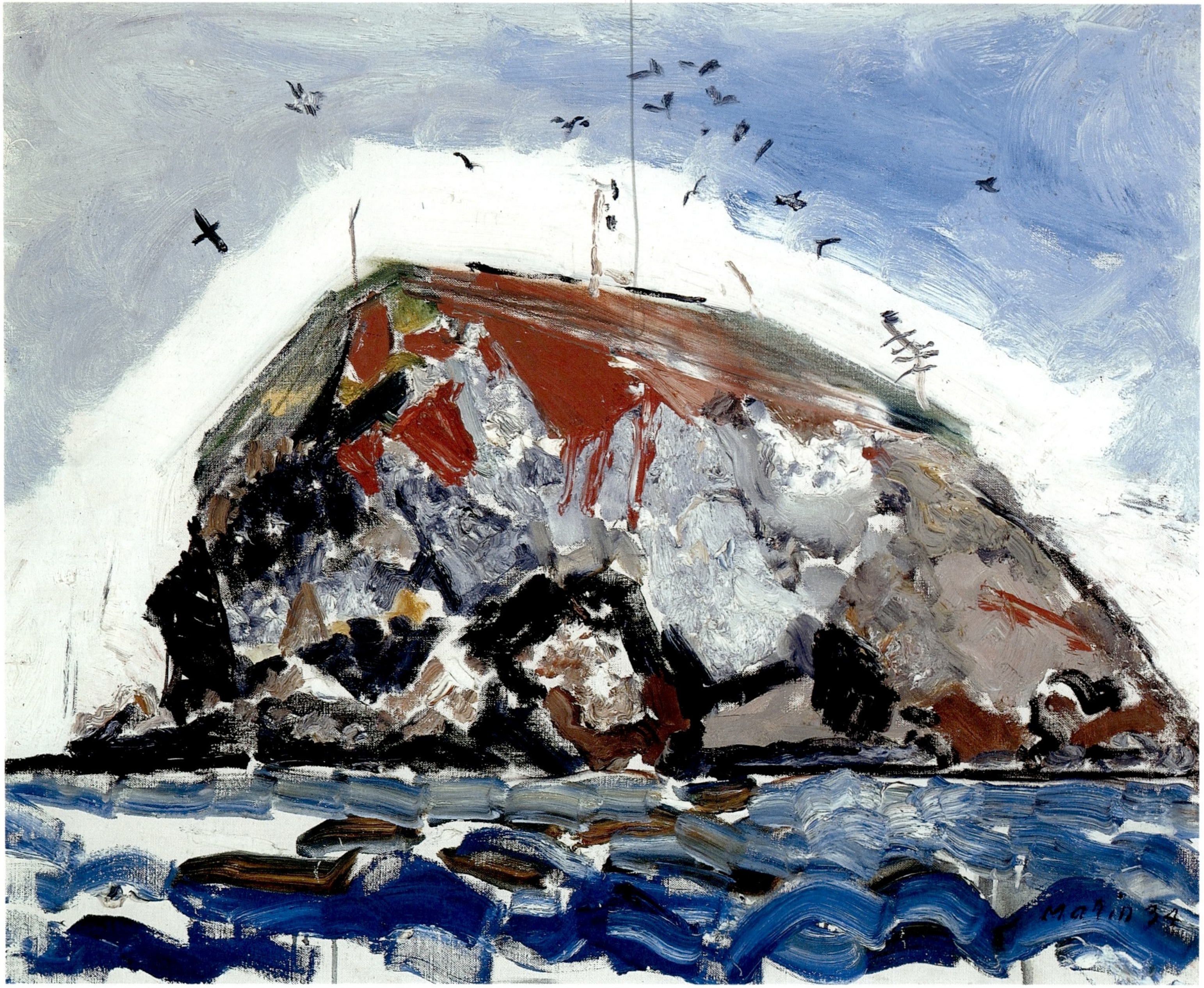

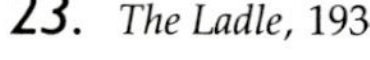

23. *The Ladle*, 1934

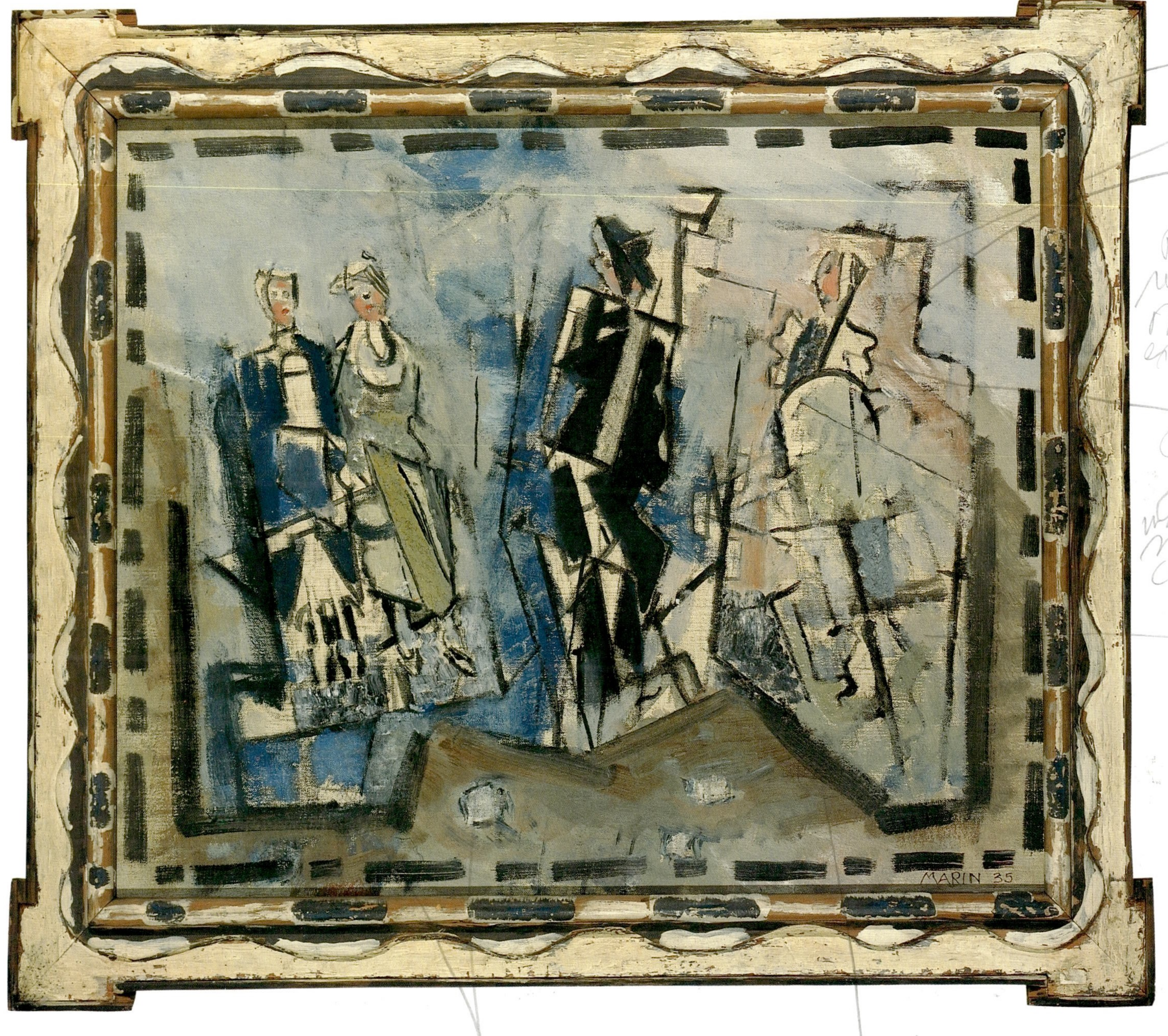

24. *Figures, Street Movement*, 1935

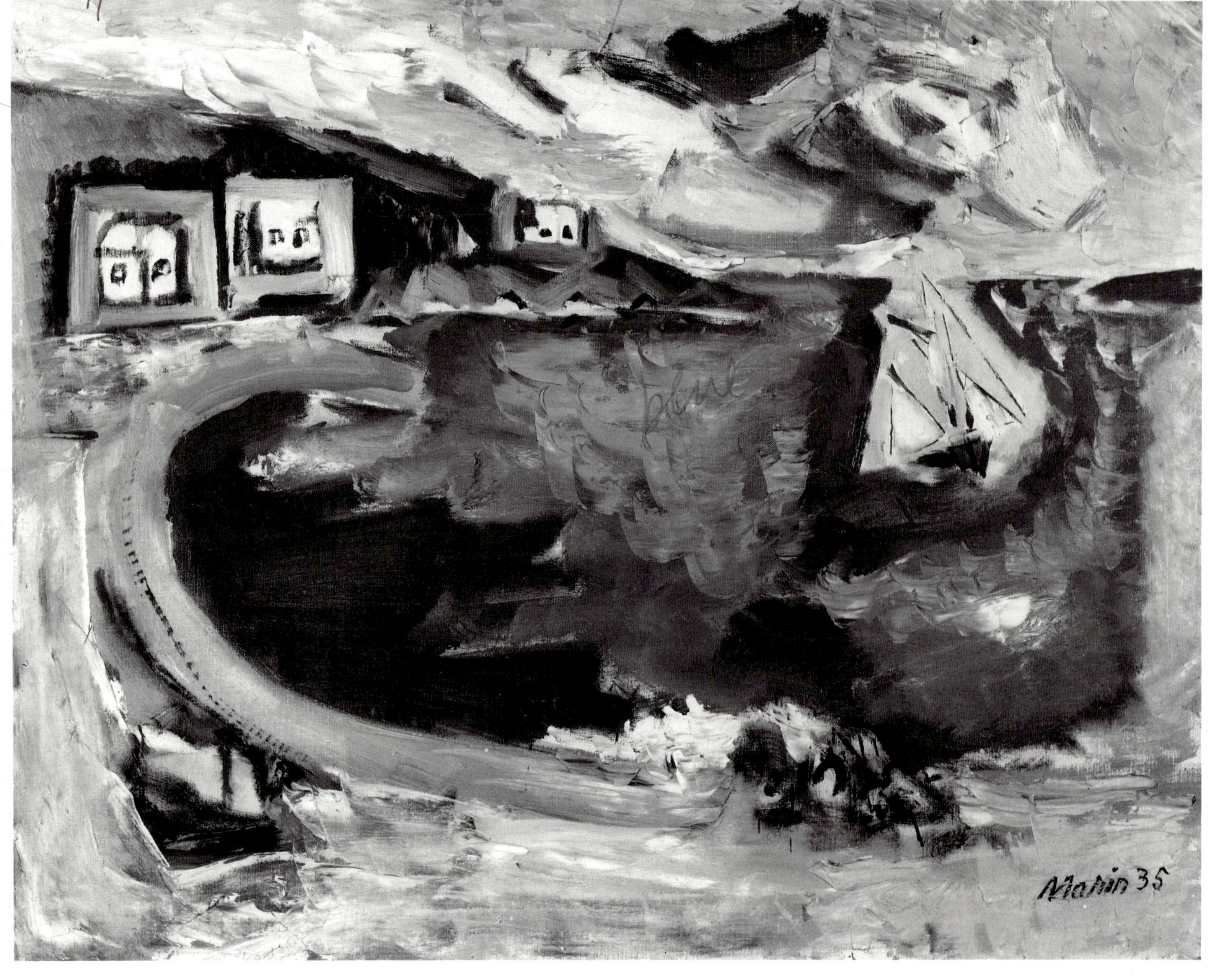

25. *From Seeing Cape Split*, 1935

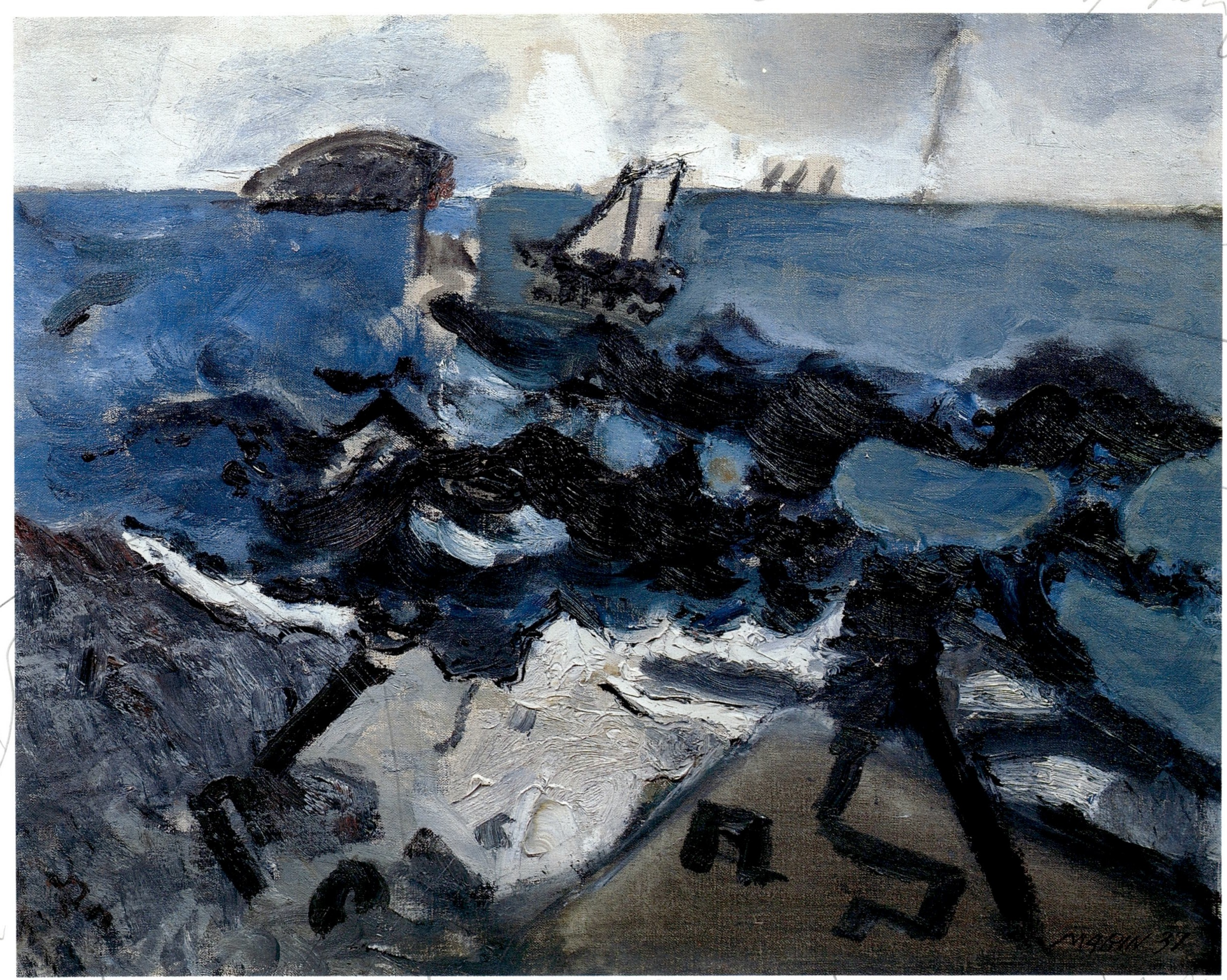

26. *The Head of the Cape, Ladle, and Boats*, 1937

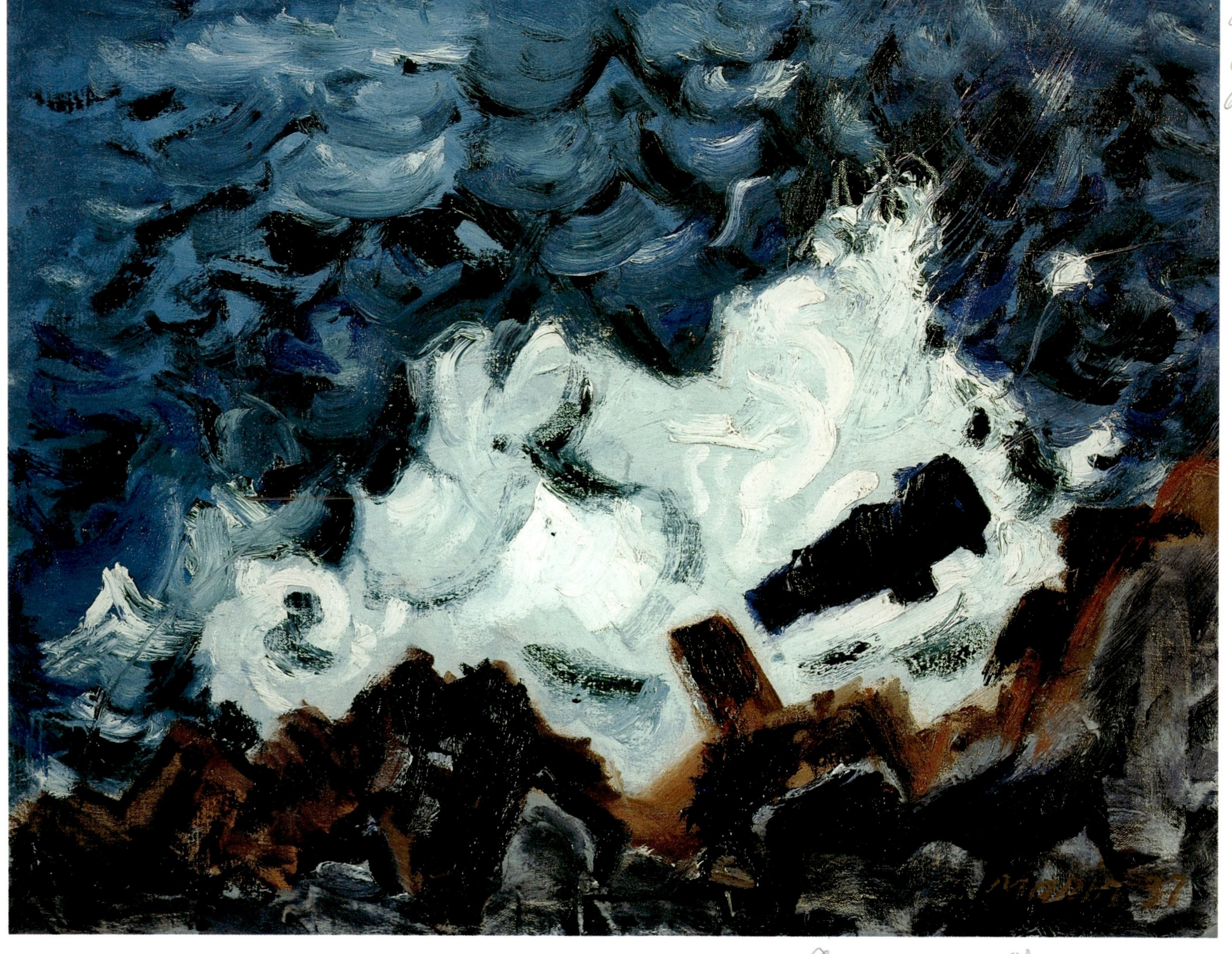

27. *Wave on Rock*, 1937

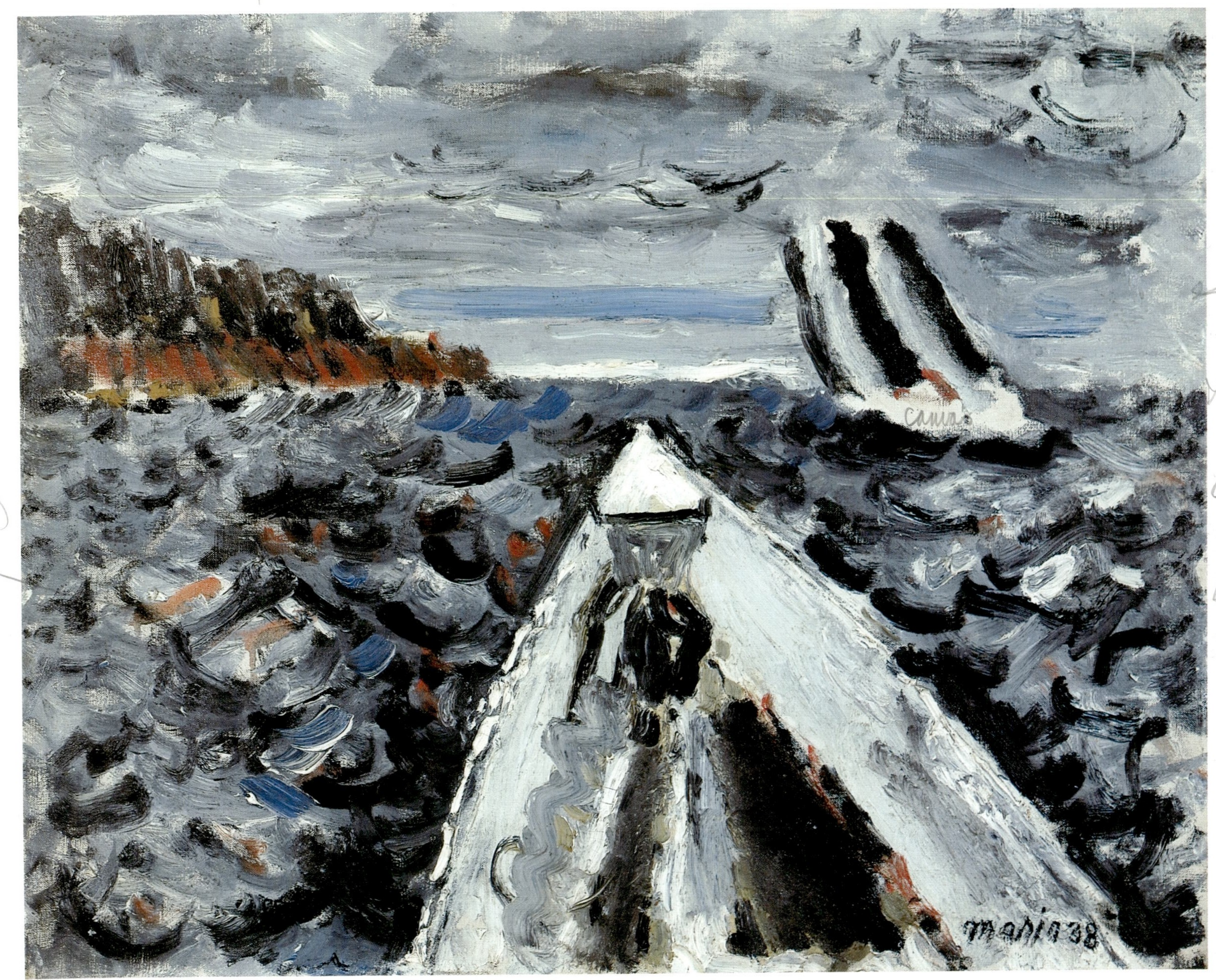

28. *Lobster Boat, Cape Split, Maine,* 1938

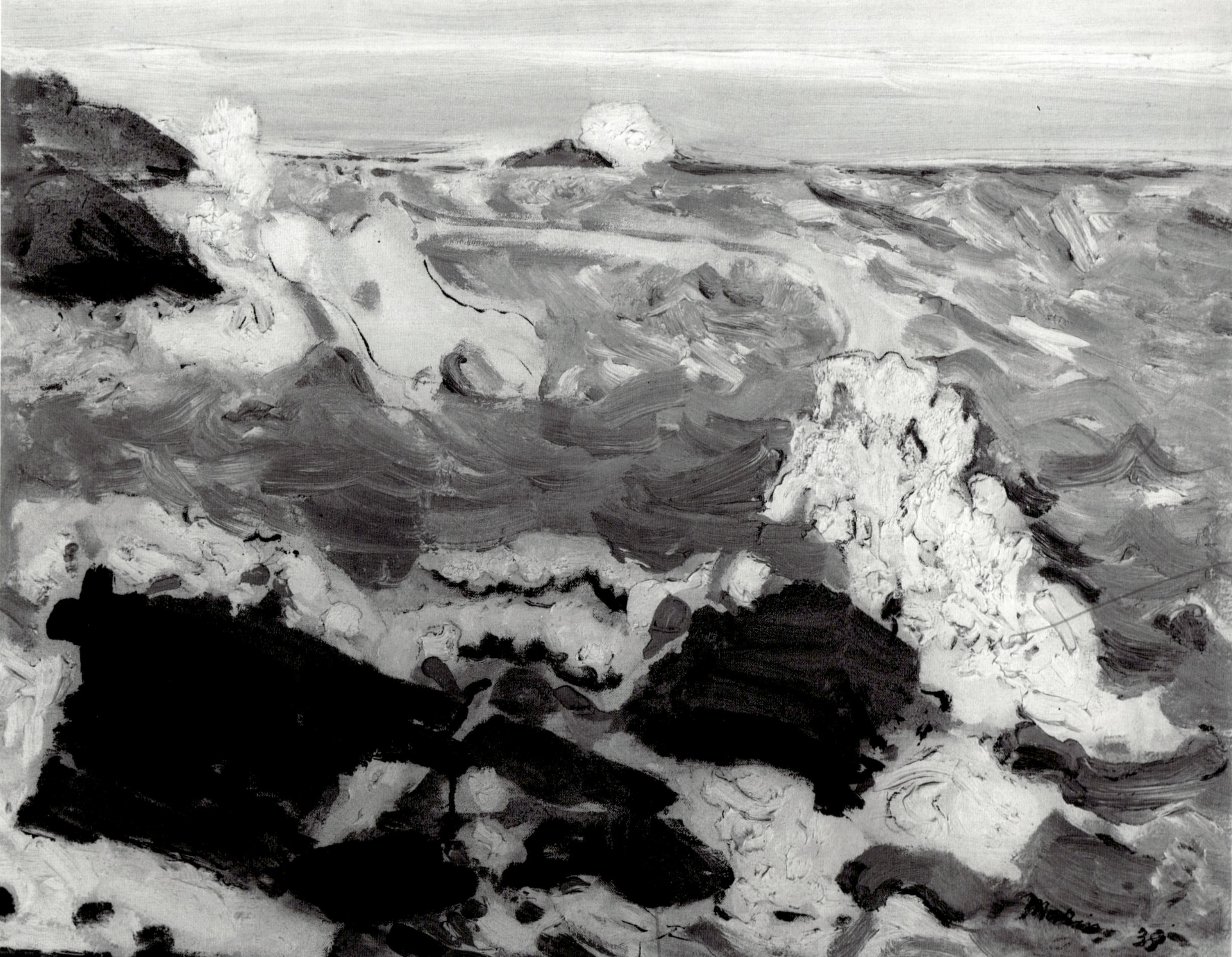

29. *The Sea, Cape Split, Maine*, 1938

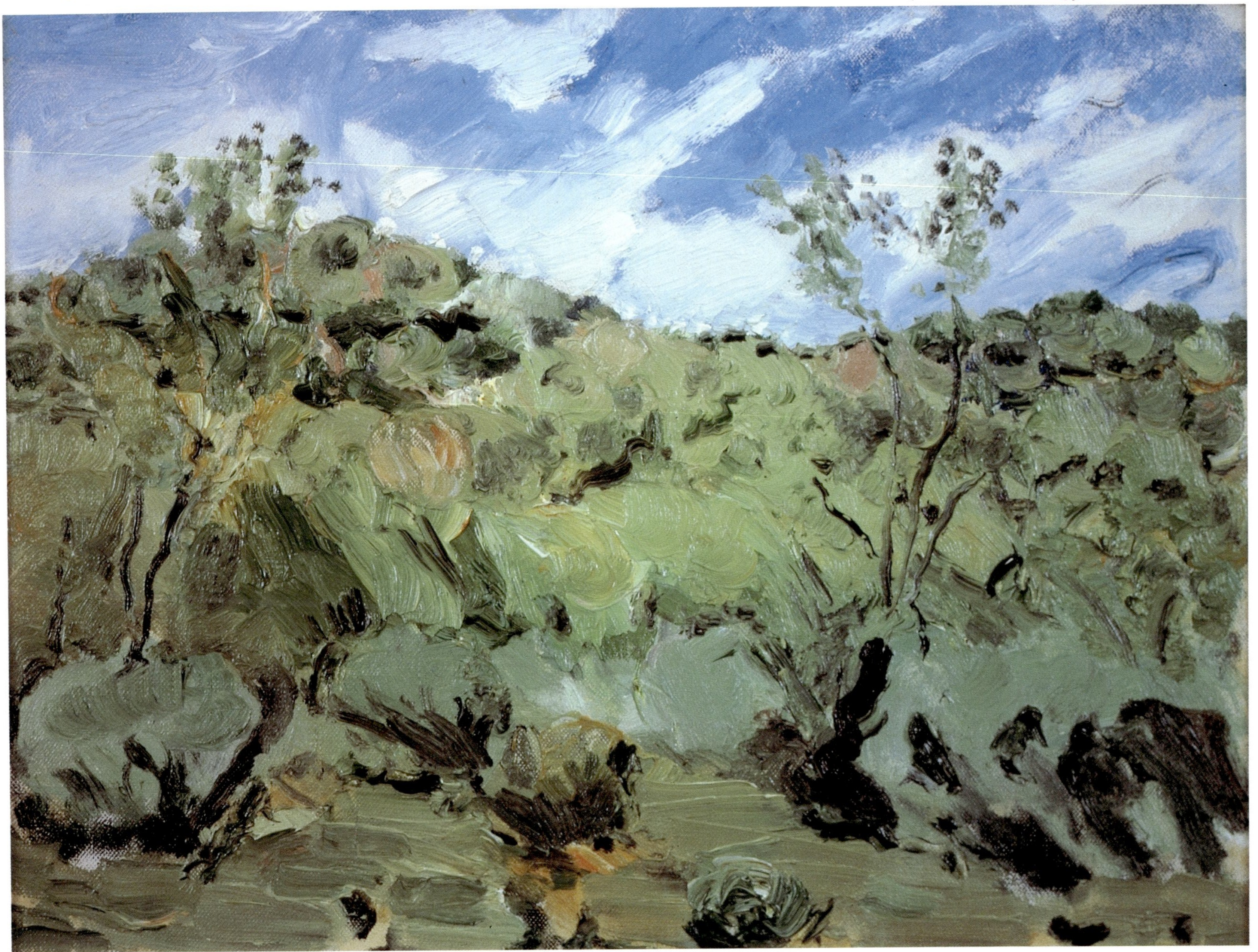

30. *No. 8, Marin Spring*, 1939

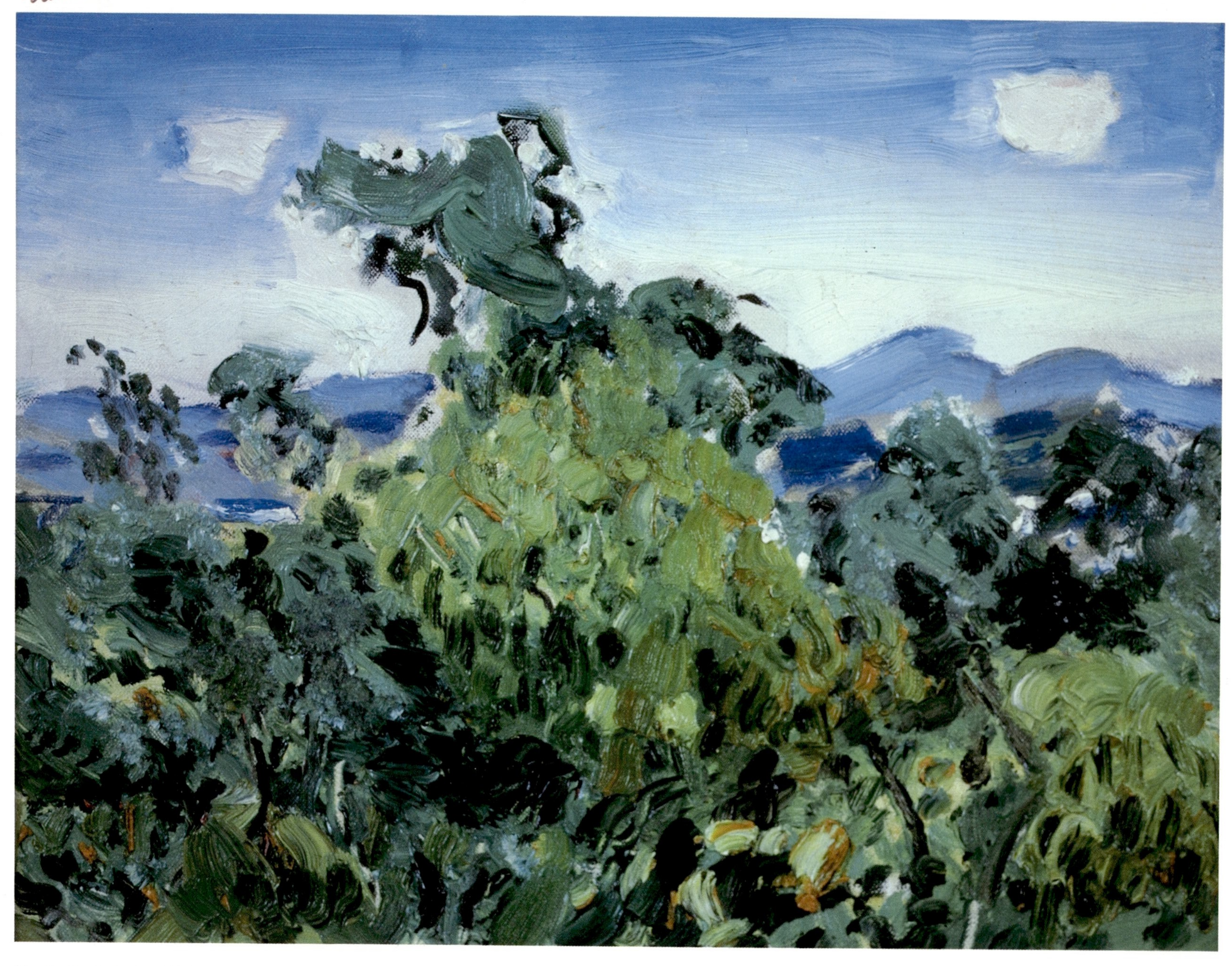

31. *No. 13, Marin Spring*, 1939

32. *The Sea, Cape Split, Maine*, 1939

33. *Maine Sea with Island*, 1940

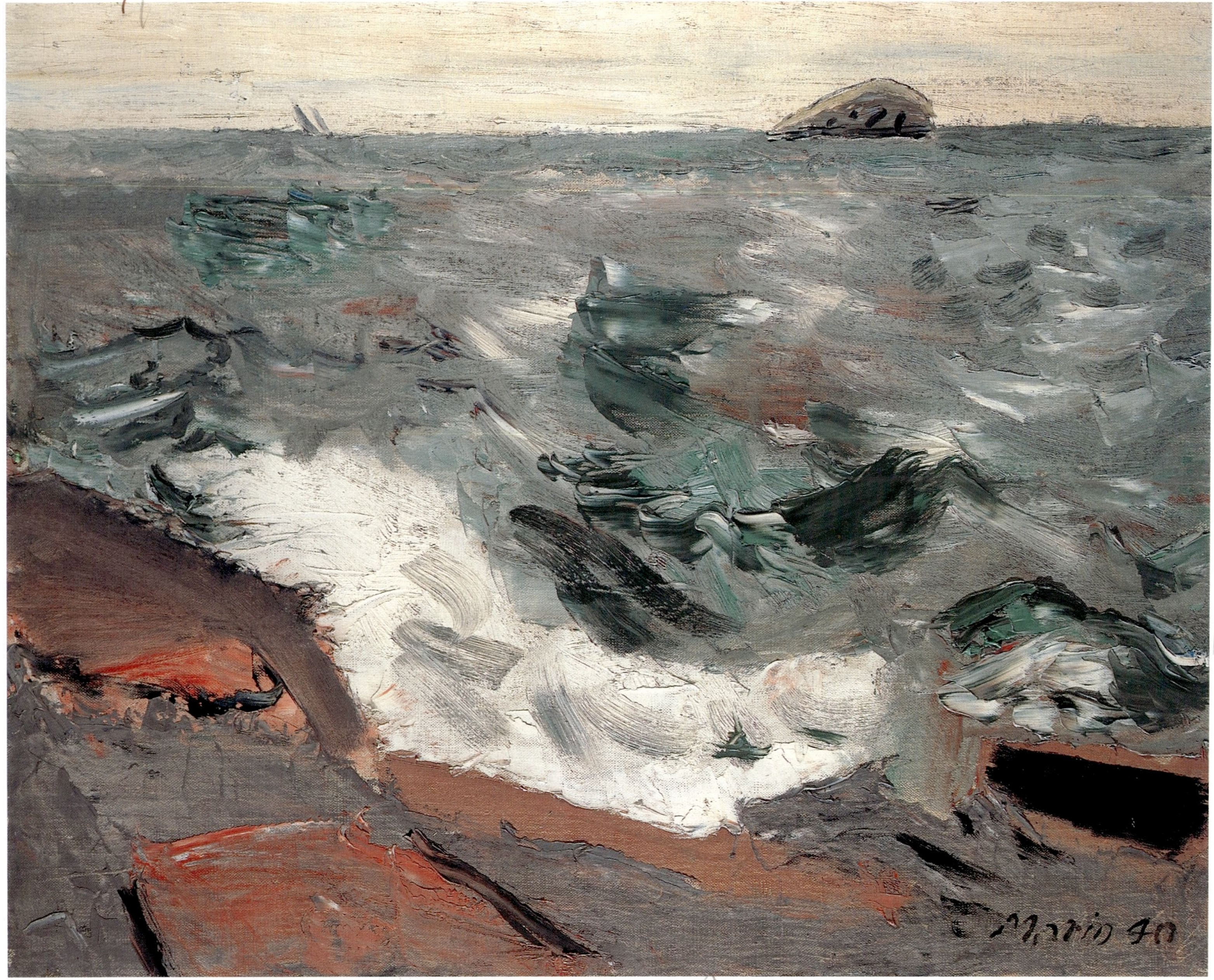

34. *Pink Rocks and Green Sea*, 1940

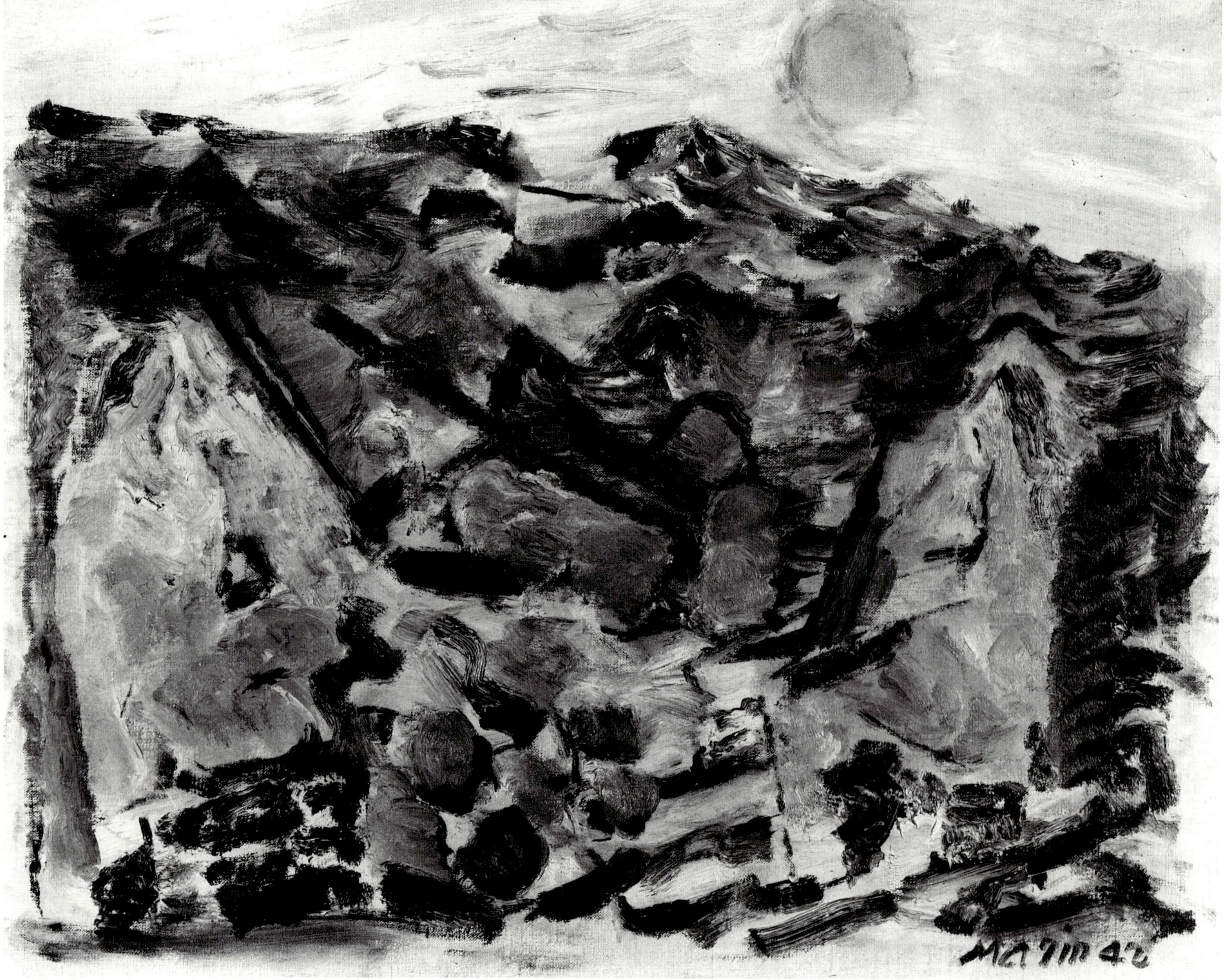

35. *Sea and Figures, Concept I,* 1942

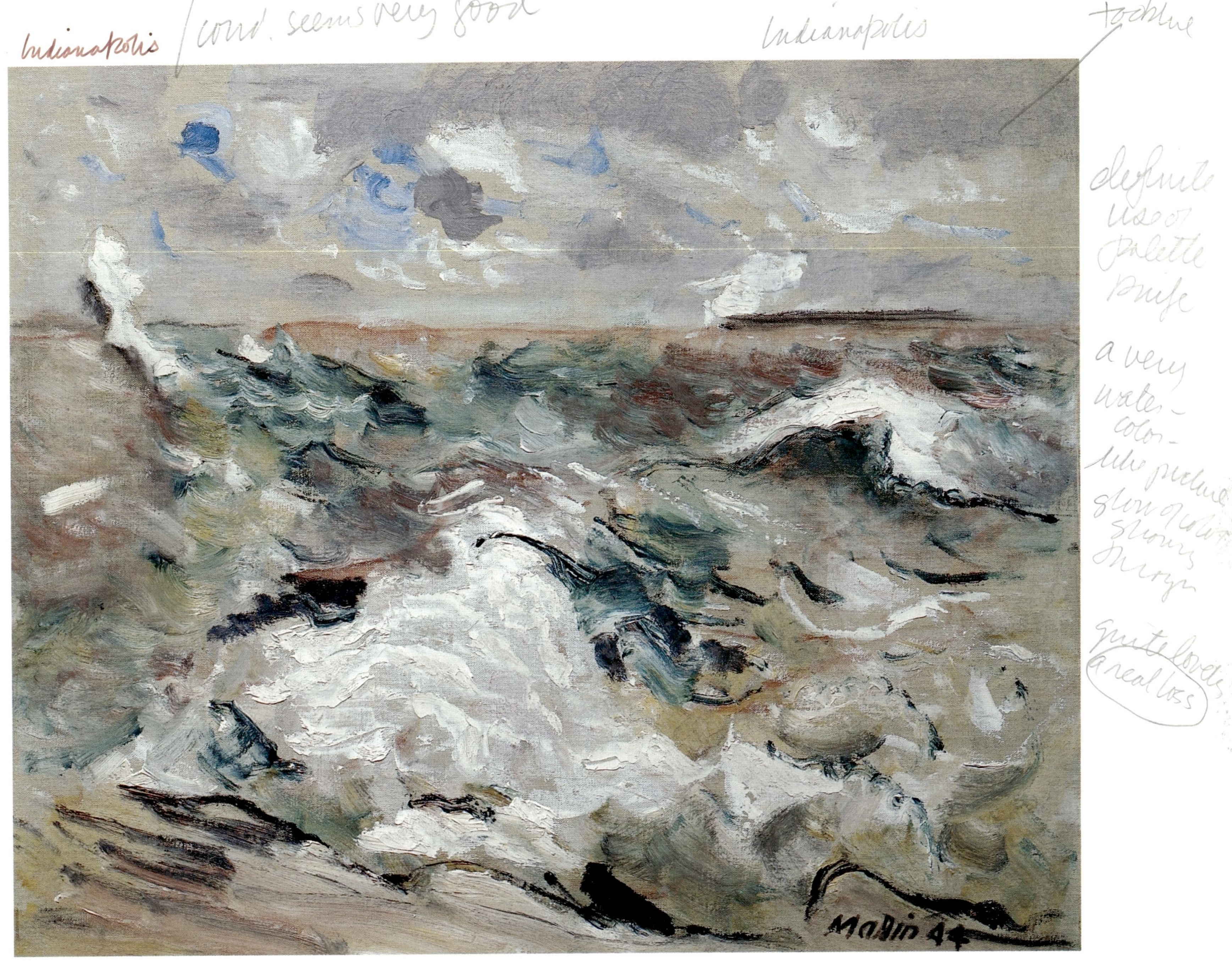

36. *Hurricane*, 1944

37. *(Seascape)*, 1944

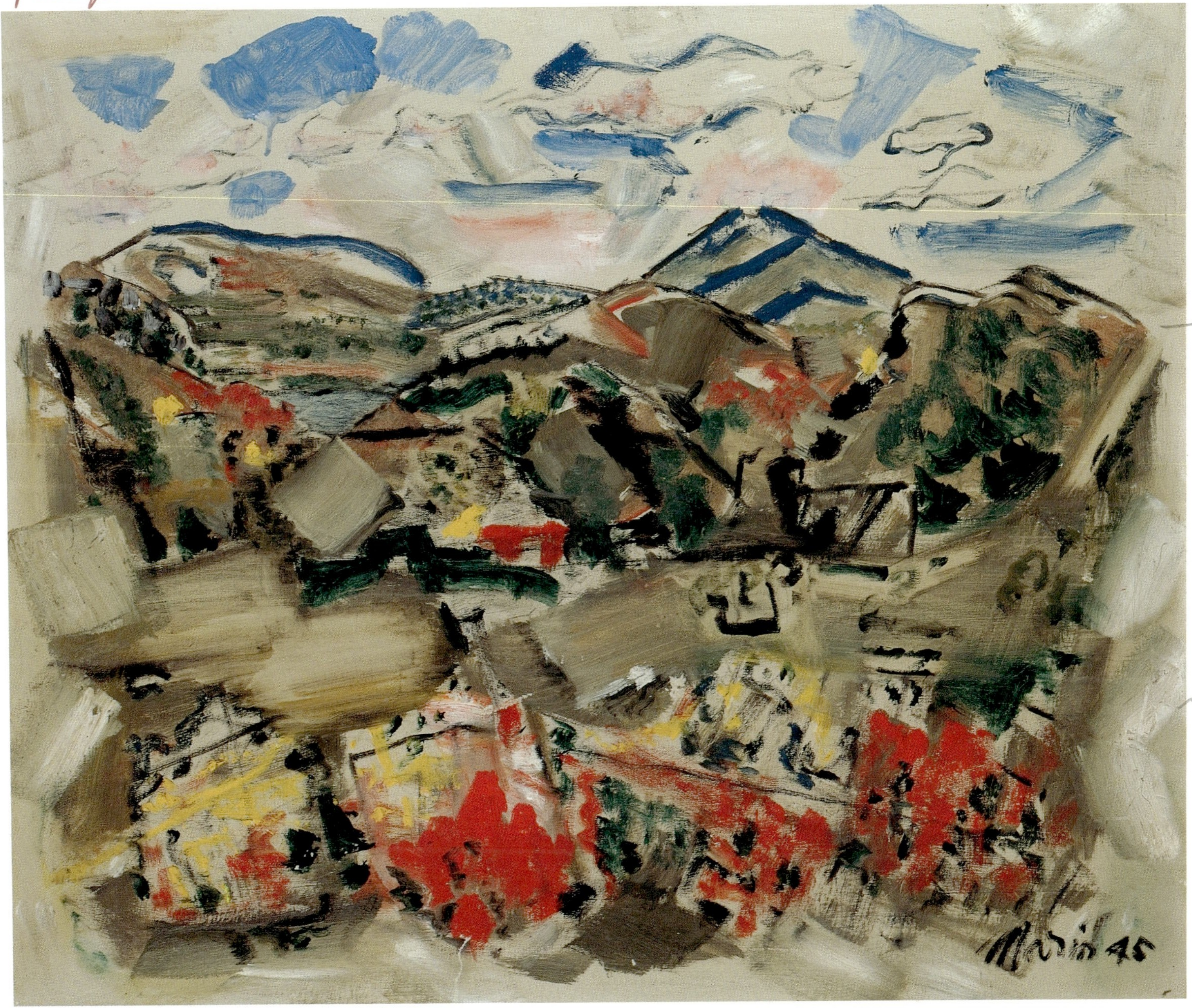

38. *Tunk Mountains, Maine*, 1945

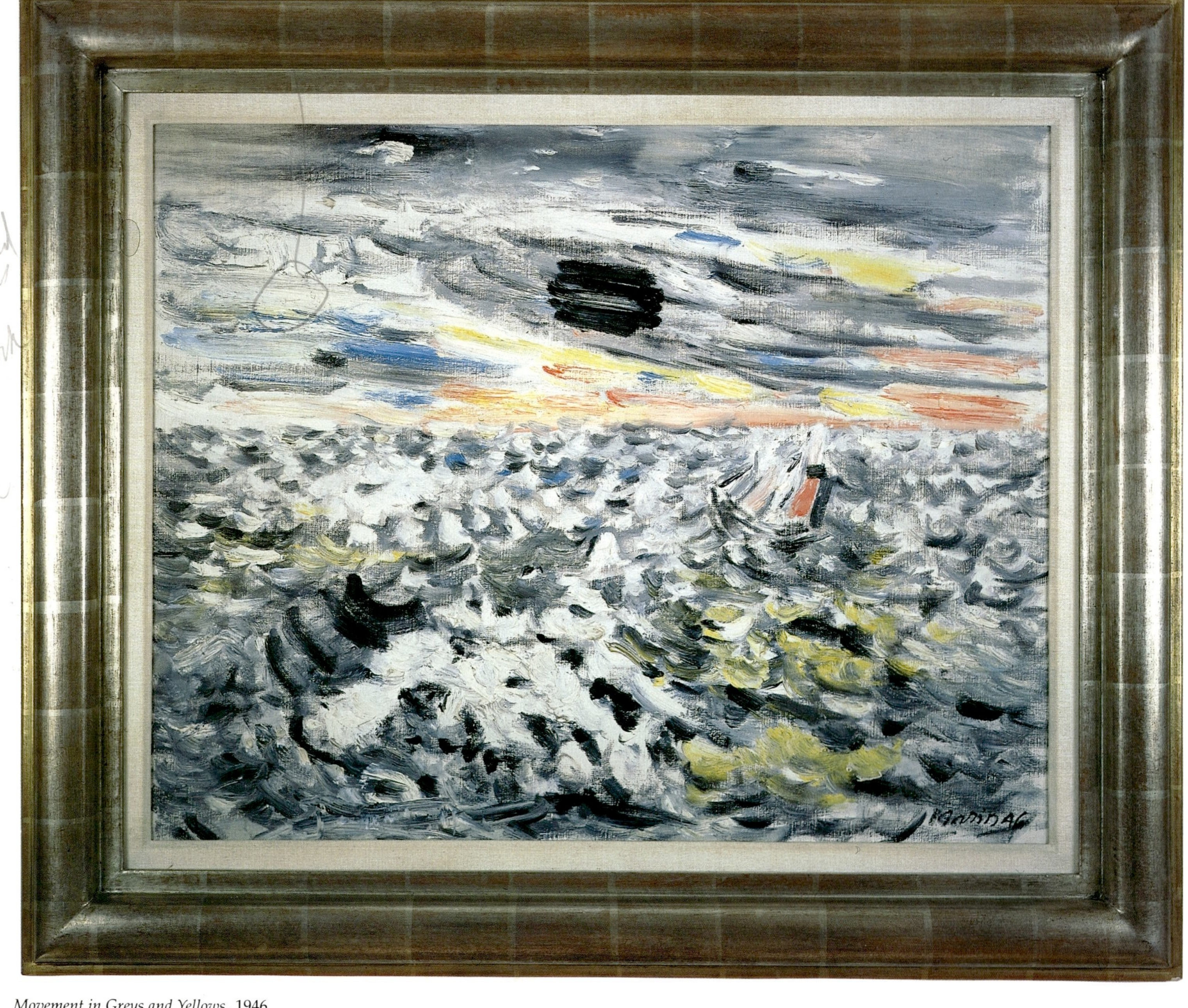

39. *Movement in Greys and Yellows*, 1946

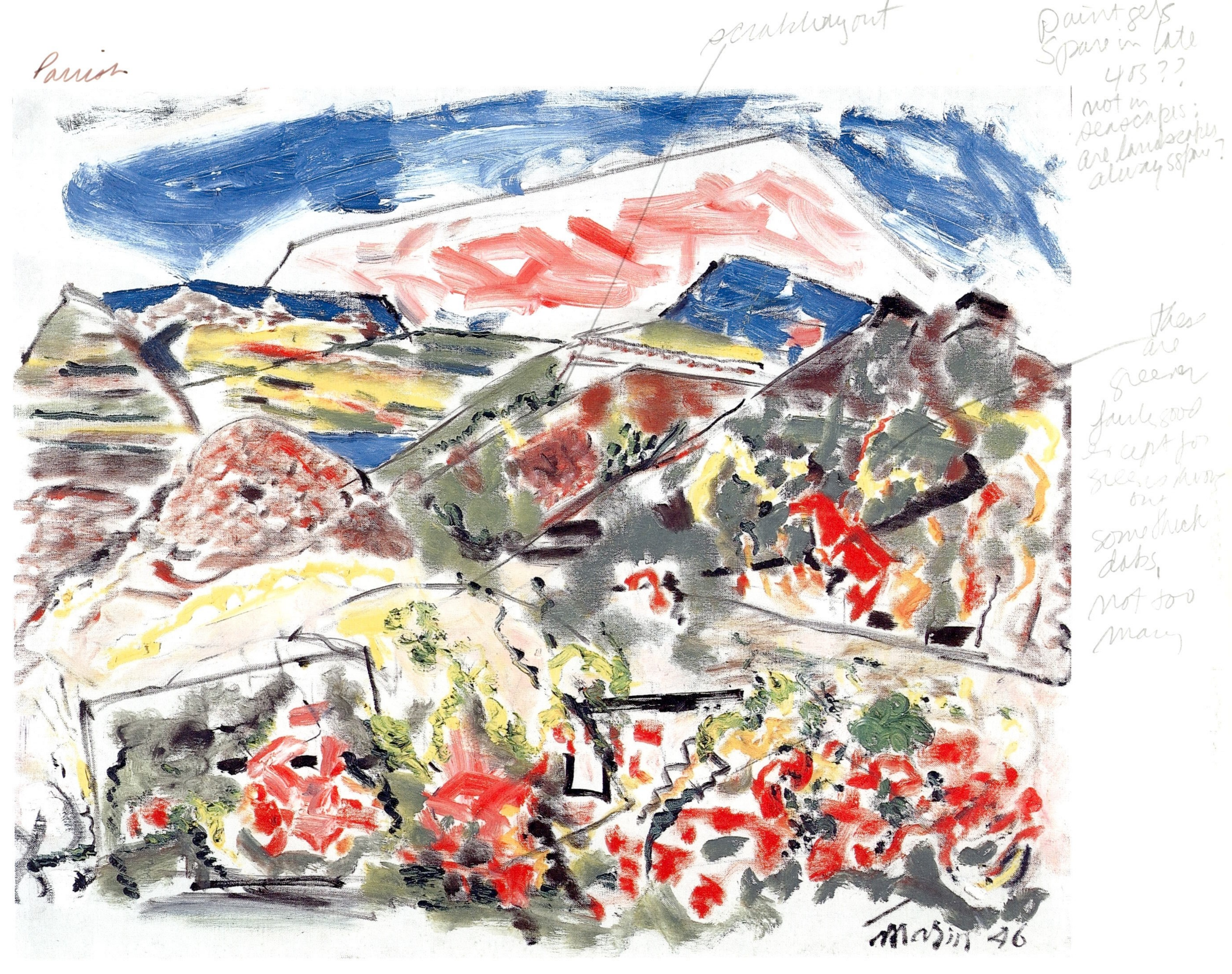

40. *Tunk Mountains, Maine,* 1946

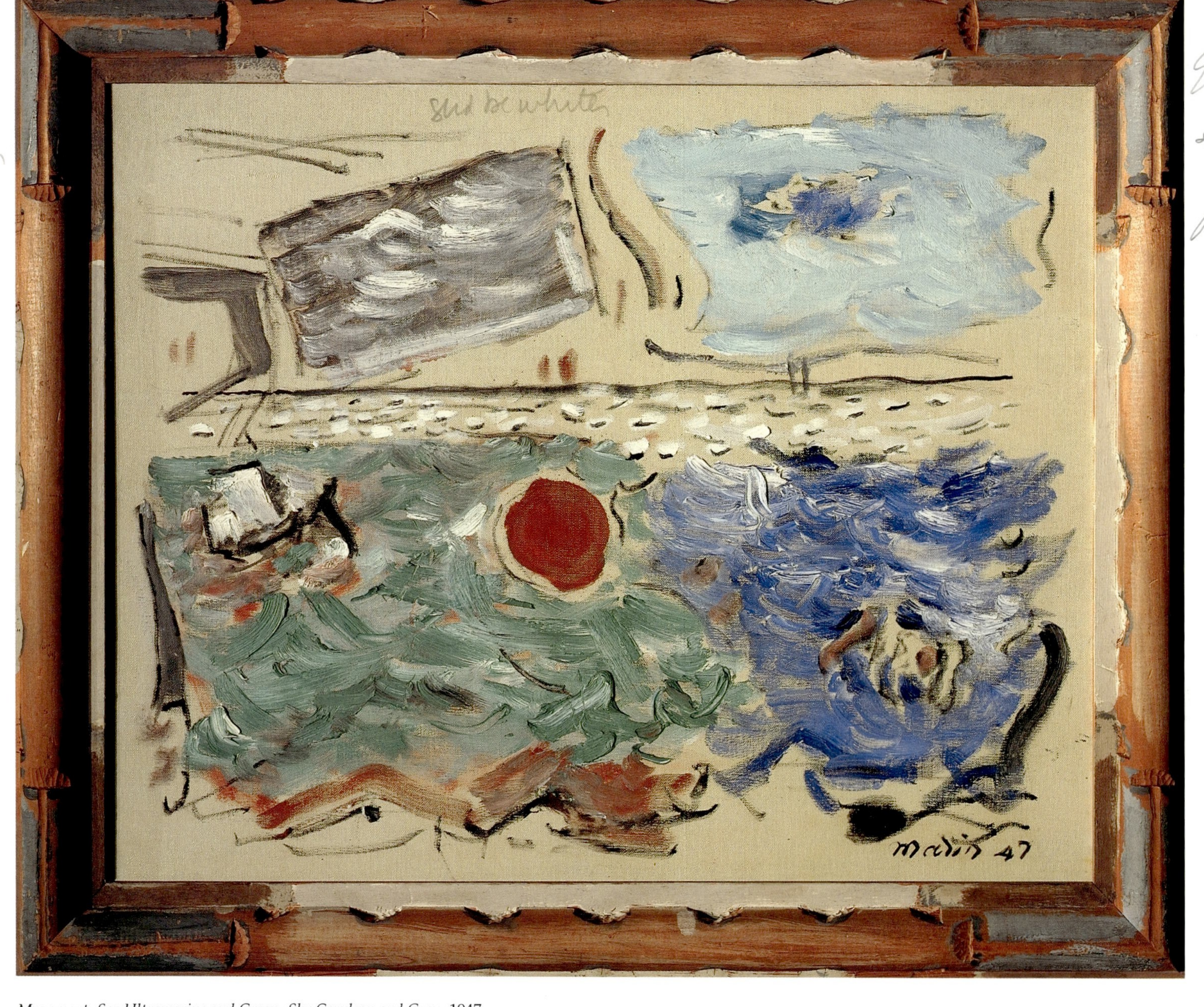

41. *Movement: Sea Ultramarine and Green, Sky Cerulean and Grey*, 1947

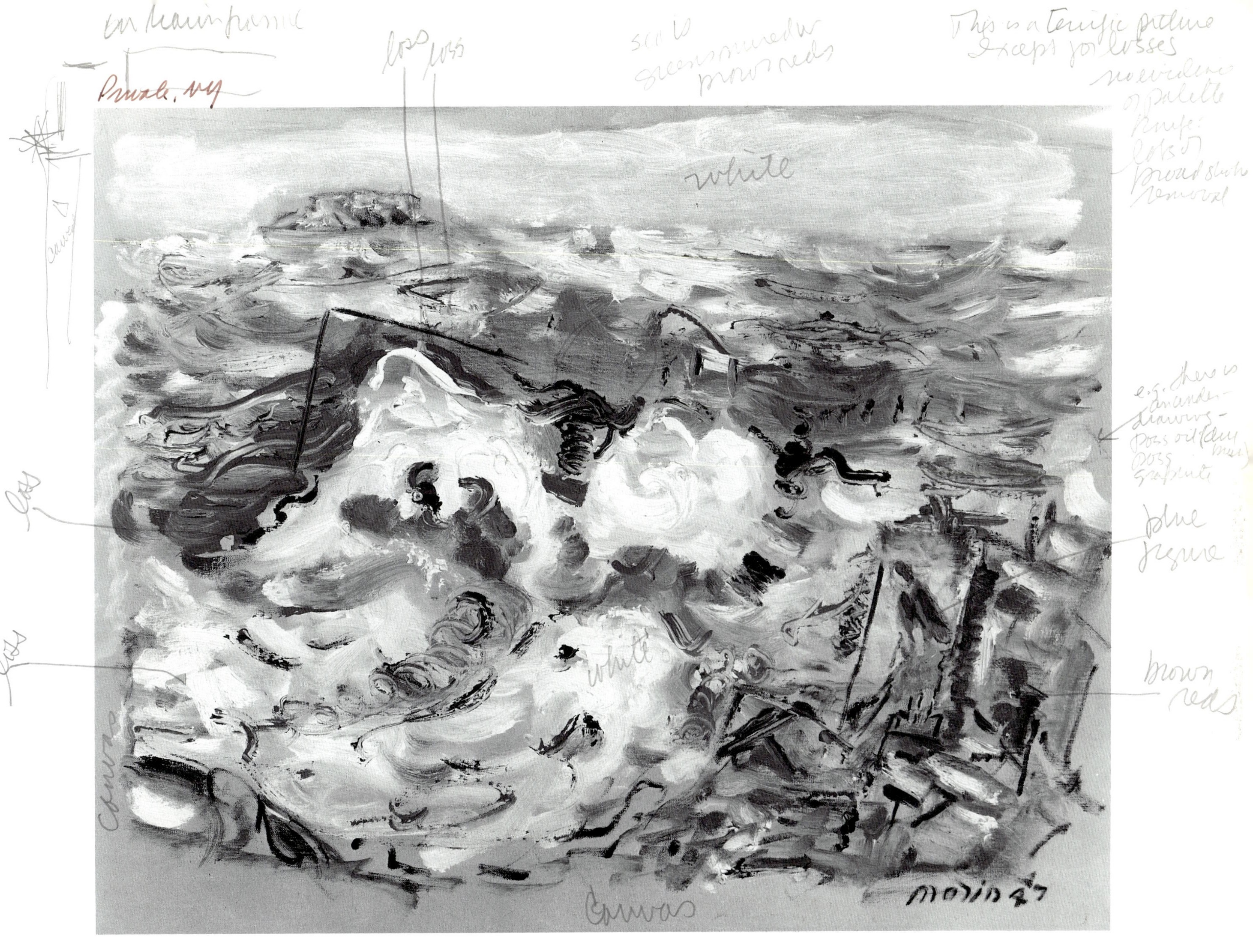

42. *Movement: Seas After Hurricane, Red, Green, and White, Figure in Blue, Maine,* 1947

43. *Movement: Wind Southwest*, 1947

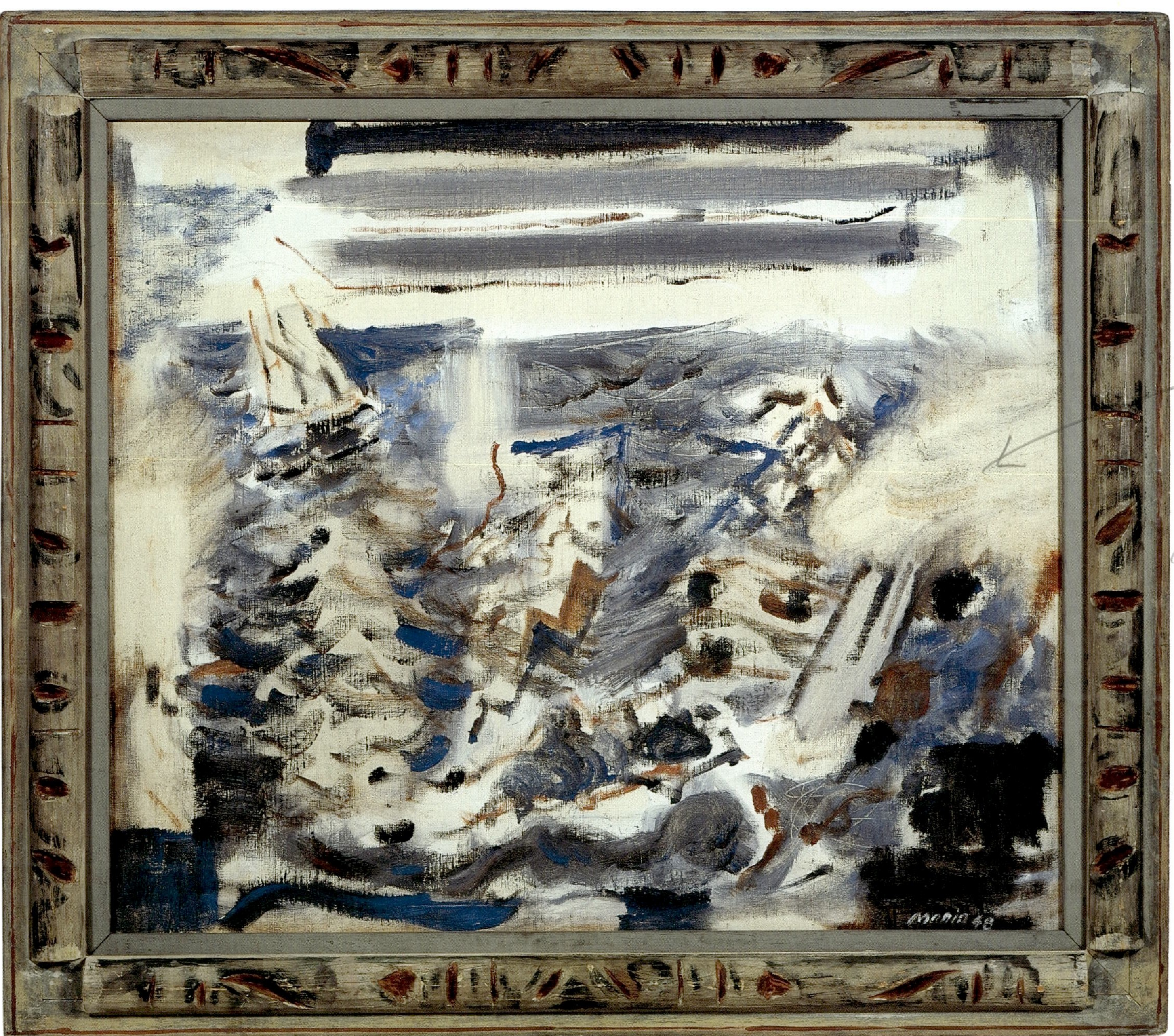

44. *Sea in Blue, Greys, and Light Red*, 1948

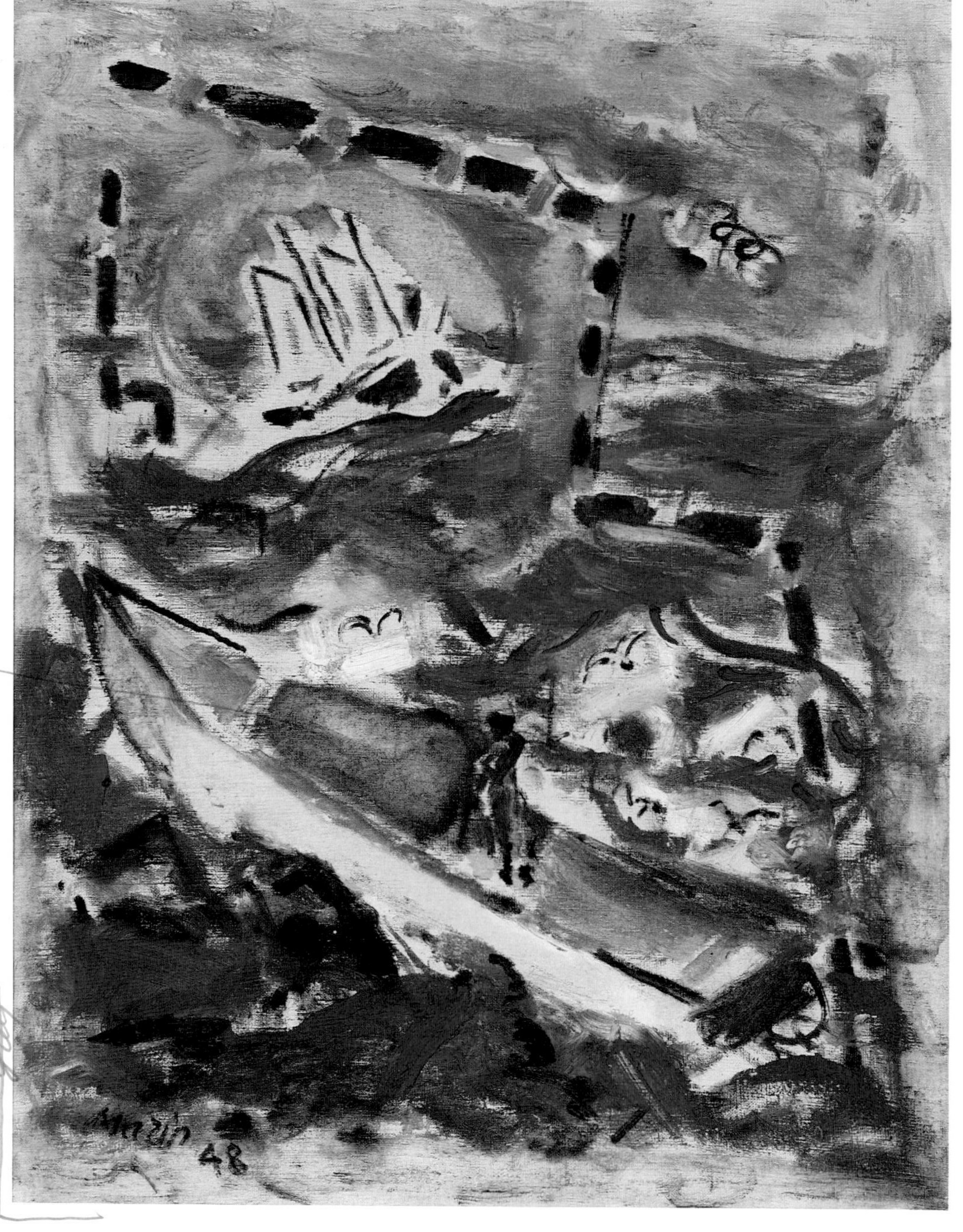

45. *The Lobster Fisherman*, 1948

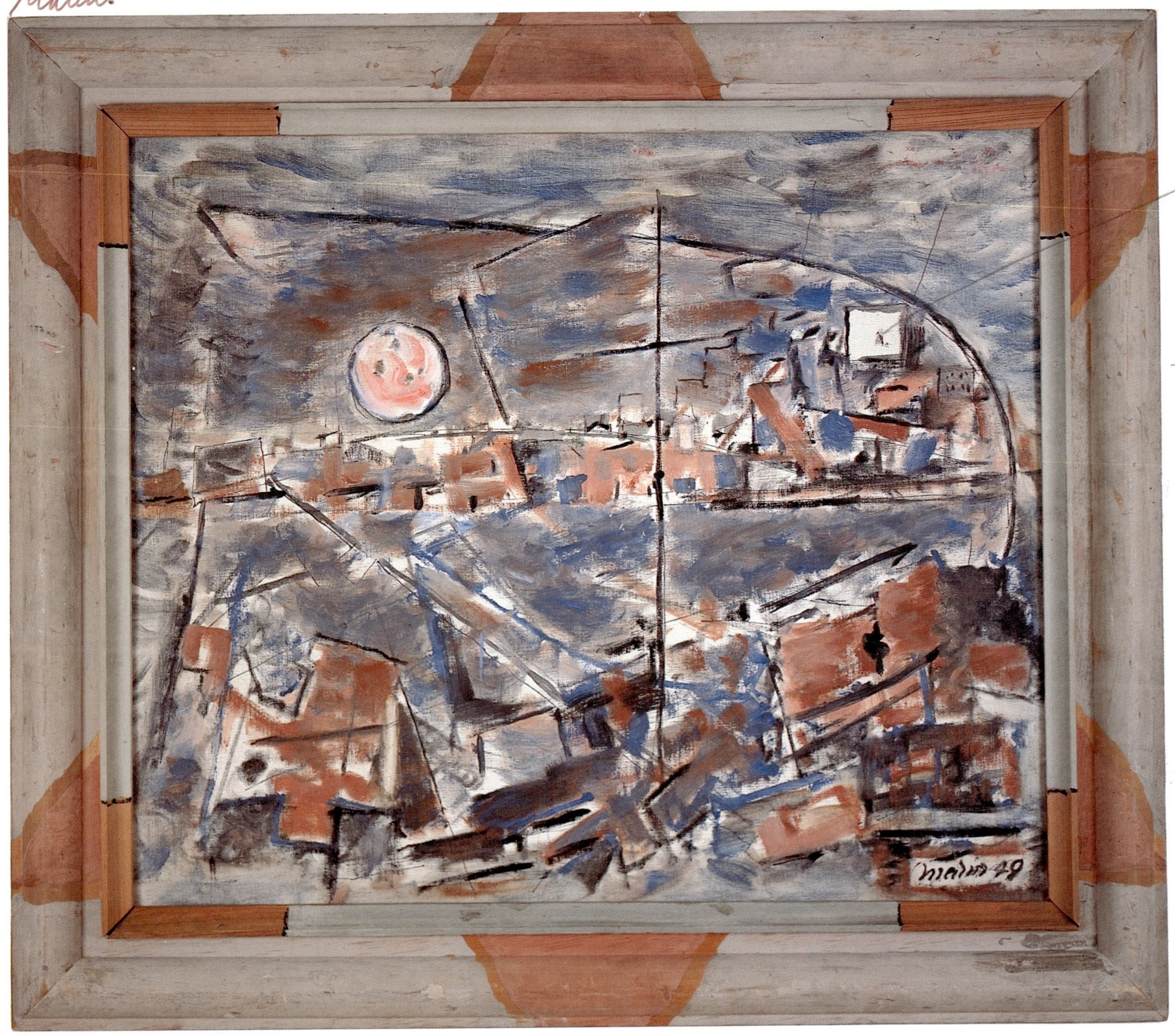

46. *Full Moon Over the City No. 2*, 1949

47. *Movement in Brown Ochre, Cobalt Green, and Umber*, 1950

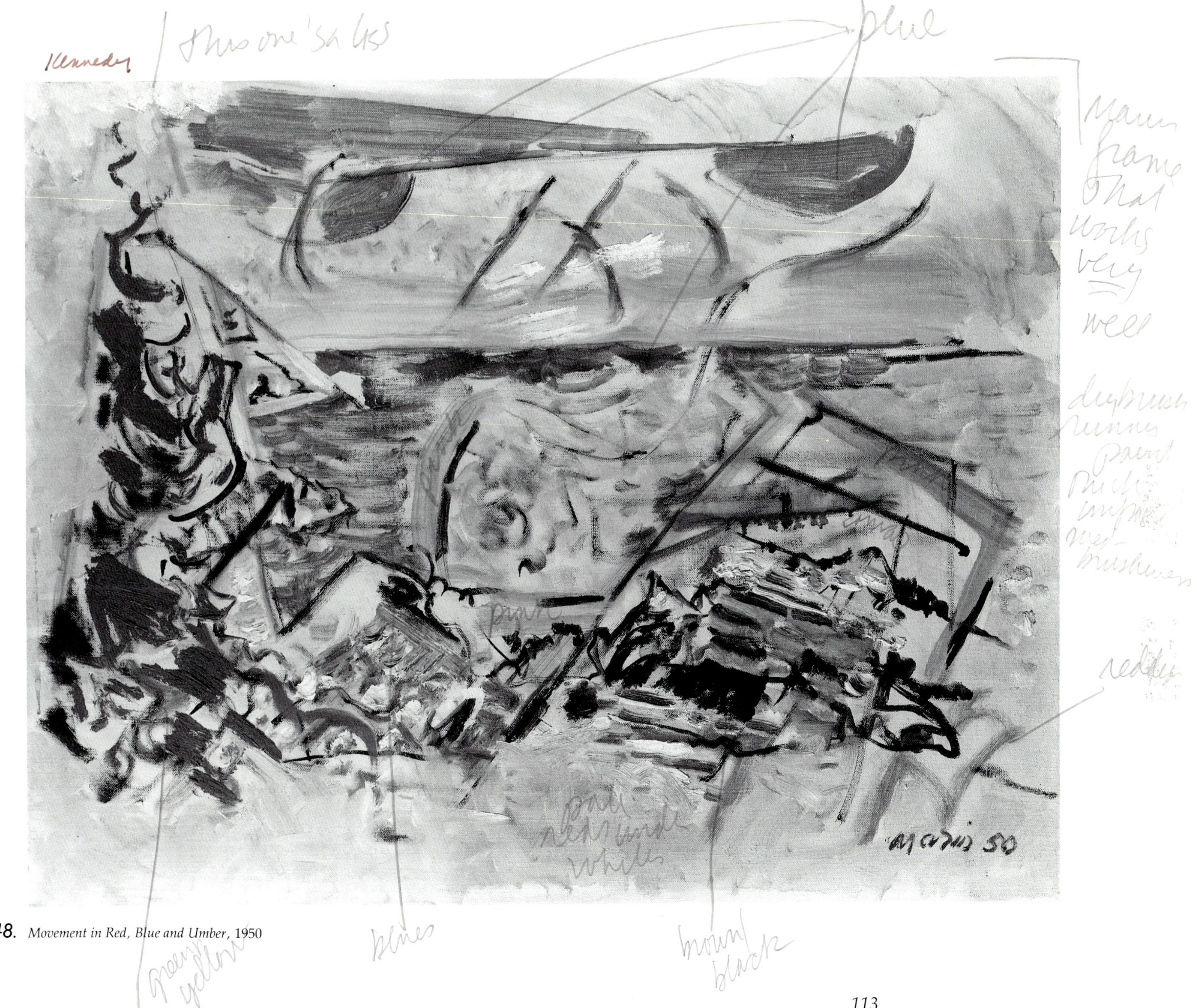

48. *Movement in Red, Blue and Umber*, 1950

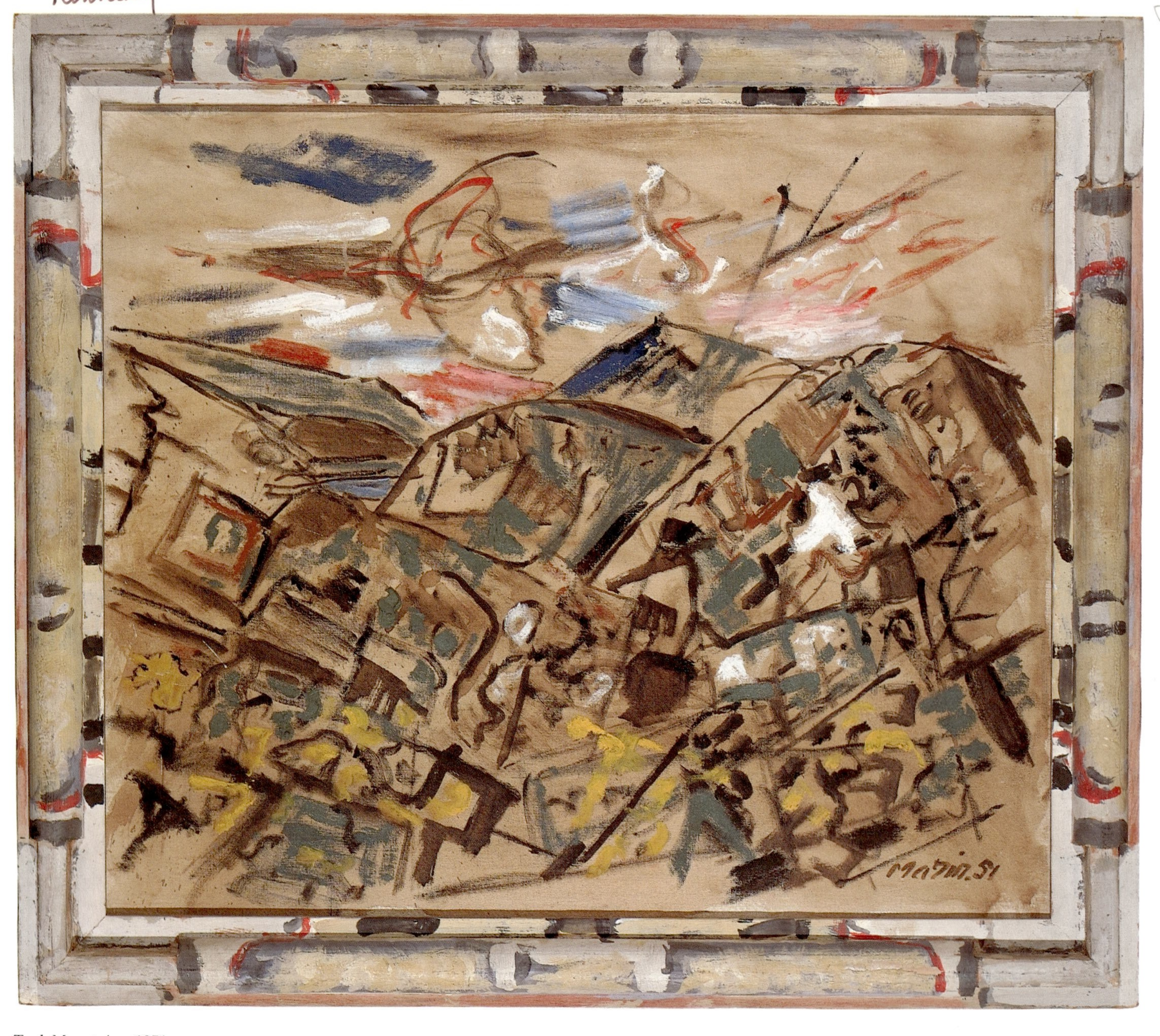

49. *Tunk Mountains*, 1951

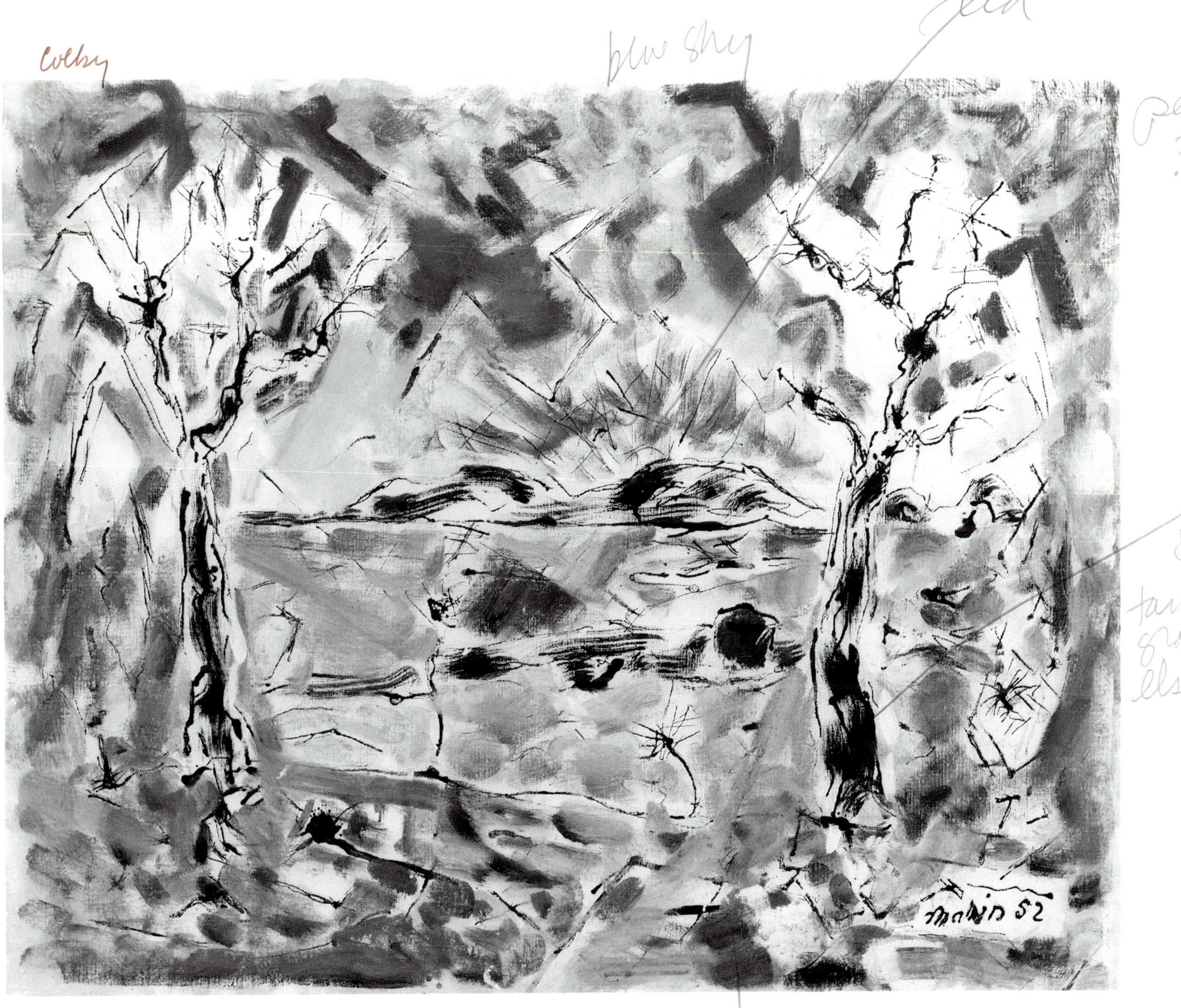

50. *Huntington Long Island No. 2,* 1952

Private, NY

color fairly good: mm-print except for blue

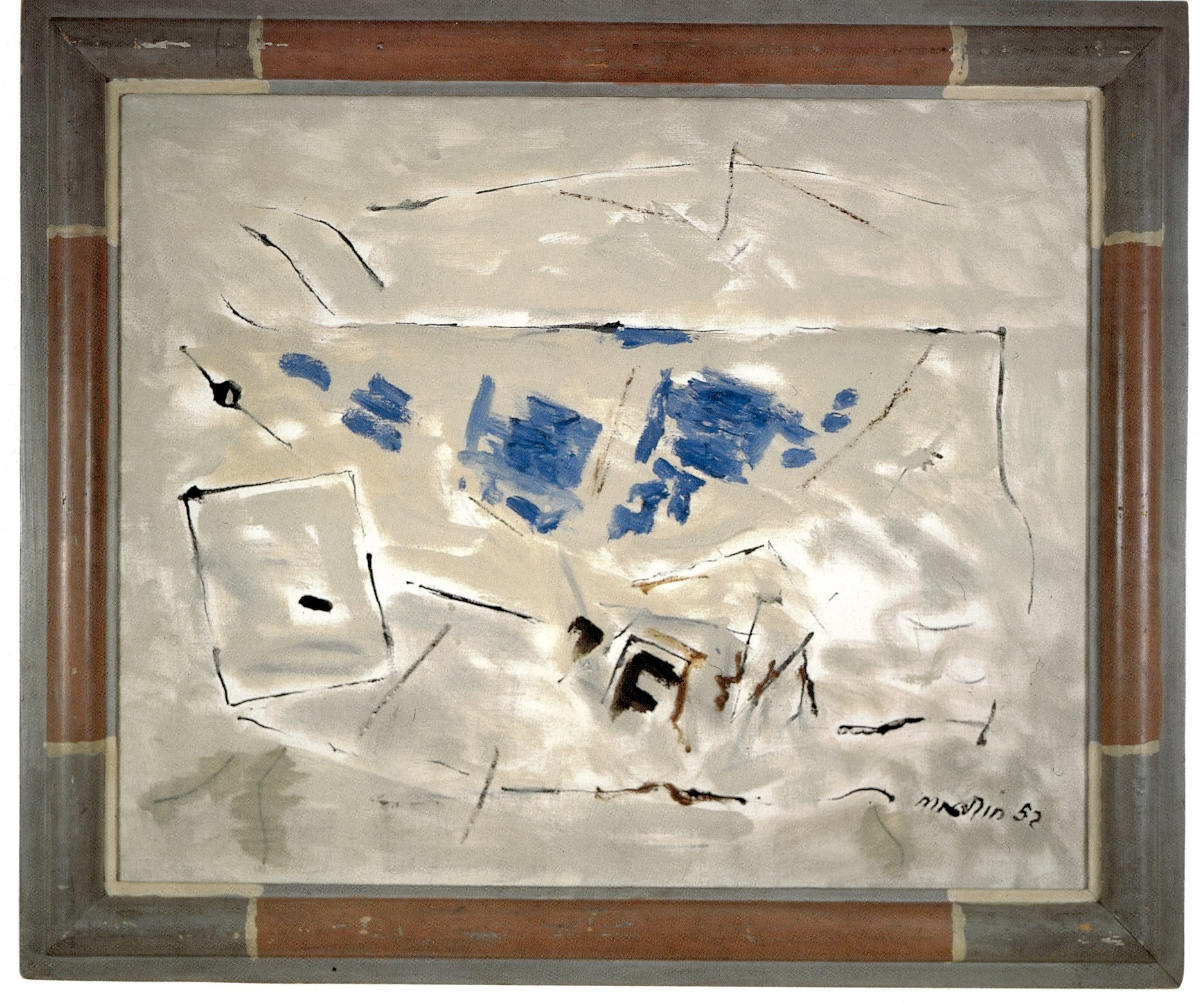

51. *Movement: Grey and Blue*, 1952

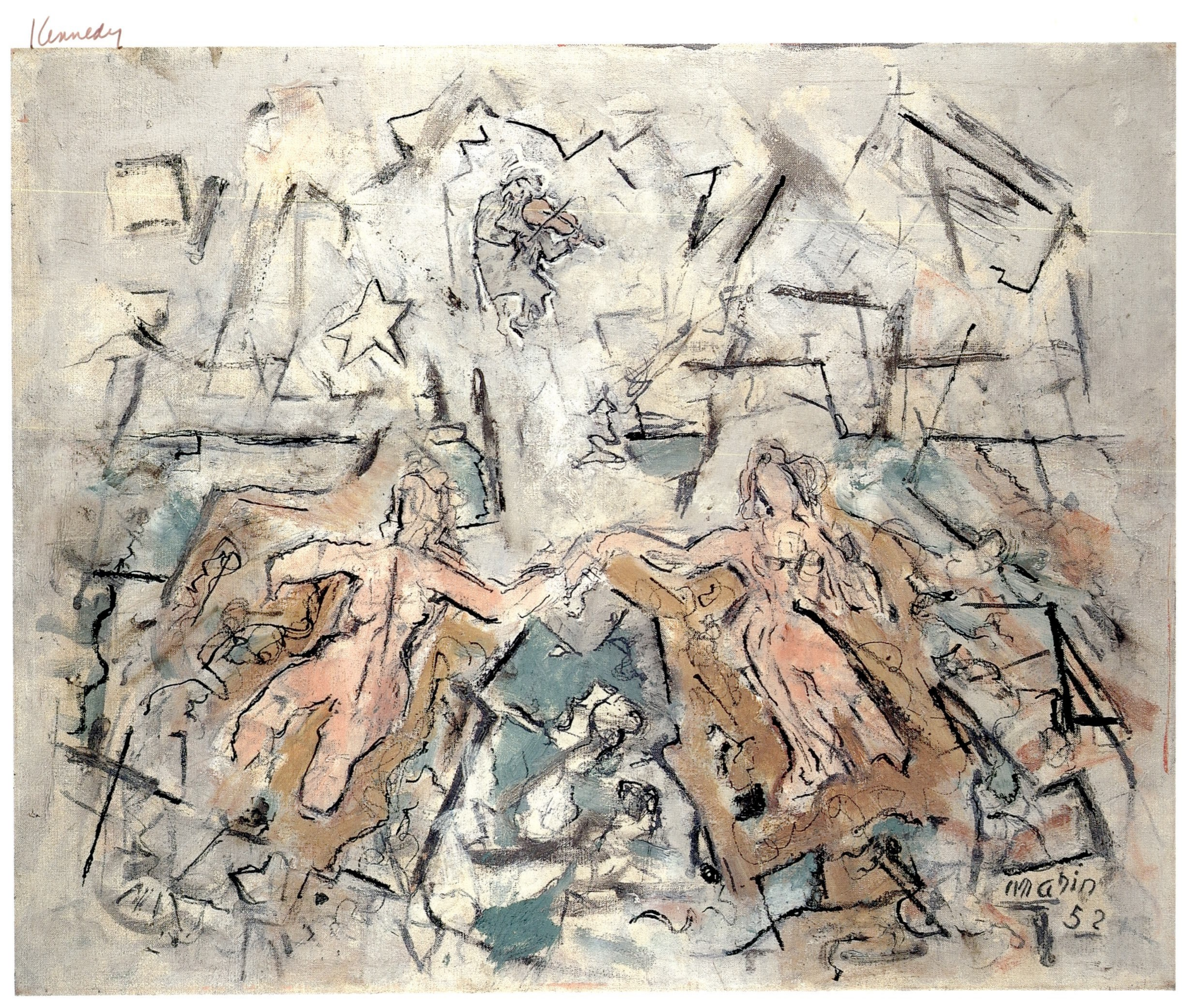

52. *Sea Fantasy*, 1952

a major loss

53. *The Written Sea*, 1952

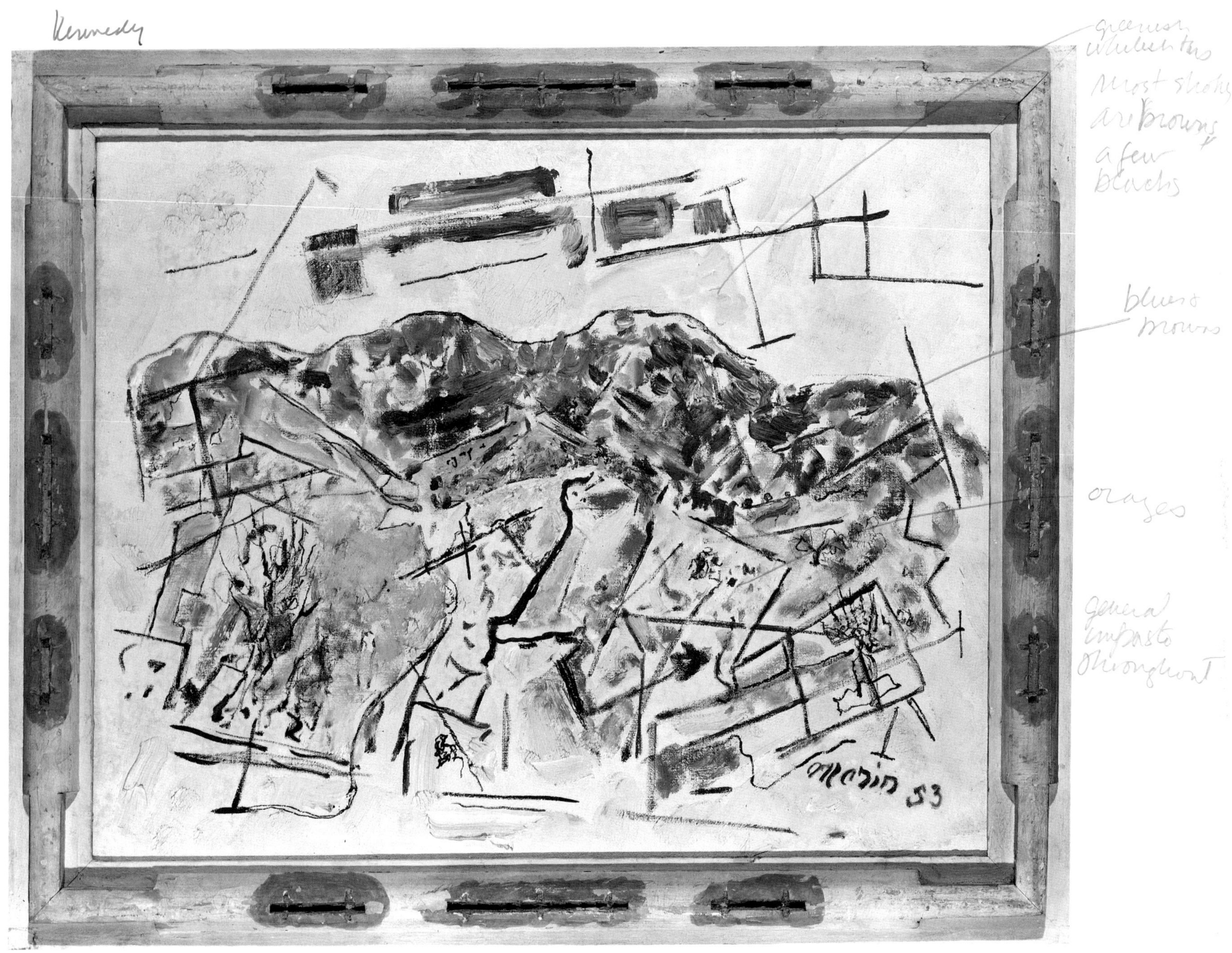

54. *Spring No. 2*, 1953

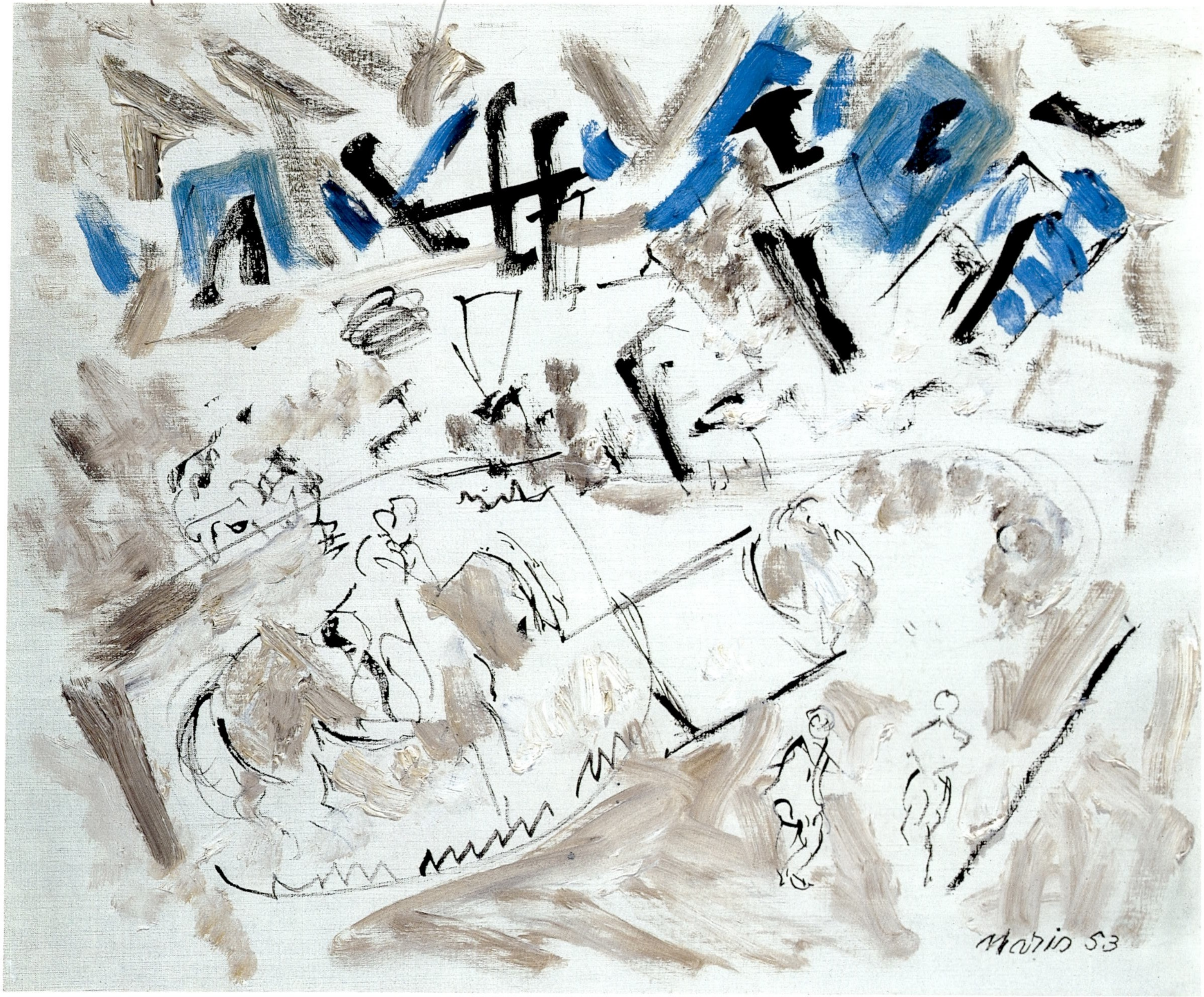

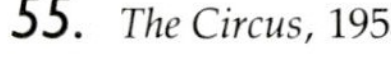

55. *The Circus*, 1953

CATALOGUE

1. *Autumn, Castorland, New York*. 1913.
Oil on canvas, 28¼ x 22 in.
Collection Mr. and Mrs. Irving Moskovitz, New York

2. *The Little Maple Tree, Castorland, New York*. 1913.
Oil on canvas, 26¾ x 22 in.
Courtesy Kennedy Galleries, Inc., New York

3. *Landscape*. 1914.
Oil on canvas, 22 x 25 in.
Private Collection

4. *River Scene from Weehawken, New Jersey*. 1916.
Oil on canvas, 19¾ x 23¼ in.
Collection Dr. and Mrs. Norman Rosenberg,
East Brunswick, N.J.

5. *Weehawken Sequence*. ca. 1916.
Oil on canvas board, 10 x 12½ in.
Courtesy Kennedy Galleries, Inc., New York

6. *Weehawken Sequence (No. 65)*. ca. 1916.
Oil on canvas board, 12¼ x 9½ in.
Colby College Museum of Art, Waterville, Maine,
Gift of Mr. and Mrs. John Marin, Jr.

7. *Weehawken Sequence (No. 5)*. ca. 1916.
Oil on canvas board, 9½ x 12½ in.
Whitney Museum of American Art, New York,
Gift of Mr. and Mrs. John Marin, Jr.

8. *Weehawken Sequence (No. 80)*. ca. 1916.
Oil on canvas board, 9½ x 12¼ in.
University of Maine at Machias

9. *Weehawken Sequence (No. 68)*. ca. 1916.
Oil on canvas board, 9 x 12 in.
Collection Mr. and Mrs. William Janss, Sun Valley, Idaho

10. *Weehawken Sequence*. ca. 1916.
Oil on canvas board, 9½ x 12½ in.
Courtesy Kennedy Galleries, Inc., New York

11. *Sea, Tree, and Boat*. 1921.
Oil on canvas, 27 x 22 in.
Courtesy Kennedy Galleries, Inc., New York

12. *Region of Sparkill, New York No. 2*. 1928.
Oil on canvas, 22 x 27 in.
Courtesy Kennedy Galleries, Inc., New York

13. *No. 1, Fall of 1930*.
Oil on canvas board, 14 x 17¾ in.
The Farber Collection, New York

14. *Lower Manhattan from Tip End*, ca. 1931
Oil on canvas, 22 x 27 in.
Private Collection, Dallas

15. *Rocks and Sea, Small Point, Maine*. 1931.
Oil on canvas, 22$\frac{1}{16}$ x 27$\frac{15}{16}$ in.
The Cleveland Museum of Art, Norman O. Stone and
Ella A. Stone Memorial Fund

16. *Bathers*. 1932.
Oil on canvas, 22 x 28 in.
Dallas Museum of Art, Gift of Mr. and Mrs. Algur H.
Meadows and the Meadows Foundation Incorporated

17. *Looking Up Fifth Avenue from Thirtieth Street*. 1932.
Oil on canvas, 27⅛ x 22⅛ in.
Norton Gallery of Art, West Palm Beach, Florida

18. *Composition, Cape Split, Maine No. 1*. 1933.
Oil on canvas, 22 x 28 in.
Courtesy Kennedy Galleries, Inc., New York

19. *Composition, Cape Split, Maine No. 3*. 1933.
Oil on canvas, 22 x 28 in.
The Santa Barbara Museum of Art, Santa Barbara,
California,
Gift of Mrs. Sterling Morton to the Preston Morton
Collection

20. *New York*. ca. 1934.
Oil on canvas board, 9½ x 11⅞ in.
Courtesy Kennedy Galleries, Inc., New York

21. *Off Cape Split, Maine 1*. 1934.
Oil on canvas, 22⅛ x 28 in.
Collection Douglass and Fredrica Carmichael,
Washington, D.C.

22. *Study, New York*. ca. 1934.
Oil on canvas, 22 x 28 in.
Collection Mr. and Mrs. William Janss, Sun Valley, Idaho

23. *The Ladle*. 1934.
Oil on canvas, 22 x 28 in.
Collection Norma Boom Marin, New York

24. *Figures, Street Movement*. 1935.
Oil on canvas, 22 x 28 in.
Collection Joseph M. Klein, M.D., Longboat Key, Florida

25. *From Seeing Cape Split*. 1935.
Oil on canvas, 23 x 29½ in.
Colby College Museum of Art, Waterville, Maine,
Gift of Mr. and Mrs. John Marin, Jr.

26. *The Head of the Cape, Ladle, and Boats*. 1937.
Oil on canvas, 23 x 30 in.
Collection Charles Simon, New York

27. *Wave on Rock*. 1937.
Oil on canvas, 22¾ x 30 in.
Whitney Museum of American Art, New York,
Purchase, with funds from Charles Simon and the Painting and Sculpture Committee

28. *Lobster Boat, Cape Split, Maine*. 1938.
Oil on canvas, 22 x 28 in.
Collection Mr. and Mrs. Carl D. Lobell, New York

29. *The Sea, Cape Split, Maine*. 1938.
Oil on canvas, 25 x 30 in.
San Francisco Museum of Modern Art,
Gift of Mrs. Henry Potter Russell

30. *No. 8, Marin Spring*. 1939.
Oil on canvas board, 12 x 16 in.
University of Maine at Machias

31. *No. 13, Marin Spring*. 1939.
Oil on canvas board, 12 x 16 in.
University of Maine at Machias

32. *The Sea, Cape Split, Maine*. 1939.
Oil on canvas, 24 x 29 in.
The Phillips Collection, Washington, D.C.

33. *Maine Sea with Island*. 1940.
Oil on canvas, 22 x 30 in.
Courtesy Kennedy Galleries, Inc., New York

34. *Pink Rocks and Green Sea*. 1940.
Oil on canvas, 22½ x 28¼ in.
Courtesy Kennedy Galleries, Inc., New York

35. *Sea and Figures, Concept I*. 1942.
Oil on canvas, 22 x 28 in.
Colby College Museum of Art, Waterville, Maine
Gift of Mr. and Mrs. John Marin, Jr.

36. *Hurricane*. 1944.
Oil on canvas, 25 x 30 in.
Indianapolis Museum of Art,
Estate of Mrs. James W. Fesler

37. (*Seascape*). 1944.
Oil on canvas, 22 x 28 in.
Collection Mr. and Mrs. John Kluge, Charlottesville, Virginia

38. *Tunk Mountains, Maine*. 1945.
Oil on canvas, 25 x 30 in.
The Phillips Collection, Washington, D.C.

39. *Movement in Greys and Yellows*. 1946.
Oil on canvas, 22 x 28 in.
Private Collection, New York

40. *Tunk Mountains, Maine*. 1946.
Oil on canvas, 25 x 32 in.
The Parrish Art Museum, Southampton, N.Y.,
Museum Purchase, Robert Lehman Fund

41. *Movement: Sea Ultramarine and Green, Sky Cerulean and Grey*, 1947.
Oil on canvas, 22 x 28 in.
Archer M. Huntington Art Gallery, The University of Texas at Austin,
James and Mari Michener Collection

42. *Movement: Seas After Hurricane, Red, Green and White, Figure in Blue, Maine*. 1947.
Oil on canvas, 22 x 28 in.
Private Collection, New York

43. *Movement: Wind Southwest*. 1947.
Oil on canvas, 22 x 28 in.
Collection Mr. and Mrs. William C. Bahan, Fort Worth

44. *Sea in Blue, Greys, and Light Red*. 1948.
Oil on canvas, 24 x 30
Private Collection, New York

45. *The Lobster Fisherman*. 1948.
Oil on canvas, 28⅛ x 23¼ in.
Hirshhorn Museum and Sculpture Garden,
Smithsonian Institution, Washington, D.C.,
Gift of Joseph H. Hirshhorn, 1966

46. *Full Moon Over the City No. 2*. 1949.
Oil on canvas, 22 x 28 in.
Collection Mr. and Mrs. John Marin, Jr., New York

47. *Movement in Brown Ochre, Cobalt Green, and Umber*. 1950.
Oil on canvas, 22 x 28 in.
Willard Straight Hall Collection,
Cornell University, Ithaca, New York

48. *Movement in Red, Blue and Umber*. 1950
Oil on canvas, 22 x 28 in.
Courtesy Kennedy Galleries, Inc., New York

49. *Tunk Mountains*. 1951.
Oil on canvas, 25 x 30 in.
Courtesy Kennedy Galleries, Inc., New York

50. *Huntington Long Island No. 2*. 1952.
Oil on canvas, 22 x 28 in.
Colby College Museum of Art, Waterville, Maine,
Gift of Mr. and Mrs. John Marin, Jr.

51. *Movement: Grey and Blue*. 1952.
Oil on canvas, 22 x 28 in.
Private Collection, New York

52. *Sea Fantasy*. 1952.
Oil on canvas, 22 x 28 in.
Courtesy Kennedy Galleries, Inc., New York

53. *The Written Sea*. 1952.
Oil on canvas, 22 x 28 in.
Collection Norma Boom Marin, New York

54. *Spring No. 2*. 1953
Oil on canvas, 22 x 28 in.
Courtesy Kennedy Galleries, Inc., New York

55. *The Circus*. 1953.
Oil on canvas, 18 x 22 in.
Courtesy Kennedy Galleries, Inc., New York

BIBLIOGRAPHY

General

The Advent of Modernism/Post-Impressionism and North American Art, 1900–1918. Essays by Peter Morrin, Judith Zilczer, William C. Agee. Atlanta, Georgia: High Museum of Art, 1986.

Atkinson, D. Scott, and Homer, William Inness. *The New Society of American Artists in Paris, 1908–1912.* Queens, New York: Queens County Art and Cultural Center, 1986.

Brown, Milton, *The Story of the Armory Show.* New York: Joseph H. Hirshhorn Foundation, 1963.

Craven, Thomas. *Modern Art: The Men, the Movements, the Meaning.* New York: Simon & Schuster, 1934.

Goodrich, Lloyd. *American Watercolor and Winslow Homer.* Minneapolis, Minnesota: Walker Art Center, 1945.

Hobbs, Robert Carlton, and Levin, Gail. *Abstract Expressionism: The Formative Years.* New York: Whitney Museum of American Art, 1978.

Homer, William Inness. *Alfred Stieglitz and the American Avant-Garde.* London: Secker and Warburg, 1977.

Lowe, Sue Davidson. *Stieglitz: A Memoir/Biography.* New York: Farrar, Straus & Giroux, 1983.

Mellquist, Jerome. *The Emergence of an American Art.* New York: Charles Scribner's Sons, 1942.

Rose, Barbara, ed. *Readings in American Art Since 1900.* New York: Frederick A. Praeger, 1968.

Rosenblum, Robert. *Cubism and Twentieth-Century Art.* New York: Harry N. Abrams, 1960.

Wang, Wan-go. *Chinese Paintings and Calligraphy.* New York: Dover Publications, 1978.

Marin

Baur, John I. H. *John Marin's Oils.* New York: Kennedy Galleries, 1984.

Benson, E. M. *John Marin: The Man and His Work.* Washington, D.C.: The American Federation of Arts, 1935.

Finkelstein, Louis. "Marin and de Kooning." *Magazine of Art,* vol. 43, no. 6 (October 1950).

Grey, Cleve, ed. *John Marin.* New York: Holt, Rinehart & Winston, 1977.

Helm, MacKinley. *John Marin* (Foreword by John Marin). Boston: Pellegrini & Cudahy in association with the Institute of Contemporary Art, 1948.

John Marin. Essays by Henry McBride, Marsden Hartley, and E. M. Benson. New York: The Museum of Modern Art, 1936.

John Marin, 1870–1953. Essay by Larry Curry, Foreword by Sheldon Reich. Los Angeles: Los Angeles County Museum of Art, 1970.

John Marin, 1870–1953. Essays by MacKinley Helm and Sheldon Reich. Tucson: University of Arizona Art Gallery, 1963.

John Marin Memorial Exhibition. Essays by William Carlos Williams, Dorothy Norman, MacKinley Helm, and Frederick S. Wight; Foreword by Duncan Phillips; Los Angeles: The Art Galleries, University of California, 1955.

John Marin, a Retrospective Exhibition. Essays by John Marin, MacKinley Helm, and Frederick S. Wight. Boston: Institute of Modern Art, 1947.

Josephson, Matthew. "Leprechaun on the Palisades." *The New Yorker,* March 14, 1942.

Norman, Dorothy, ed. *The Selected Writings of John Marin.* New York: Pellegrini & Cudahy, 1949.

Reich, Sheldon. *John Marin: Part I, A Stylistic Analysis; Part II, Catalogue Raisonné.* Tucson: University of Arizona Press, 1970.

Reich, Sheldon. *John Marin Drawings, 1886–1951.* University of Utah Press, 1969.

Rosenblum, Robert. "Marin's Dynamism." *Art Digest,* vol. 28 (February 1954).

Zigrosser, Carl. *The Complete Etchings of John Marin.* Philadelphia: Philadelphia Museum of Art, 1969.

PHOTOGRAPHY CREDITS

The majority of the photographs have been provided by the owners or custodians of the works reproduced. The following list applies to those photographs for which a separate acknowledgement is due.

Geoffrey Clements, New York (cat. nos. 4, 7)
Roy Elkind (cat. no. 27)
Emil Ghinger (cat. no. 47)
Carmelo Guadagno (fig. 11)
Joseph Haroutunian (cat. no. 51)
Richard Hurley (cat. no. 40)
Kennedy Galleries, Inc., New York (cat. nos. 3, 9, 13, 21, 22, 24)
Otto E. Nelson, New York (cat. nos. 6, 25, 35, 44, 50)
Pollitzer, Strong, & Meyer, New York (figs. 16, 23; cat. nos. 1, 14, 26, 37)
Adam Reich (fig. 31; cat. nos. 23, 39, 42, 46, 51, 53)
Joseph Szaszfai (fig. 13)
Wharton Photography, Fort Worth (cat. no. 43)

BOARD OF TRUSTEES

MUSEUM STAFF

Trudy C. Kramer, *Director*
Maureen C. O'Brien, *Associate Director for Curatorial Affairs*
Anke Jackson, *Associate Director for Budget and Operations*
Melissa Patton, *Associate Director for Education*
Janine Veto, *Associate Director for Development and Public Relations*
Klaus Kertess, *Robert Lehman Curator*
Alicia Longwell, *Registrar*
Robin Box Klopfer, *Building Manager*
Nina Madison, *Development Coordinator*
Marsha Kenny, *Public Relations Consultant*
Lorne Singh, *Director of Merchandising*
Lisa Cresson, *Education Assistant*
Susan Swiatocha, *Assistant for Finance*
Peggy Gillis, *Secretary to the Director*
Mary McNeirney, *Membership Secretary*
Norma Loehner, *Curatorial Secretary*
Christine Engel, *Curatorial Intern*
Judy Williams, *Security*
Virginia Grean, *Receptionist*
Patricia Farre, *Receptionist*
Virginia Drucker, *Volunteer Coordinator*

MARIN IN OIL

was produced for
THE PARRISH ART MUSEUM, Southampton, New York
by PERPETUA PRESS, Los Angeles
Edited by SARA BLACKBURN
Designed by DANA LEVY
Typeset in Palatino and Gill Sans
by CONTINENTAL TYPOGRAPHICS, Chatsworth, CA.
Printed in Japan by DAI NIPPON PRINTING COMPANY, Tokyo